GIRLS' LAST TOUR

4

TSUKUMIZU

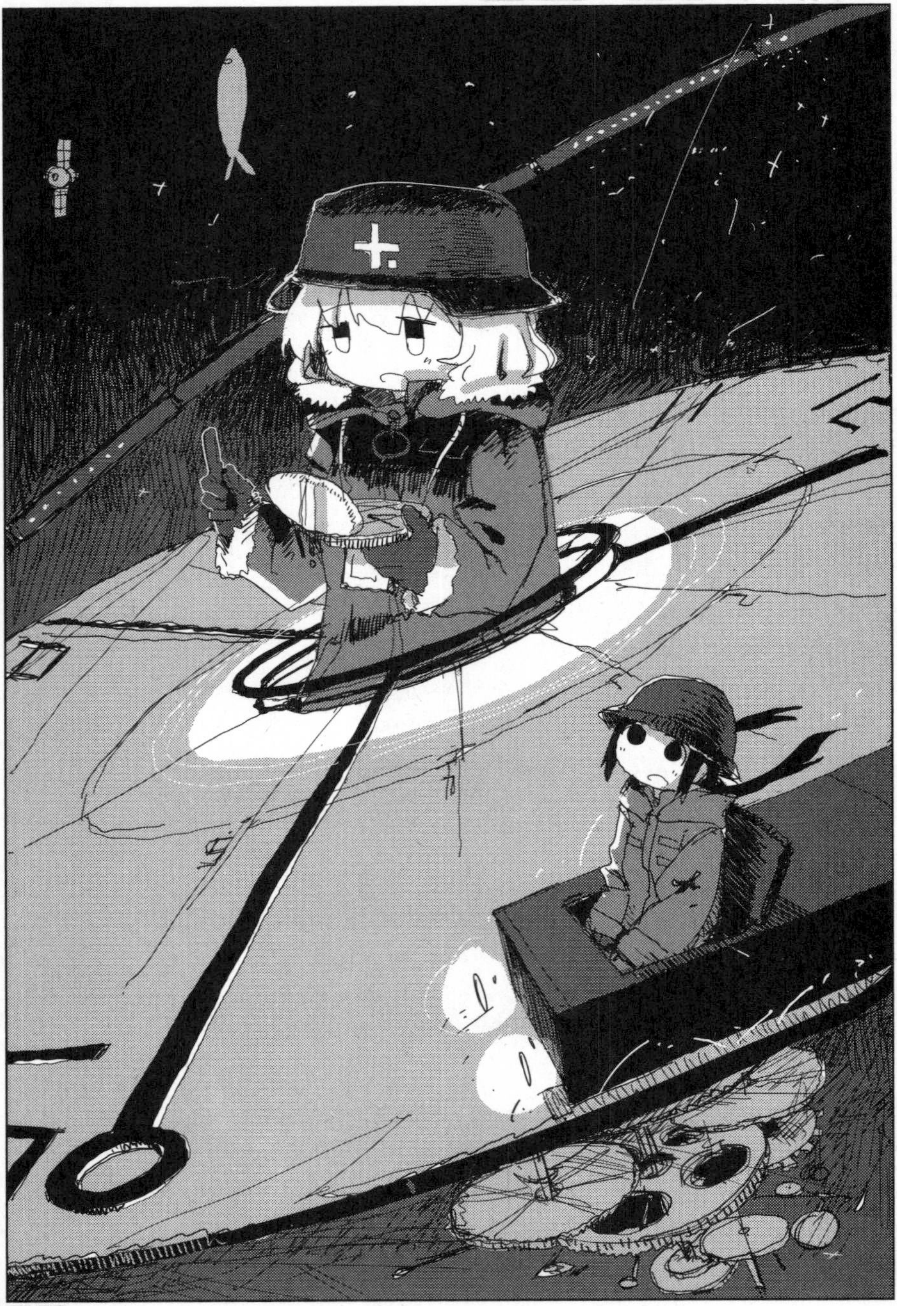

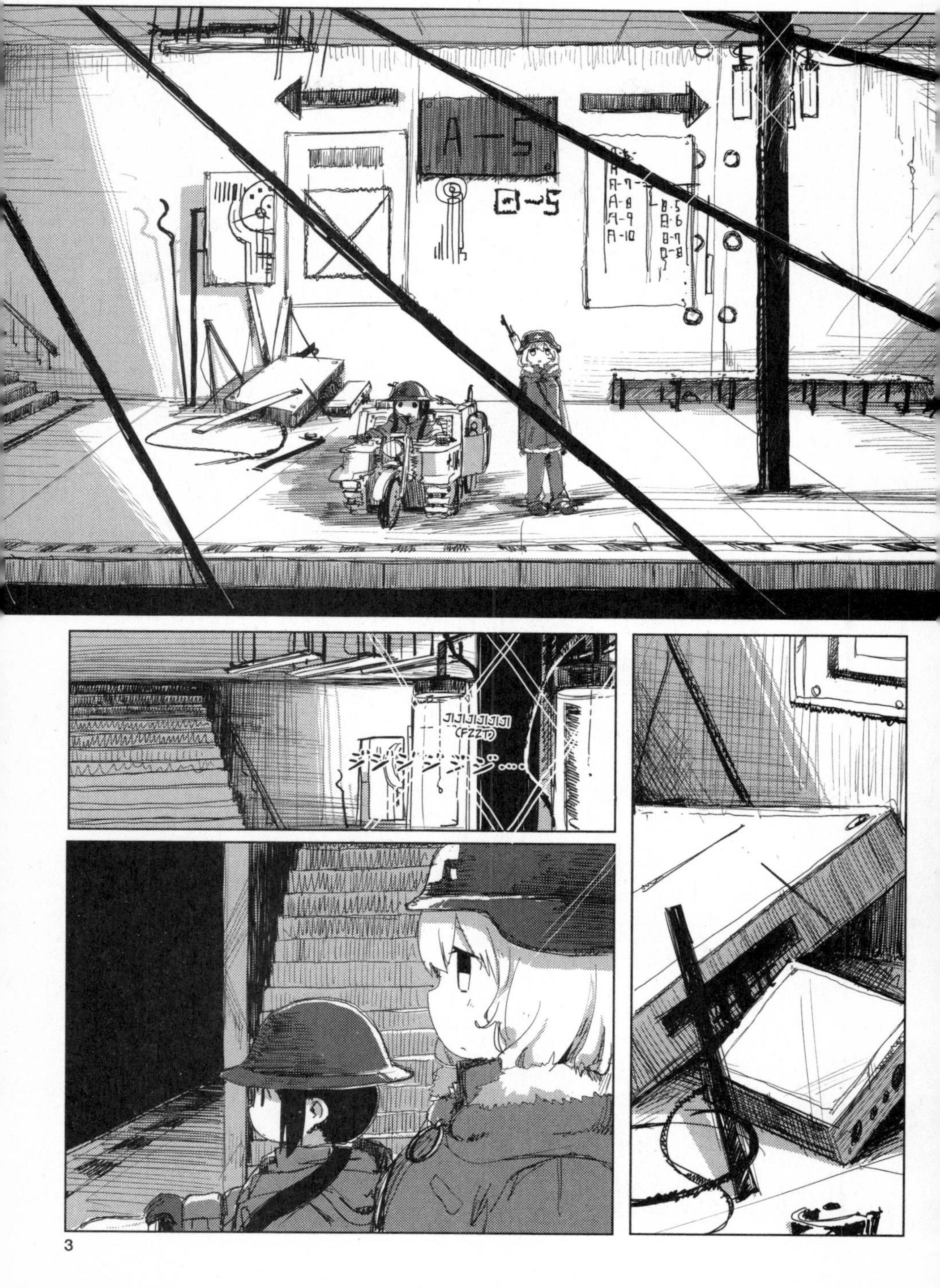
A-5
A-7
A-8
A-9
A-10
B-5
B-6
B-7
B-8
ジジジジジジ…
JIJIJIJIJIJI
(FZZT)

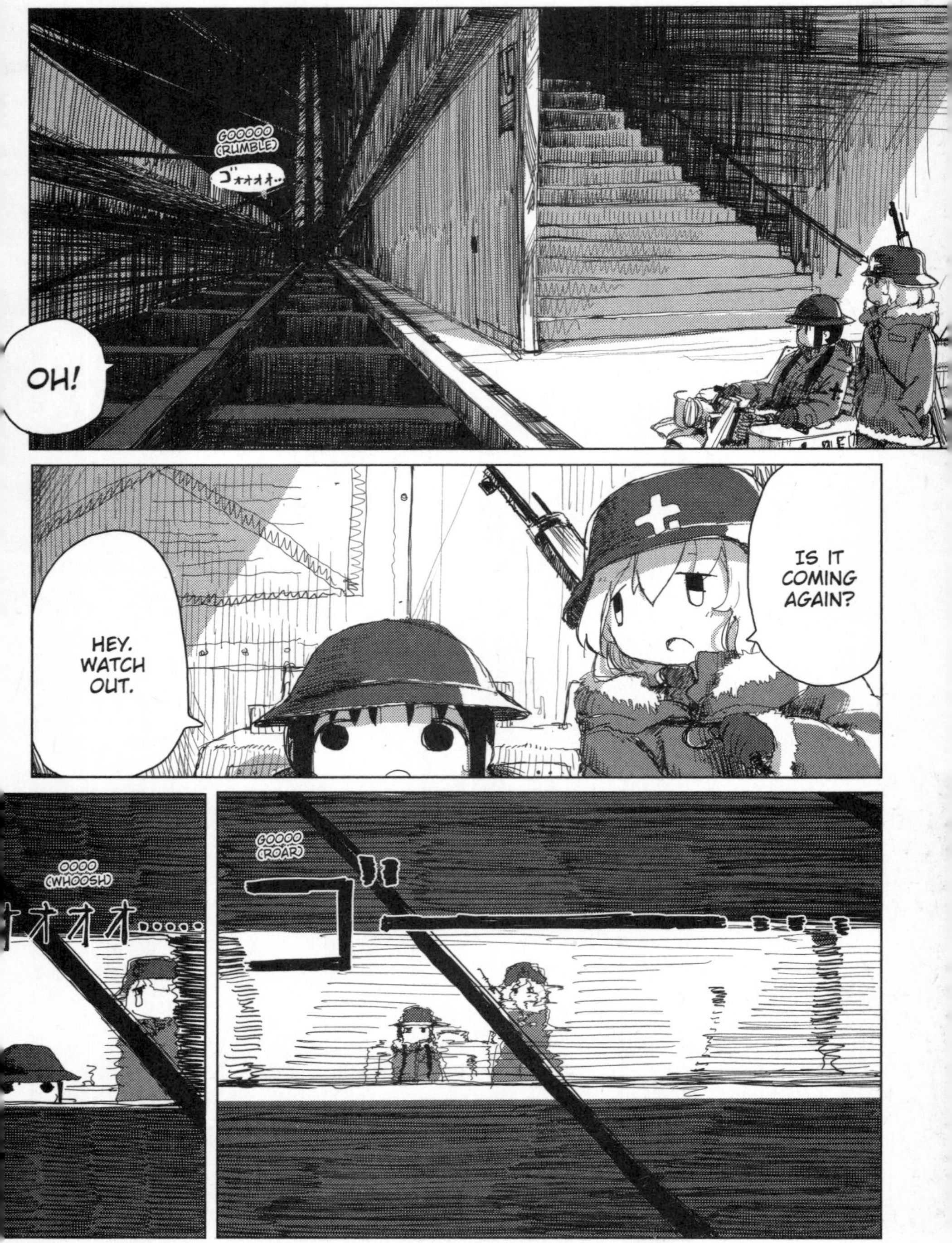
GOOOOO (RUMBLE)
ゴォォォォ…
OH!
IS IT COMING AGAIN?
HEY. WATCH OUT.
GOOOO (ROAR)
ゴー
OOOO (WHOOSH)
ォオオオ……

A-5
A-5
イイイイ
IIII (KREEE)
しゅこっ
SHUKO (SHNK)
トトトトトトト
TOTOTOTOTOTOTO (PUTTER)
しゅーこっ
SHUKO

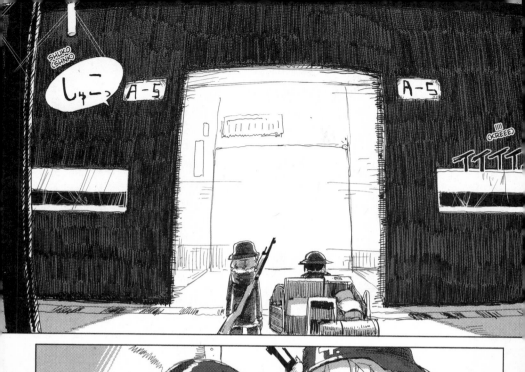

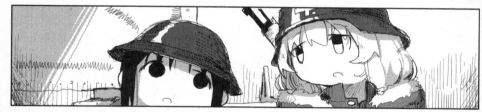

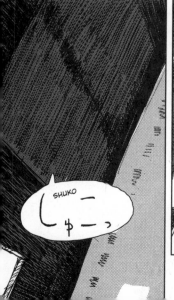

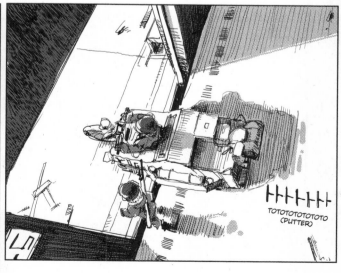

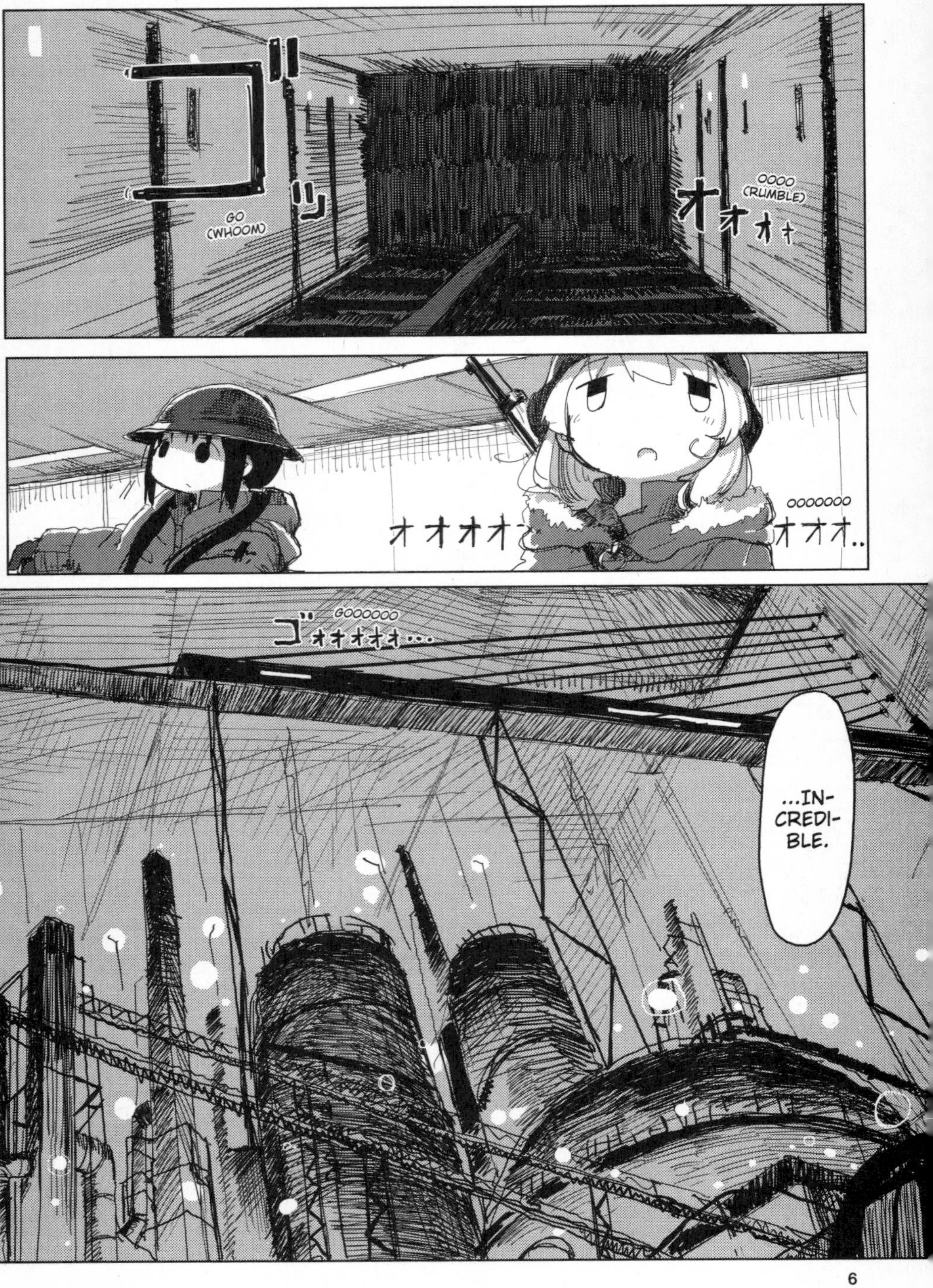
ゴッ
GO (WHOOM)
オオオォ
OOOO (RUMBLE)
OOOOOOO
オオオ..
オオオオ
ゴォォォォ...
GOOOOOO
...IN-CREDI-BLE.

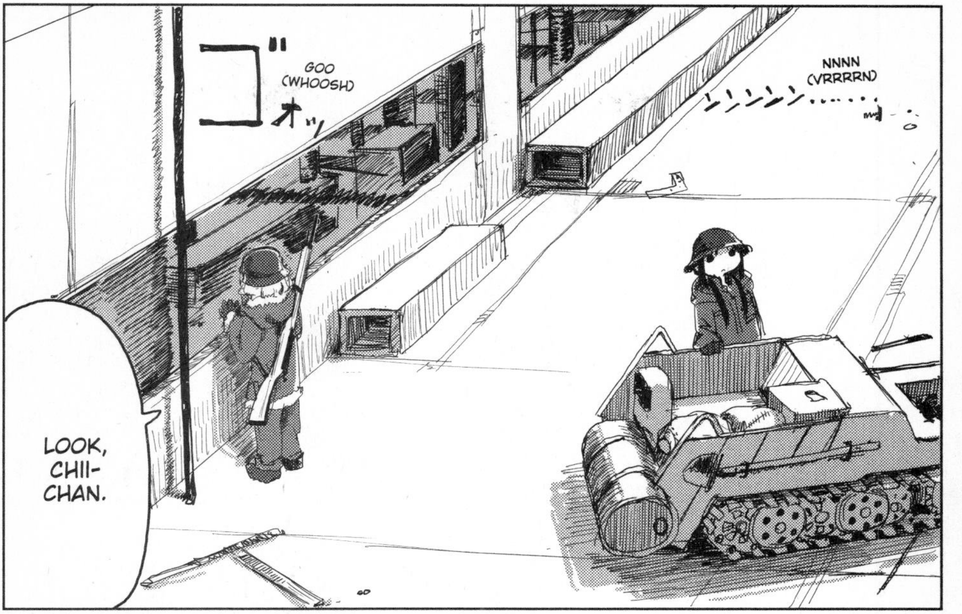
ンンンン……
NNNN (VRRRRN)
ゴオッ
GOO (WHOOSH)
LOOK, CHII-CHAN.

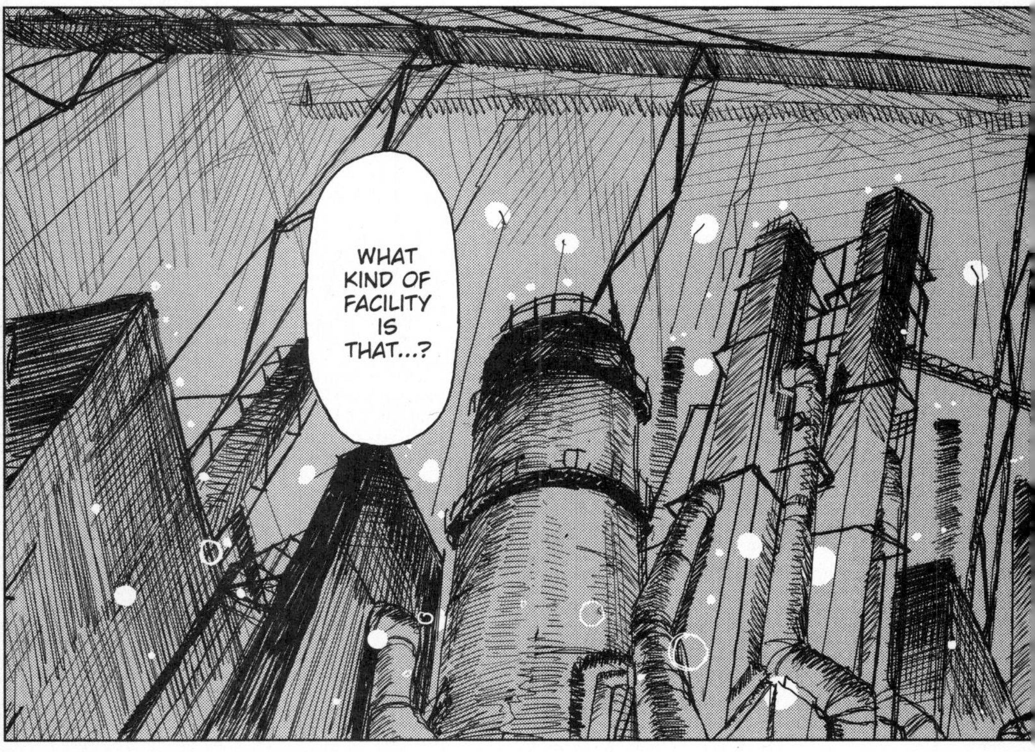
WHAT KIND OF FACILITY IS THAT...?

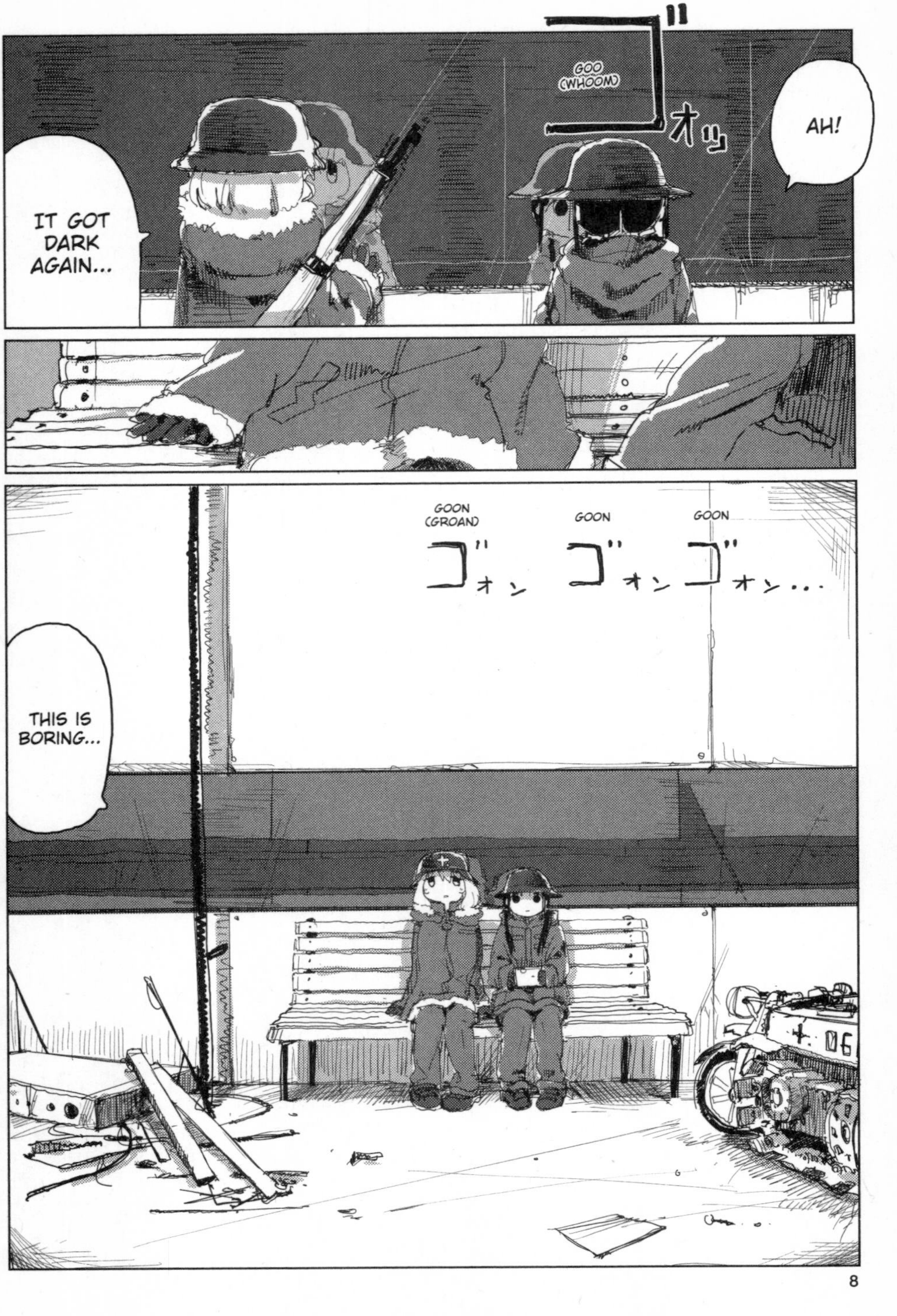
AH!
GOO (WHOOM)
ゴオッ
IT GOT DARK AGAIN...
GOON (GROAN) GOON GOON
ゴォン ゴォン ゴォン...
THIS IS BORING...

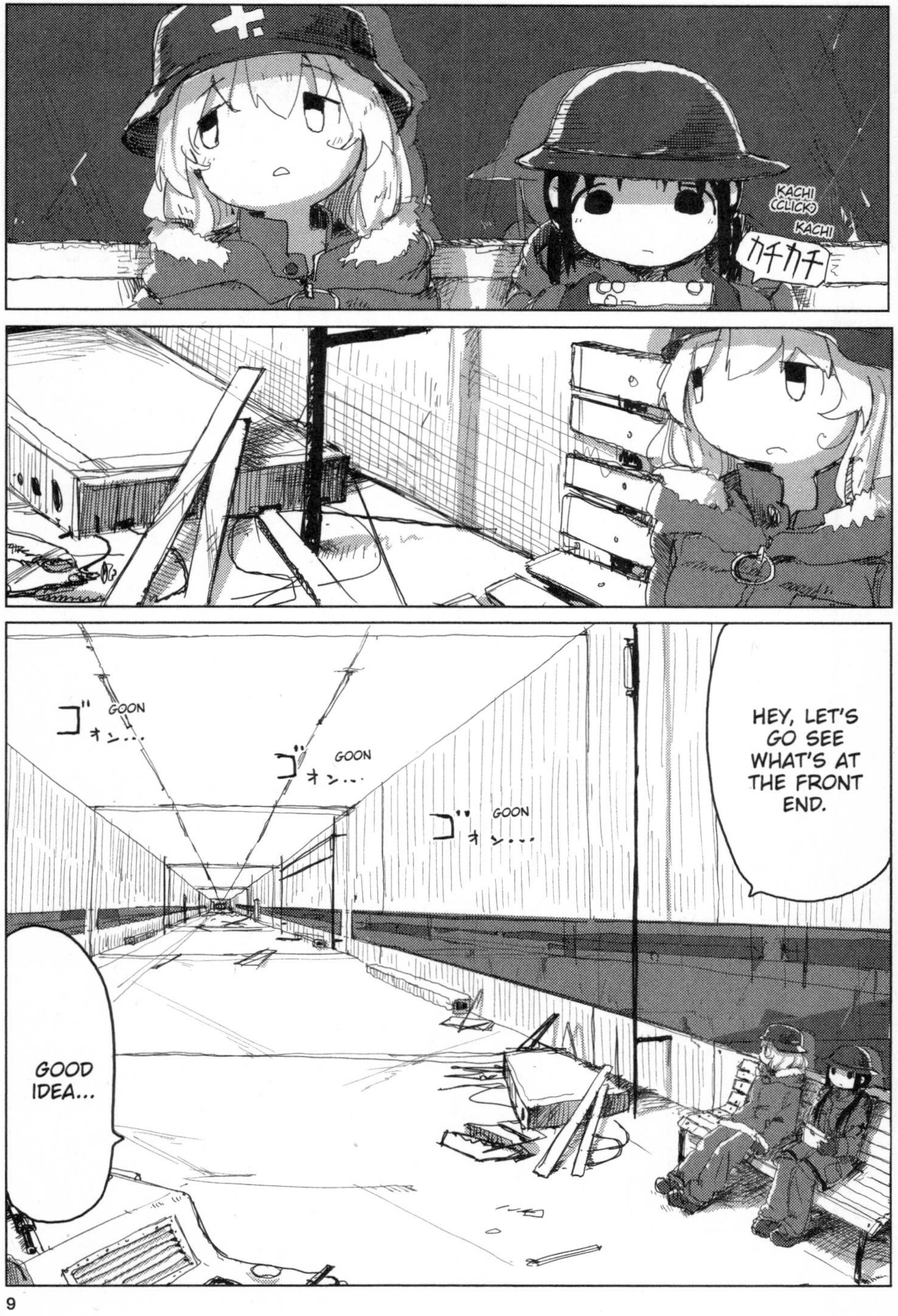
KACHI (CLICK) KACHI
カチカチ
HEY, LET'S GO SEE WHAT'S AT THE FRONT END.
ゴォン... GOON
ゴォン... GOON
ゴォン... GOON
GOOD IDEA...

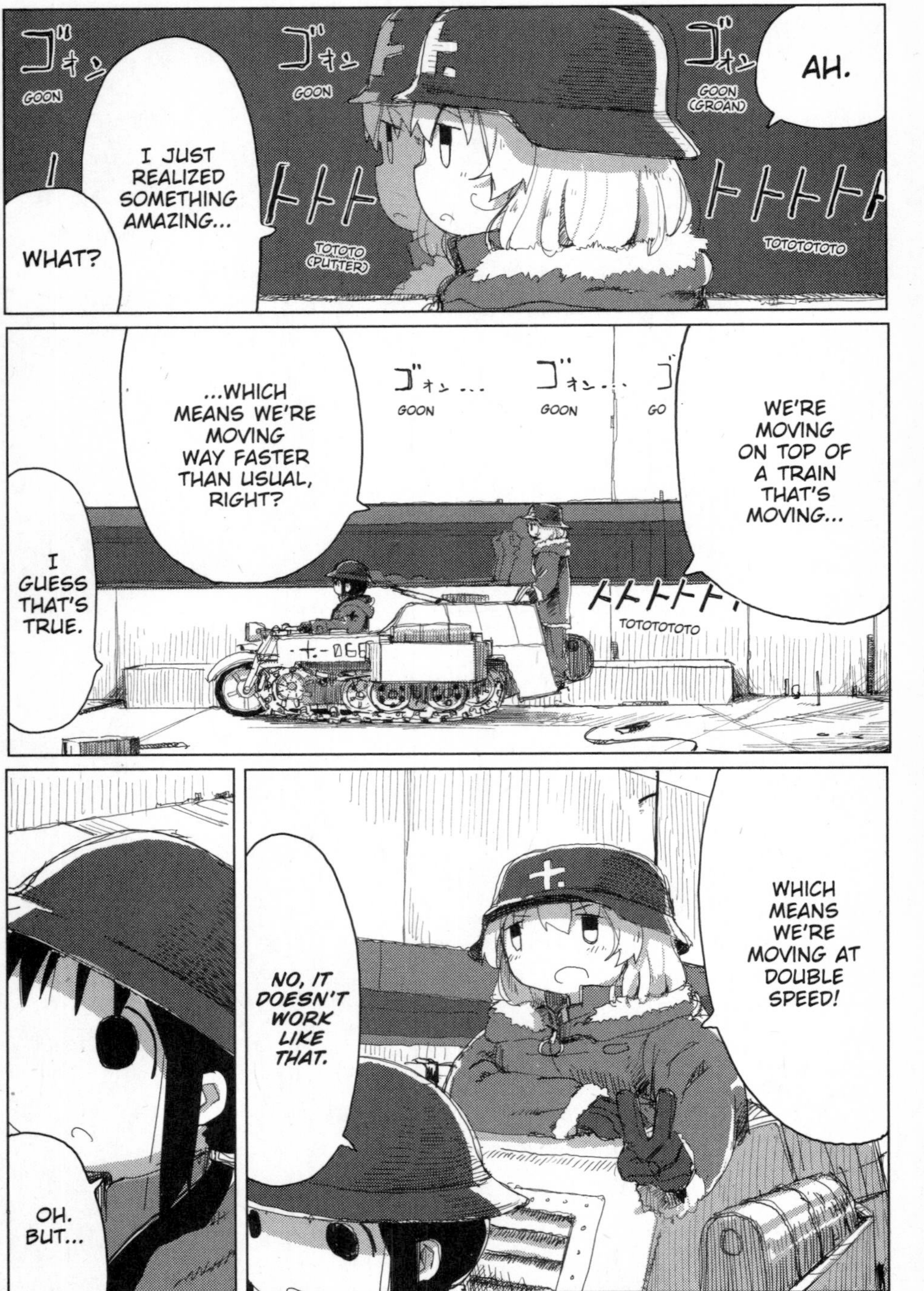
AH.
ゴォン
GOON (GROAN)
トトトトト
TOTOTOTOTO
ゴォン
GOON
トトト
TOTOTO (PUTTER)
I JUST REALIZED SOMETHING AMAZING...
ゴォン
GOON
WHAT?
WE'RE MOVING ON TOP OF A TRAIN THAT'S MOVING...
GO
ゴォン...
GOON
ゴォン...
GOON
TOTOTOTOTO
...WHICH MEANS WE'RE MOVING WAY FASTER THAN USUAL, RIGHT?
I GUESS THAT'S TRUE.
WHICH MEANS WE'RE MOVING AT DOUBLE SPEED!
NO, IT DOESN'T WORK LIKE THAT.
OH. BUT...

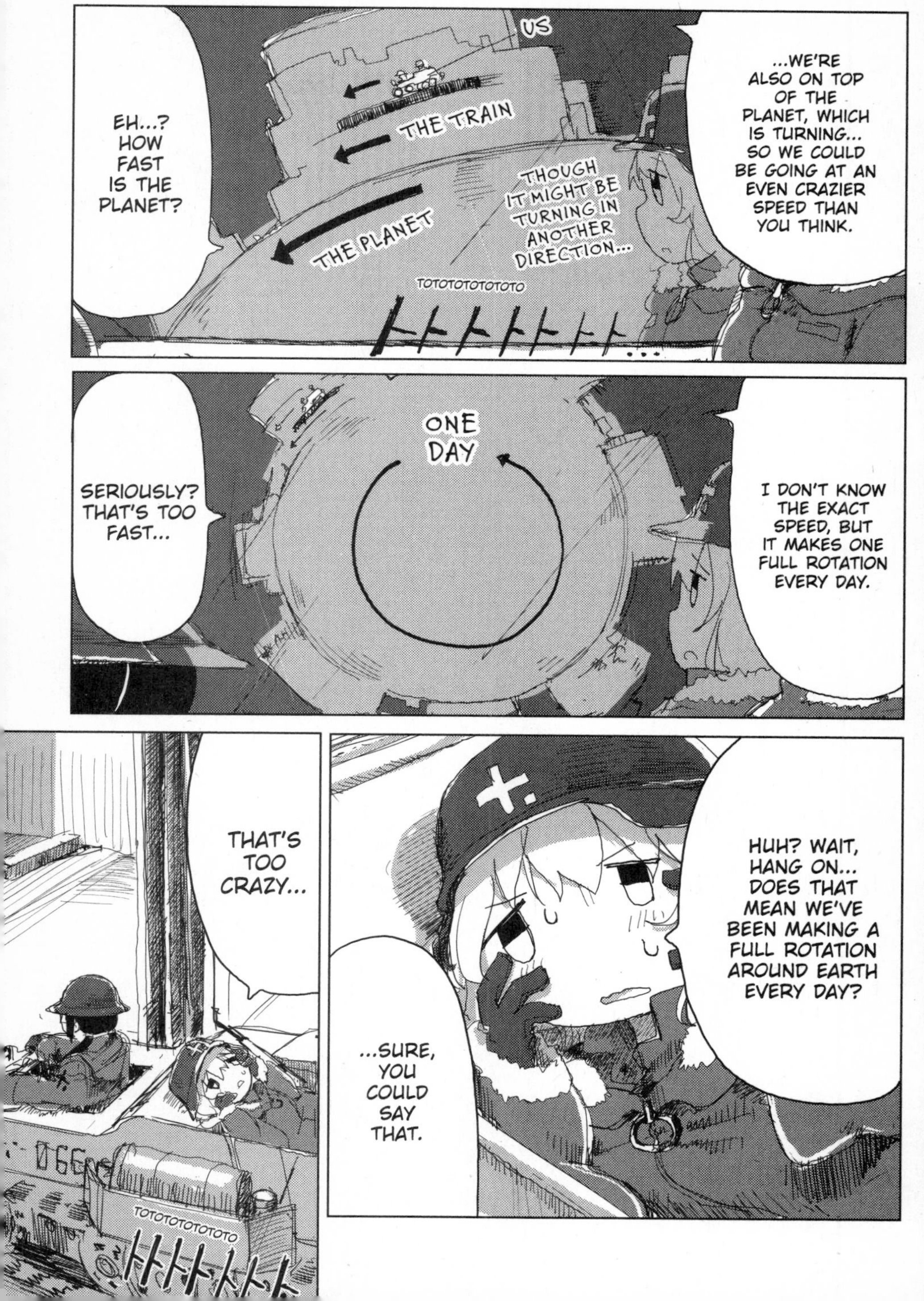

...WE'RE ALSO ON TOP OF THE PLANET, WHICH IS TURNING... SO WE COULD BE GOING AT AN EVEN CRAZIER SPEED THAN YOU THINK.
US
THE TRAIN
THE PLANET
THOUGH IT MIGHT BE TURNING IN ANOTHER DIRECTION...
TOTOTOTOTOTOTO
EH...? HOW FAST IS THE PLANET?
I DON'T KNOW THE EXACT SPEED, BUT IT MAKES ONE FULL ROTATION EVERY DAY.
ONE DAY
SERIOUSLY? THAT'S TOO FAST...
HUH? WAIT, HANG ON... DOES THAT MEAN WE'VE BEEN MAKING A FULL ROTATION AROUND EARTH EVERY DAY?
...SURE, YOU COULD SAY THAT.
THAT'S TOO CRAZY...
TOTOTOTOTOTOTO

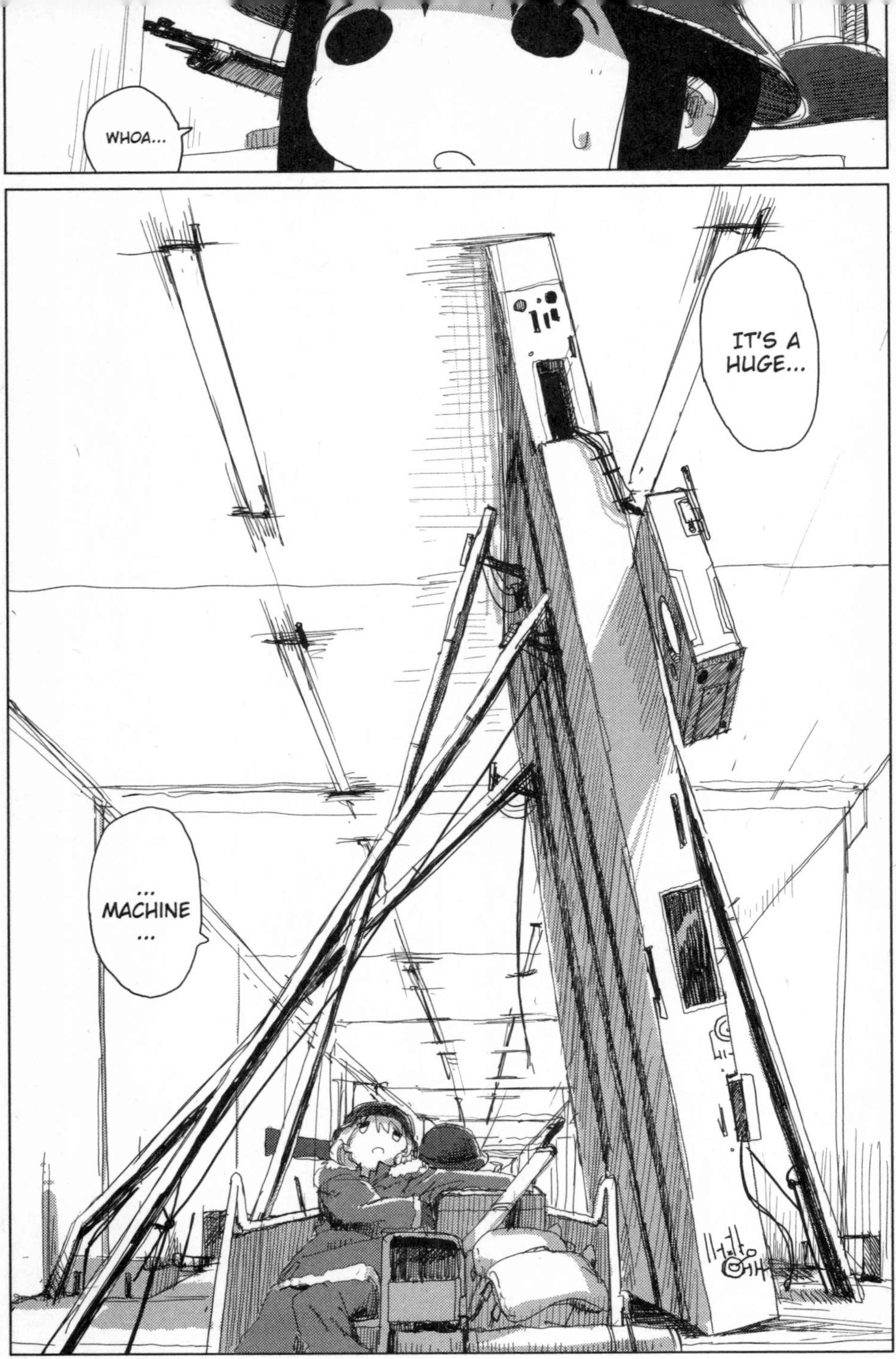
WHOA...
IT'S A HUGE...
... MACHINE ...

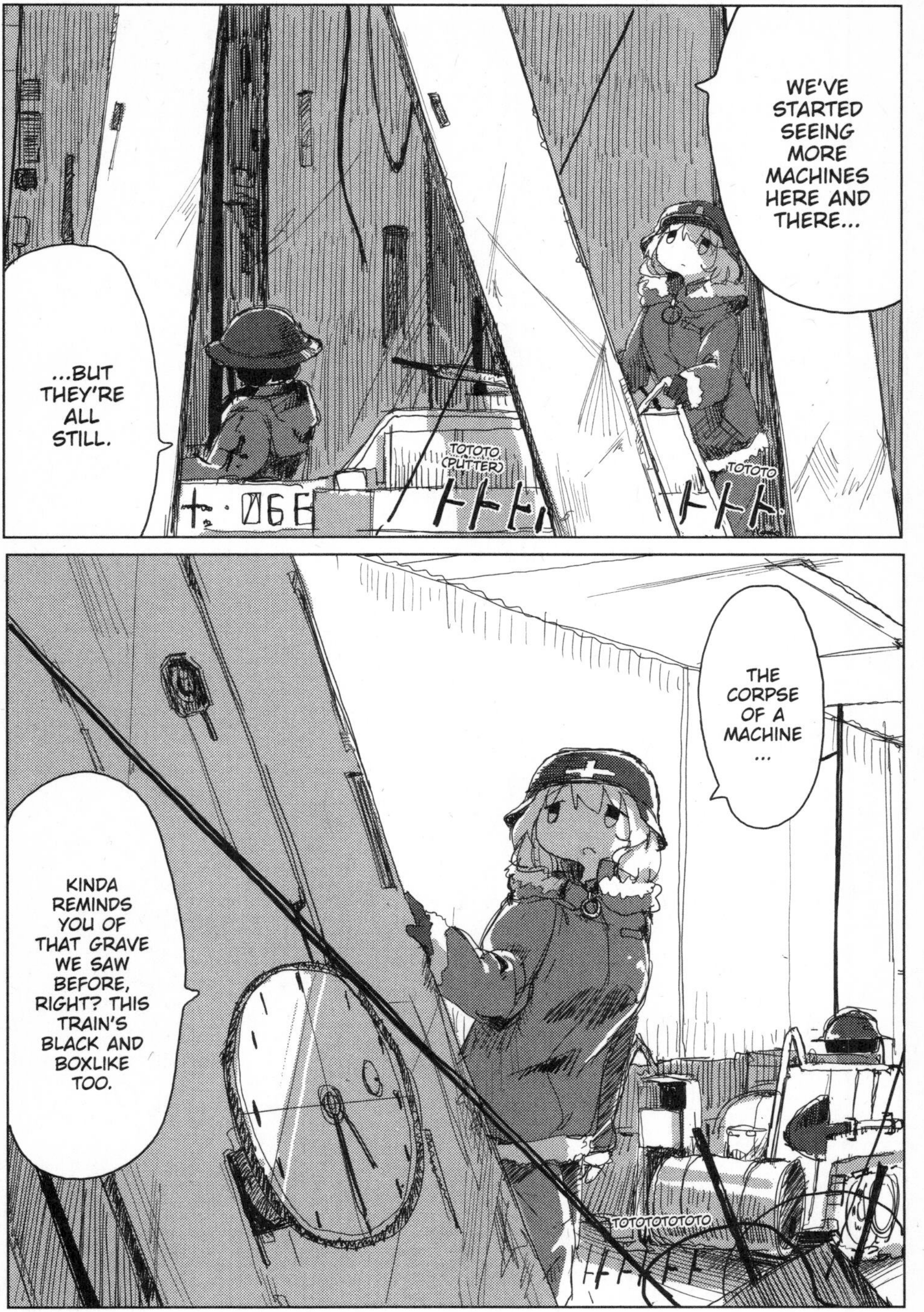
WE'VE STARTED SEEING MORE MACHINES HERE AND THERE...
...BUT THEY'RE ALL STILL.
TOTOTO
TOTOTO (PUTTER)
THE CORPSE OF A MACHINE ...
KINDA REMINDS YOU OF THAT GRAVE WE SAW BEFORE, RIGHT? THIS TRAIN'S BLACK AND BOXLIKE TOO.
TOTOTOTOTOTO

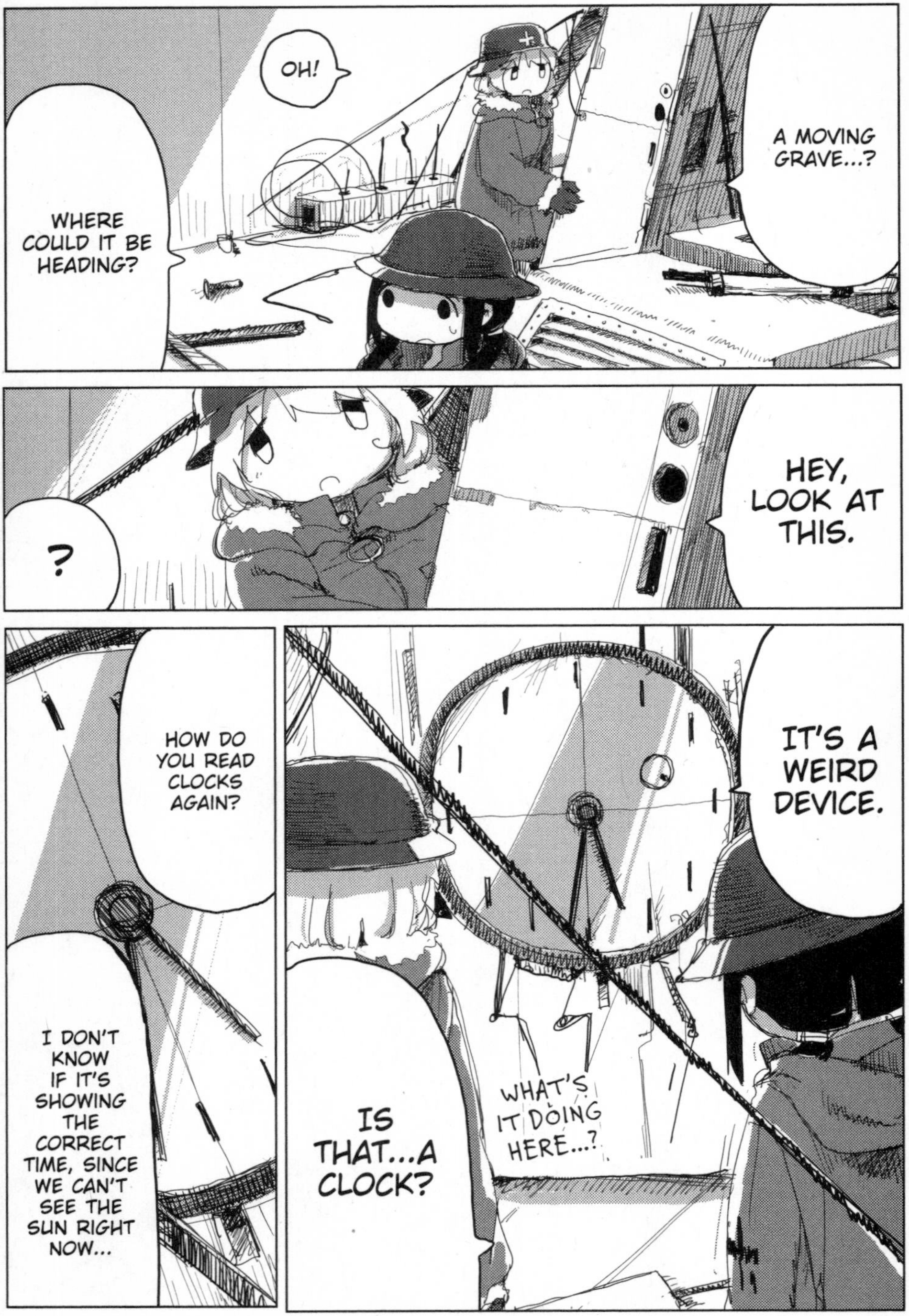
A MOVING GRAVE...?
OH!
WHERE COULD IT BE HEADING?
HEY, LOOK AT THIS.
?
IT'S A WEIRD DEVICE.
WHAT'S IT DOING HERE...?
IS THAT...A CLOCK?
HOW DO YOU READ CLOCKS AGAIN?
I DON'T KNOW IF IT'S SHOWING THE CORRECT TIME, SINCE WE CAN'T SEE THE SUN RIGHT NOW...

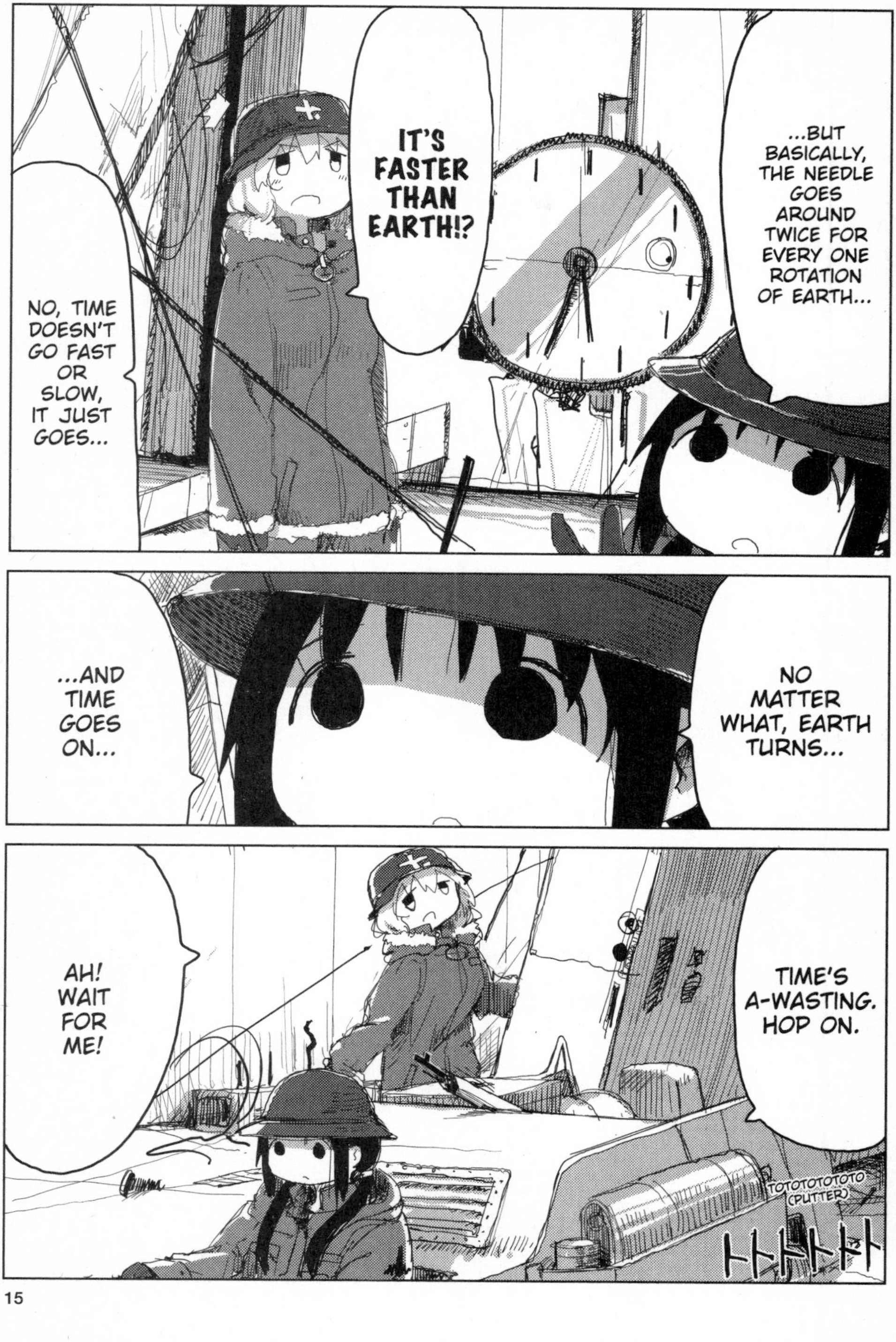
...BUT BASICALLY, THE NEEDLE GOES AROUND TWICE FOR EVERY ONE ROTATION OF EARTH...
IT'S FASTER THAN EARTH!?
NO, TIME DOESN'T GO FAST OR SLOW, IT JUST GOES...
NO MATTER WHAT, EARTH TURNS...
...AND TIME GOES ON...
TIME'S A-WASTING. HOP ON.
TOTOTOTOTOTO (PUTTER)
AH! WAIT FOR ME!

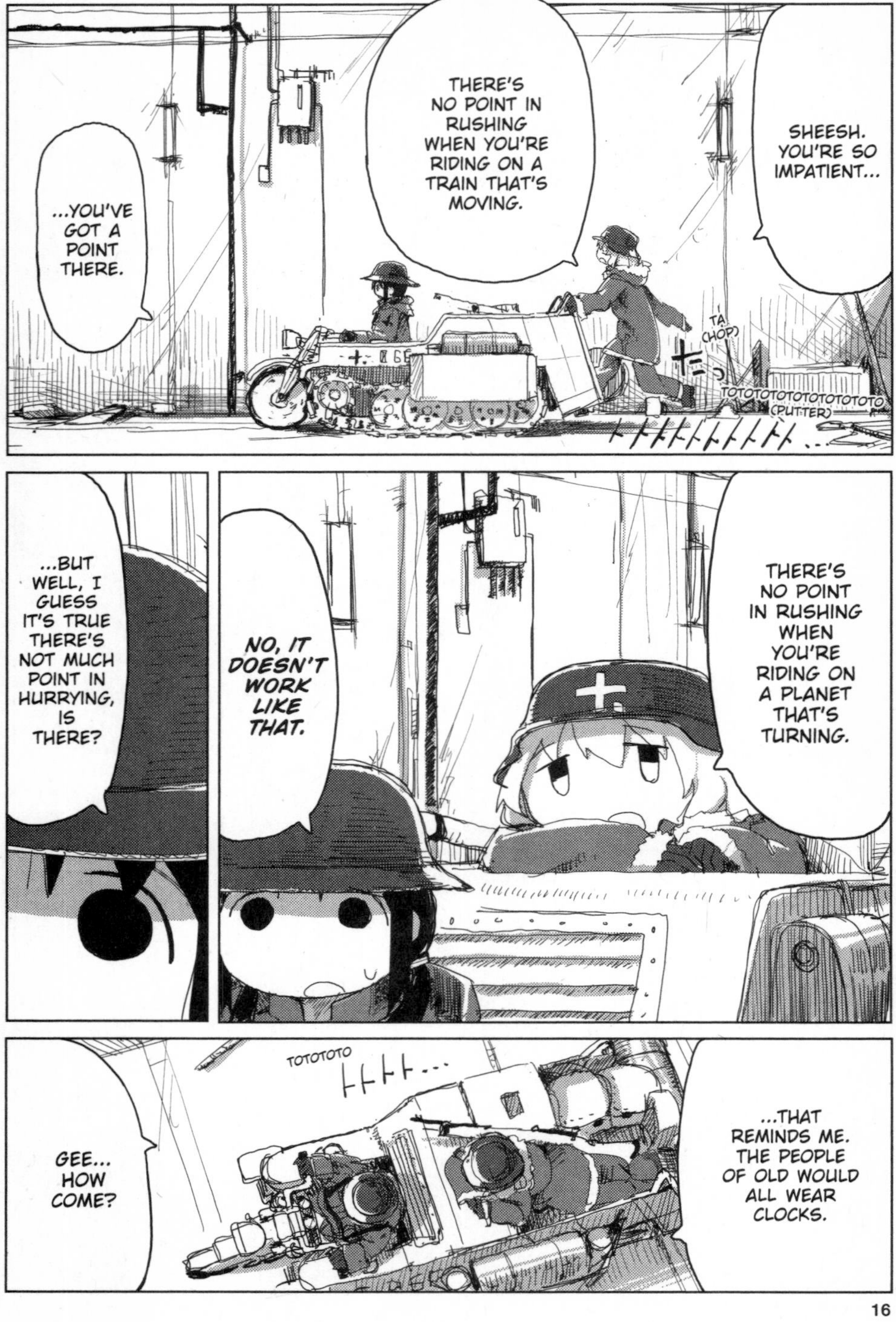
SHEESH. YOU'RE SO IMPATIENT...
THERE'S NO POINT IN RUSHING WHEN YOU'RE RIDING ON A TRAIN THAT'S MOVING.
...YOU'VE GOT A POINT THERE.
TA (CHOP)
TOTOTOTOTOTOTOTOTOTOTO (PUTTER)
THERE'S NO POINT IN RUSHING WHEN YOU'RE RIDING ON A PLANET THAT'S TURNING.
NO, IT DOESN'T WORK LIKE THAT.
...BUT WELL, I GUESS IT'S TRUE THERE'S NOT MUCH POINT IN HURRYING, IS THERE?
...THAT REMINDS ME. THE PEOPLE OF OLD WOULD ALL WEAR CLOCKS.
TOTOTOTO
GEE... HOW COME?

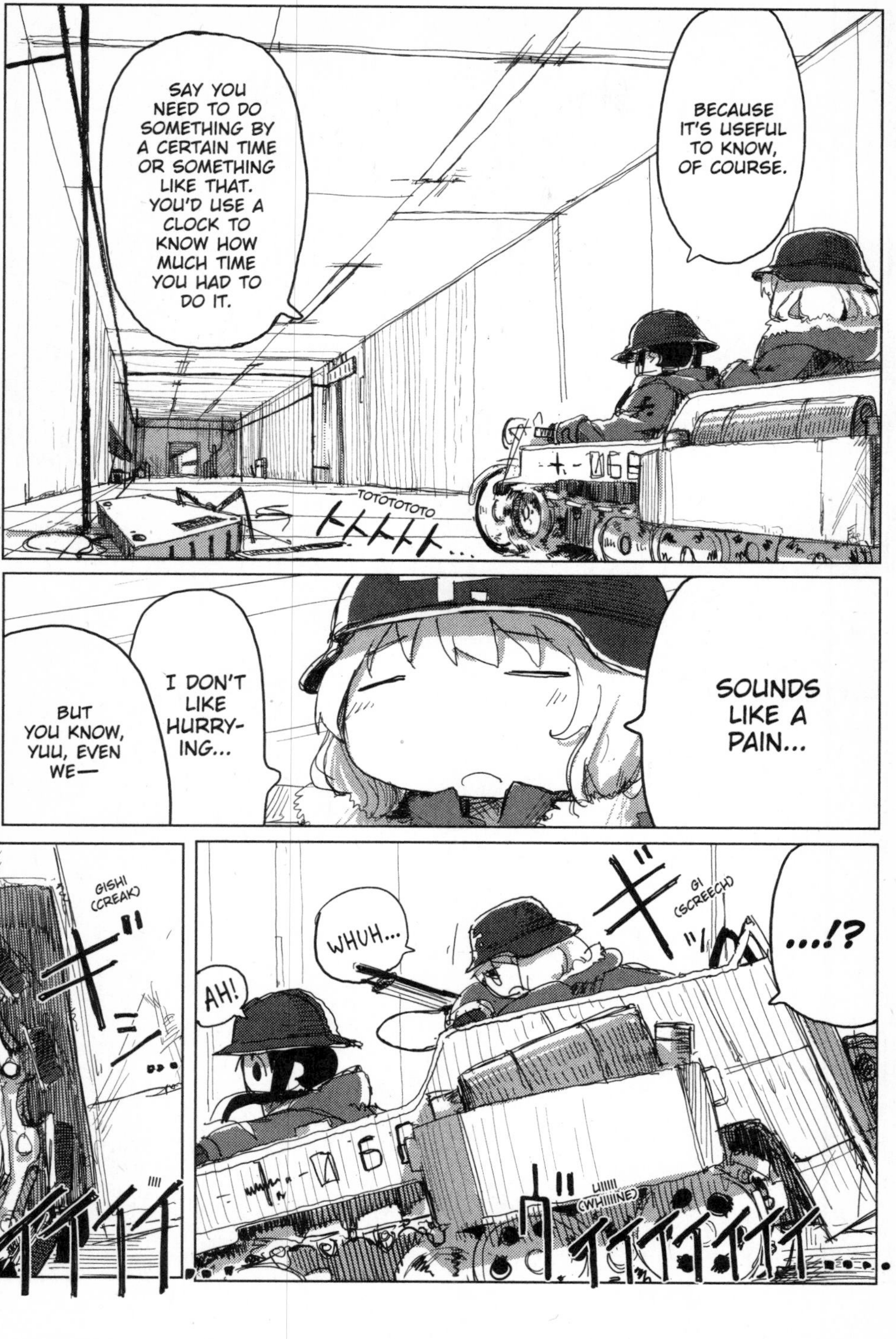
BECAUSE IT'S USEFUL TO KNOW, OF COURSE.
SAY YOU NEED TO DO SOMETHING BY A CERTAIN TIME OR SOMETHING LIKE THAT. YOU'D USE A CLOCK TO KNOW HOW MUCH TIME YOU HAD TO DO IT.
TOTOTOTOTO
SOUNDS LIKE A PAIN...
I DON'T LIKE HURRY-ING...
BUT YOU KNOW, YUU, EVEN WE—
...!?
GI (SCREECH)
WHUH...
AH!
UIIIII (WHIIIINE)
GISHI (CREAK)

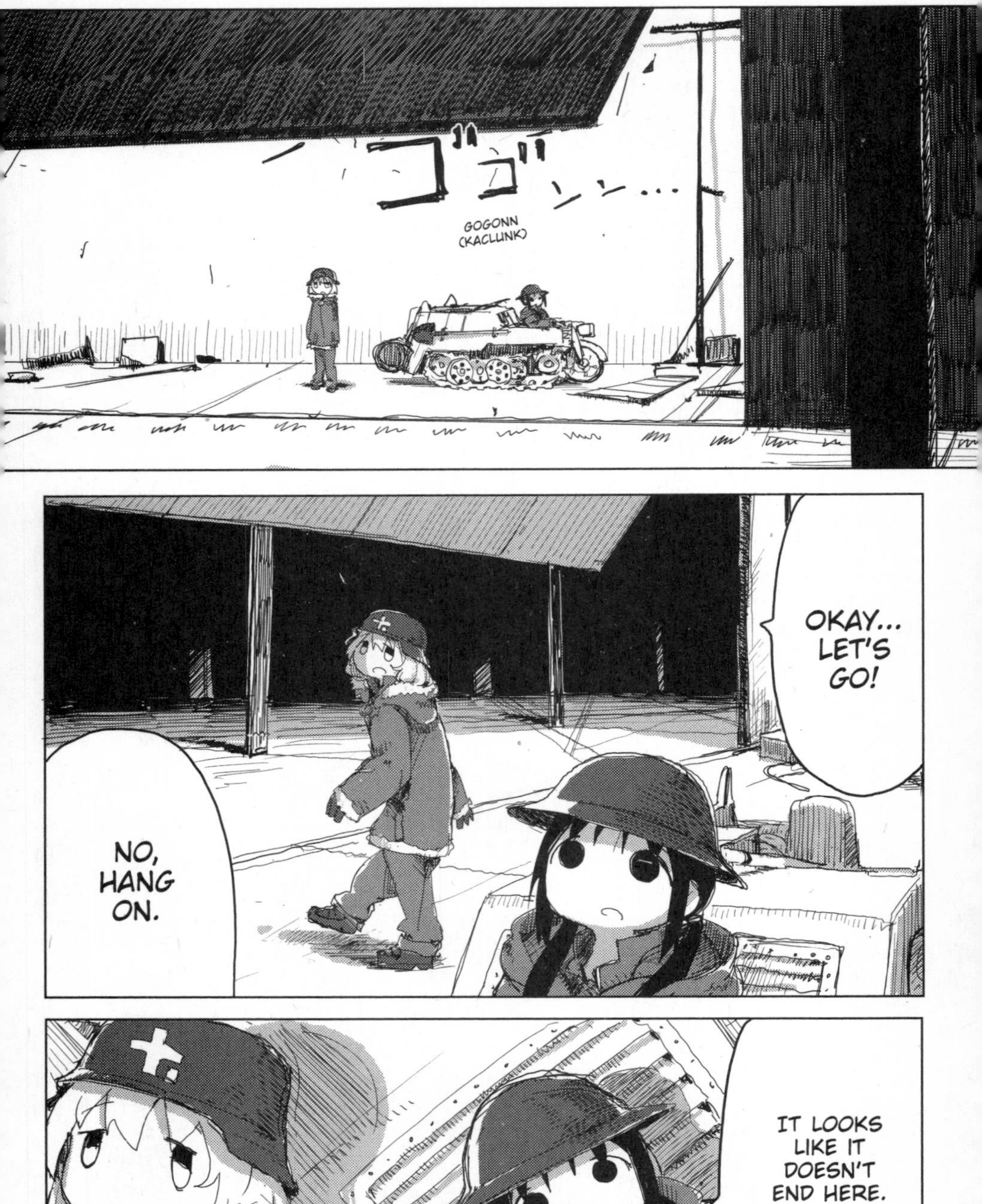
ゴゴンン…
GOGONN
(KACLUNK)
OKAY... LET'S GO!
NO, HANG ON.
IT LOOKS LIKE IT DOESN'T END HERE.

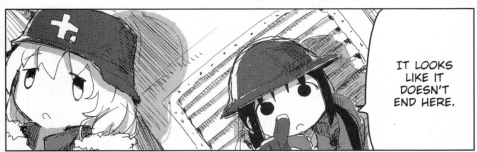

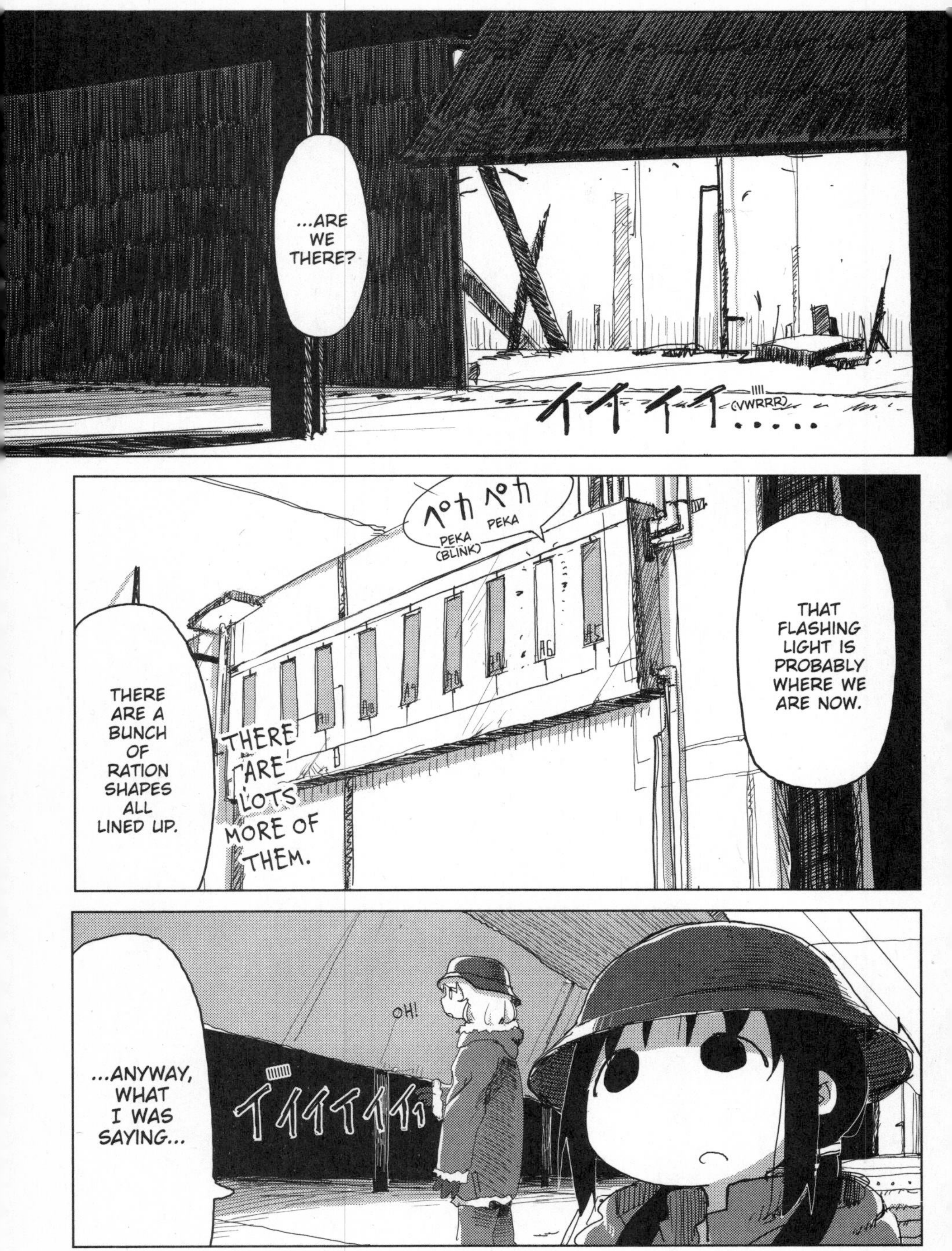
...ARE WE THERE?
イイイイ.....
(VWRRR)
THAT FLASHING LIGHT IS PROBABLY WHERE WE ARE NOW.
ペカペカ
PEKA PEKA (BLINK)
THERE ARE LOTS MORE OF THEM.
THERE ARE A BUNCH OF RATION SHAPES ALL LINED UP.
OH!
イイイイイィ
...ANYWAY, WHAT I WAS SAYING...

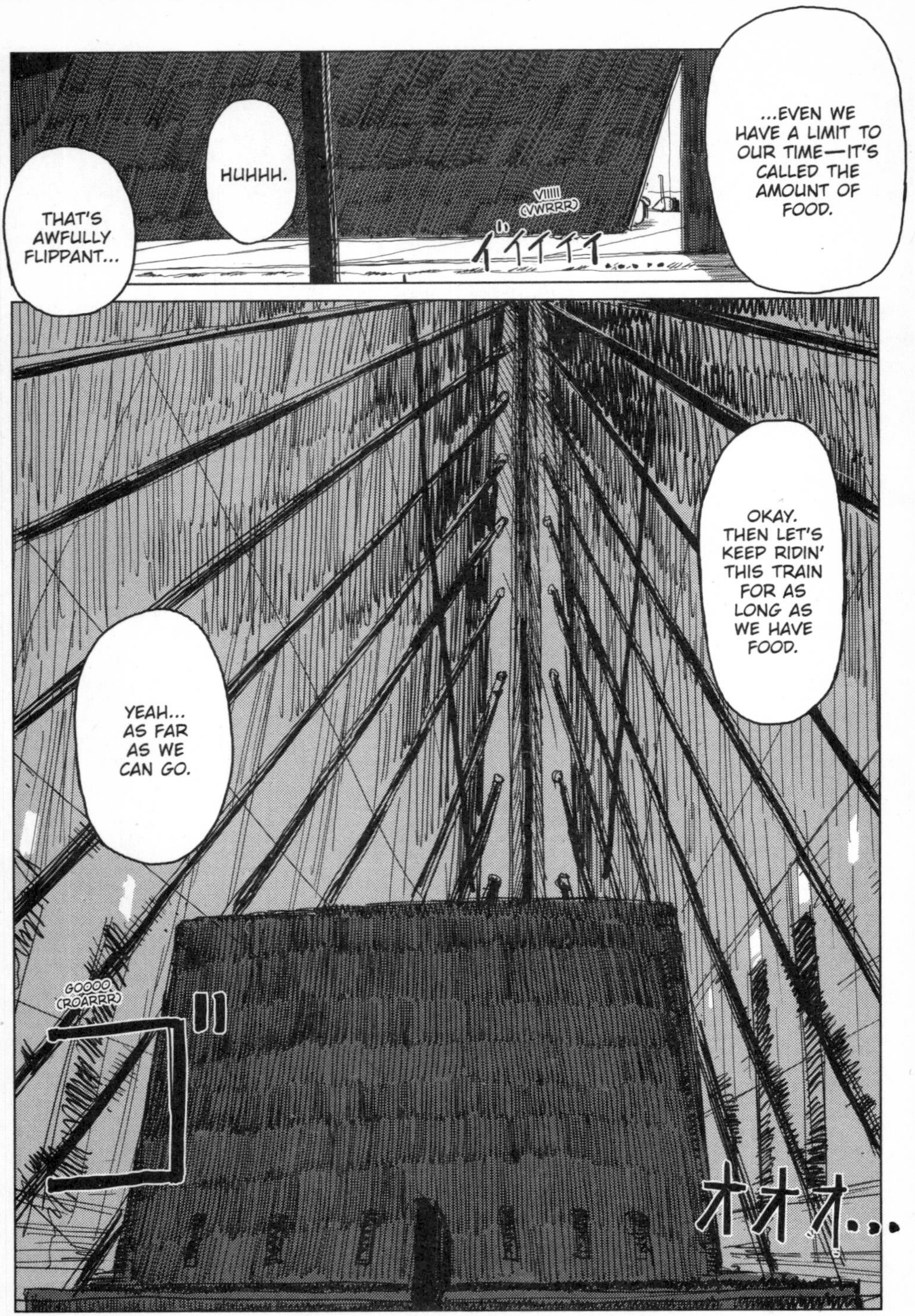

...EVEN WE HAVE A LIMIT TO OUR TIME—IT'S CALLED THE AMOUNT OF FOOD.
VIIII (VWRRR)
イイイイイイ
HUHHH.
THAT'S AWFULLY FLIPPANT...
OKAY. THEN LET'S KEEP RIDIN' THIS TRAIN FOR AS LONG AS WE HAVE FOOD.
YEAH... AS FAR AS WE CAN GO.
GOOOO (ROARRR)
ゴオオオ...

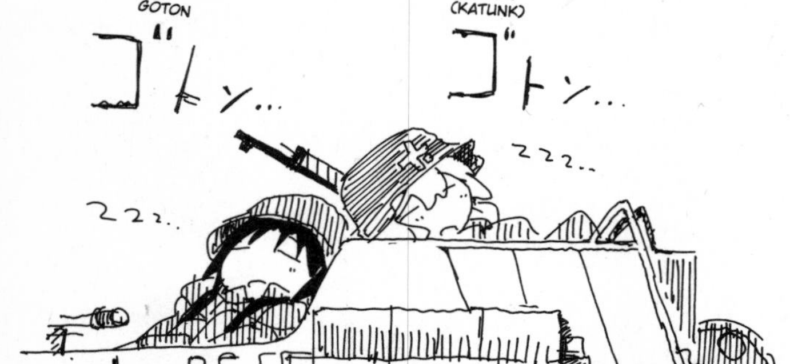
GOTON
(KATUNK)
ゴトン…
GOTON
ゴトン…
Z Z Z..
Z Z Z..

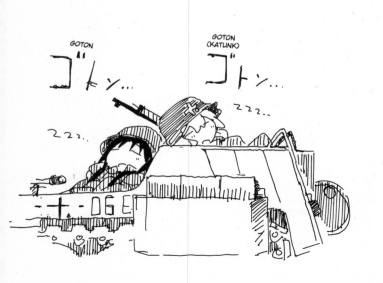

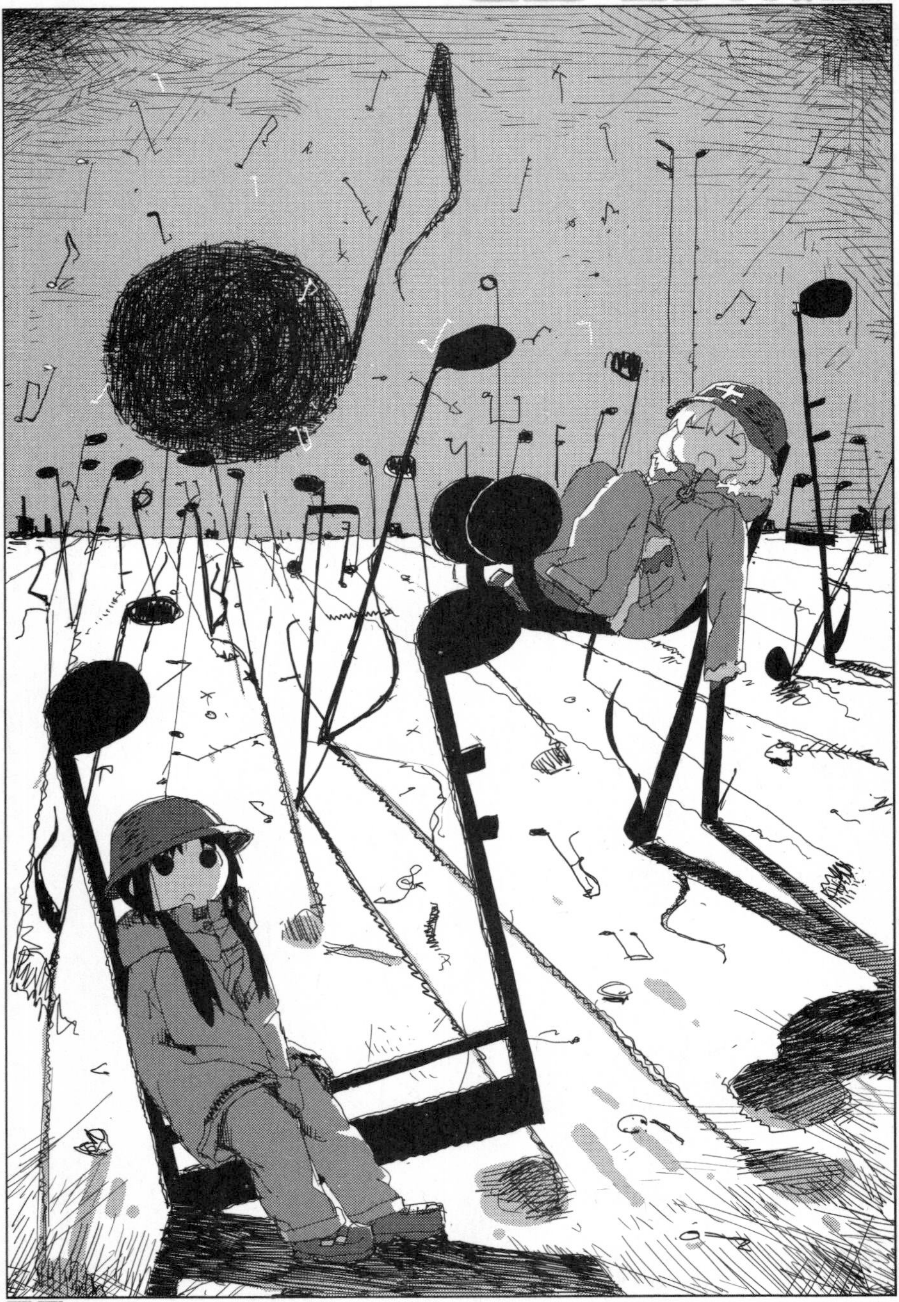

26 WAVELENGTHS

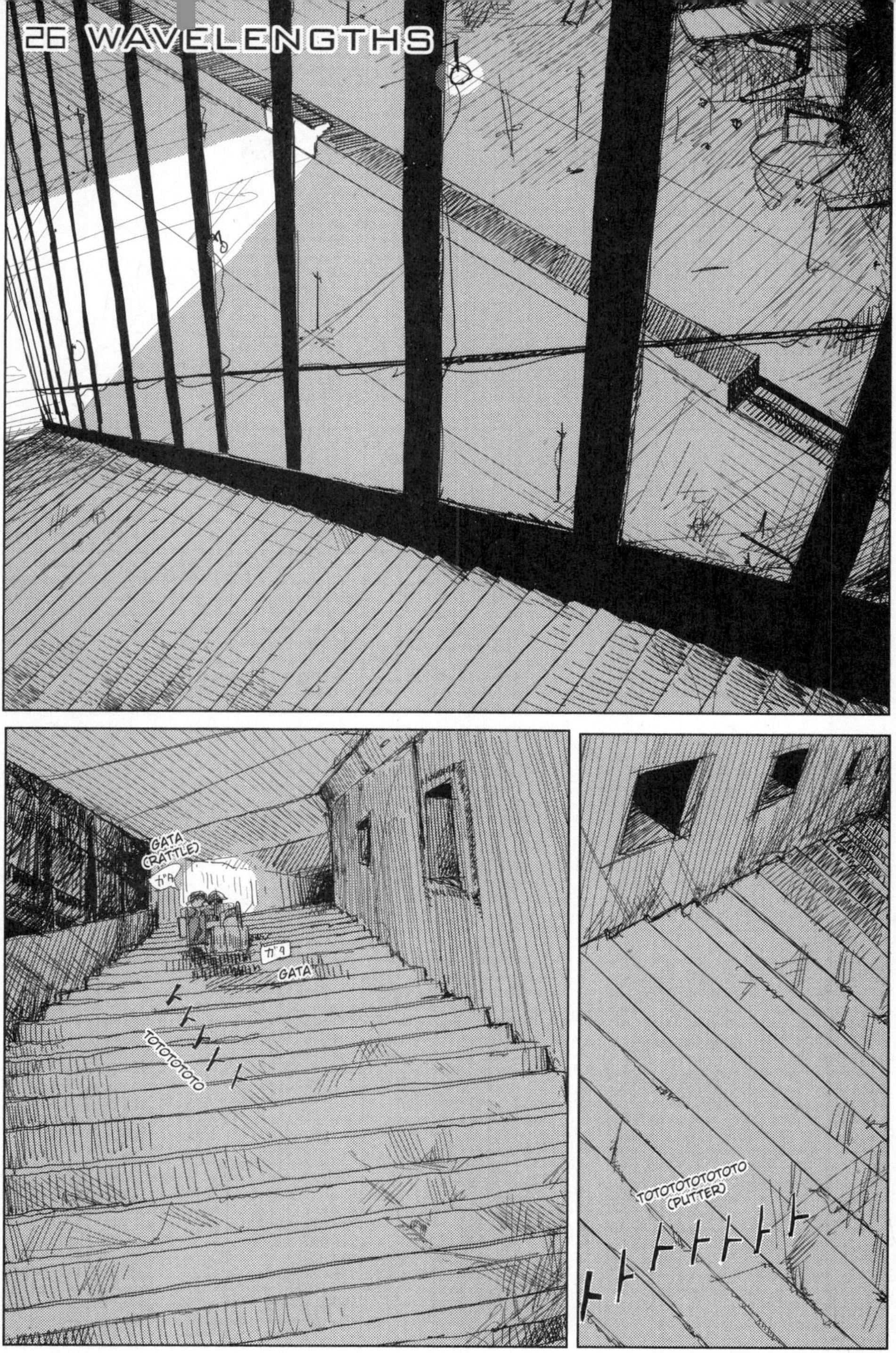
TOTOTOTOTOTOTO (PUTTER)
トトトトトトト
GATA (RATTLE)
ガタ
ガタ
GATA
トトトトト
TOTOTOTOTO

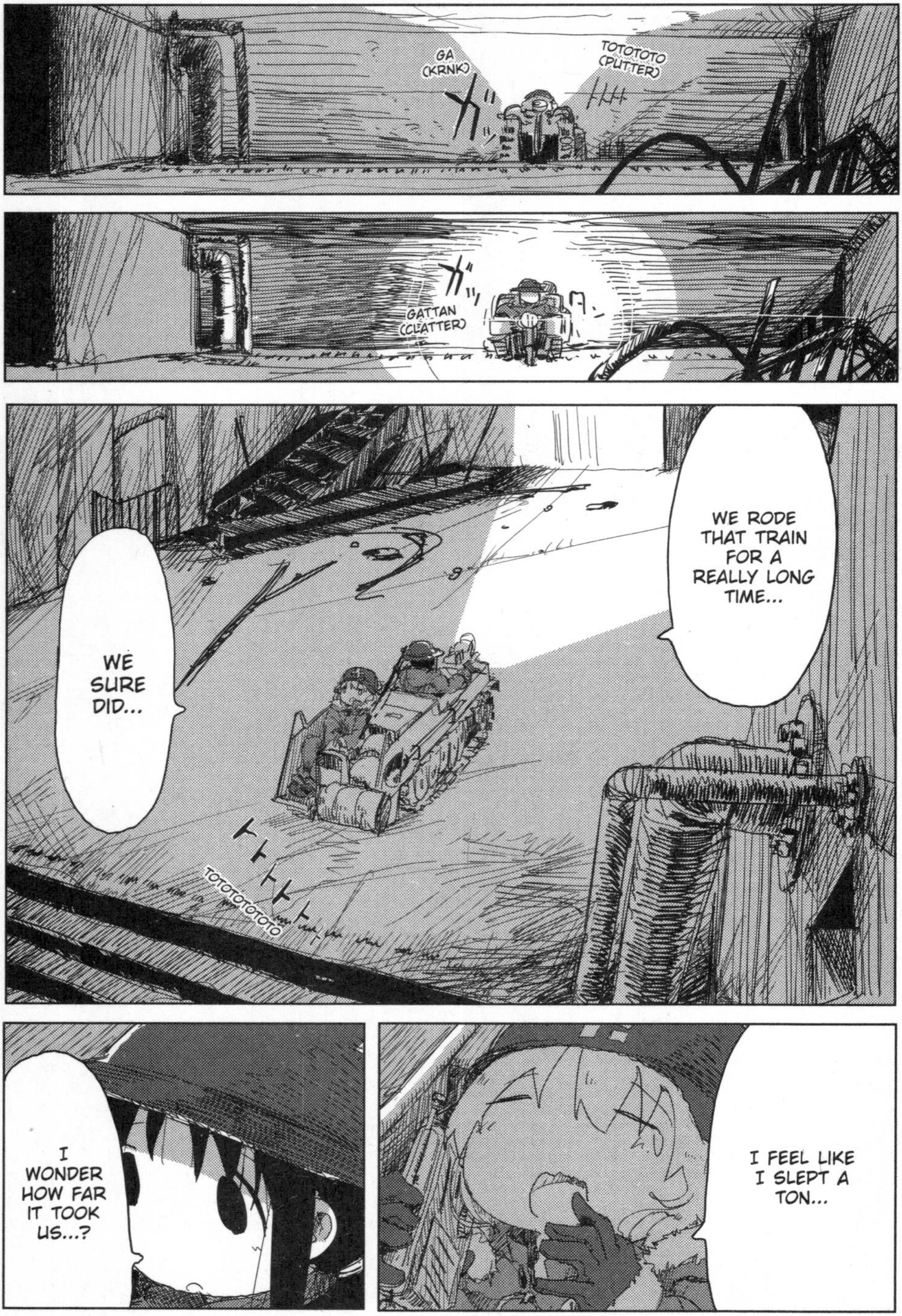
TOTOTOTO (PUTTER)
GA (KRNK)
GATTAN (CLATTER)
WE RODE THAT TRAIN FOR A REALLY LONG TIME...
WE SURE DID...
TOTOTOTOTOTO
I FEEL LIKE I SLEPT A TON...
I WONDER HOW FAR IT TOOK US...?

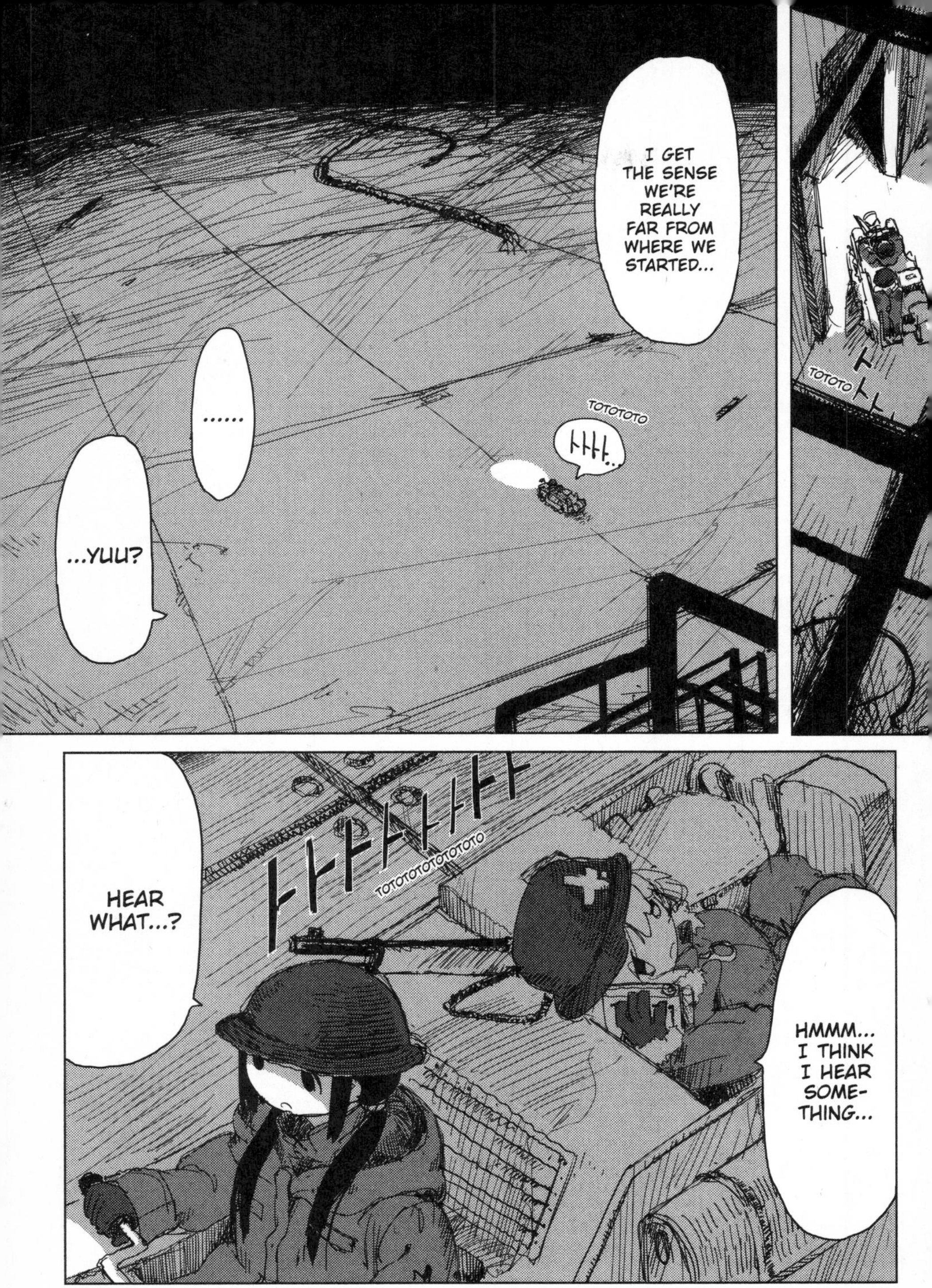
TOTOTO
トトト
I GET THE SENSE WE'RE REALLY FAR FROM WHERE WE STARTED...
TOTOTOTO
トトトト..
......
...YUU?
HMMM... I THINK I HEAR SOME-THING...
トトトトトトト
TOTOTOTOTOTOTOTO
HEAR WHAT...?

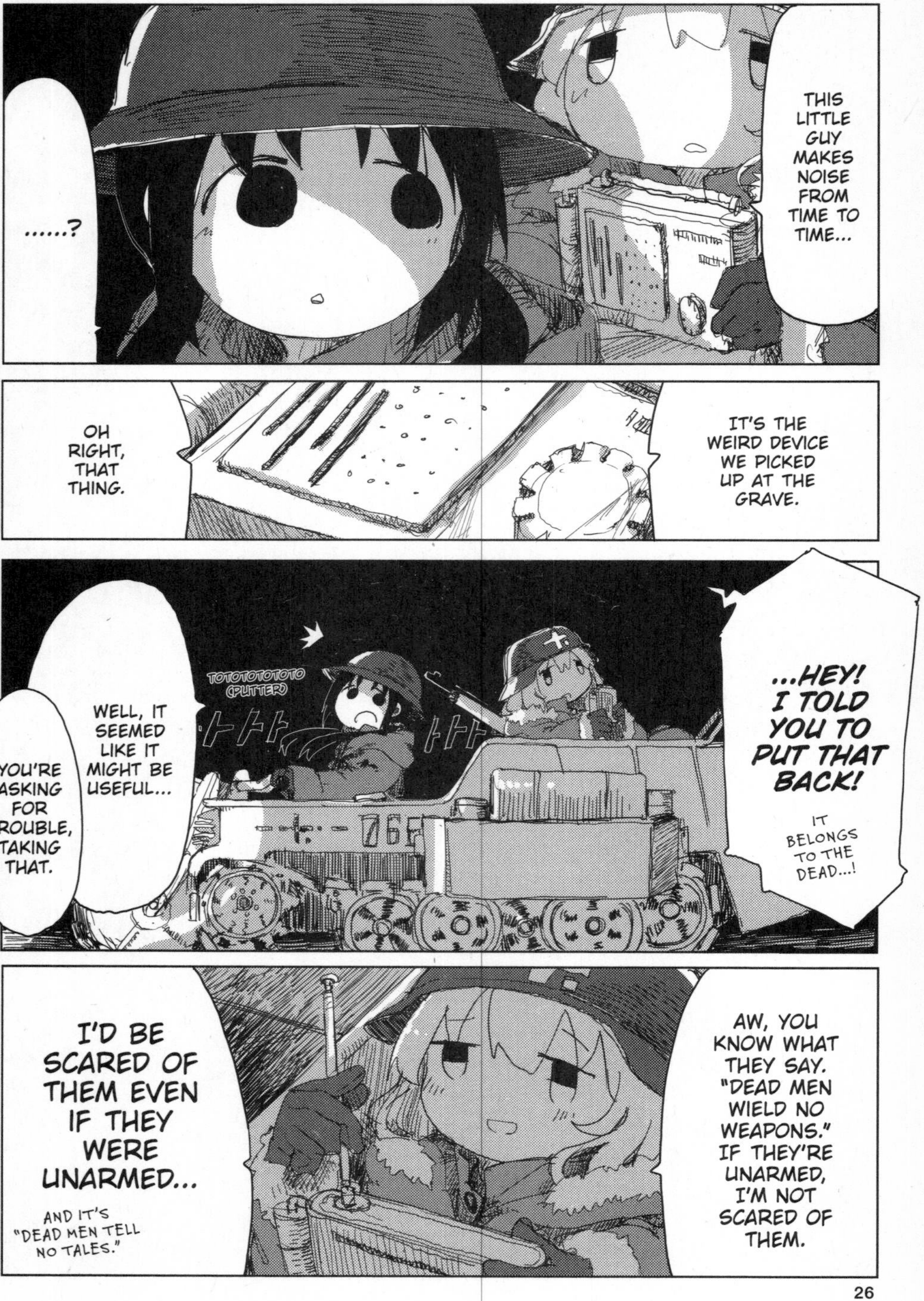
THIS LITTLE GUY MAKES NOISE FROM TIME TO TIME...
......?
IT'S THE WEIRD DEVICE WE PICKED UP AT THE GRAVE.
OH RIGHT, THAT THING.
...HEY! I TOLD YOU TO PUT THAT BACK!
IT BELONGS TO THE DEAD...!
TOTOTOTOTOTO (PUTTER)
WELL, IT SEEMED LIKE IT MIGHT BE USEFUL...
YOU'RE ASKING FOR TROUBLE, TAKING THAT.
AW, YOU KNOW WHAT THEY SAY. "DEAD MEN WIELD NO WEAPONS." IF THEY'RE UNARMED, I'M NOT SCARED OF THEM.
I'D BE SCARED OF THEM EVEN IF THEY WERE UNARMED...
AND IT'S "DEAD MEN TELL NO TALES."

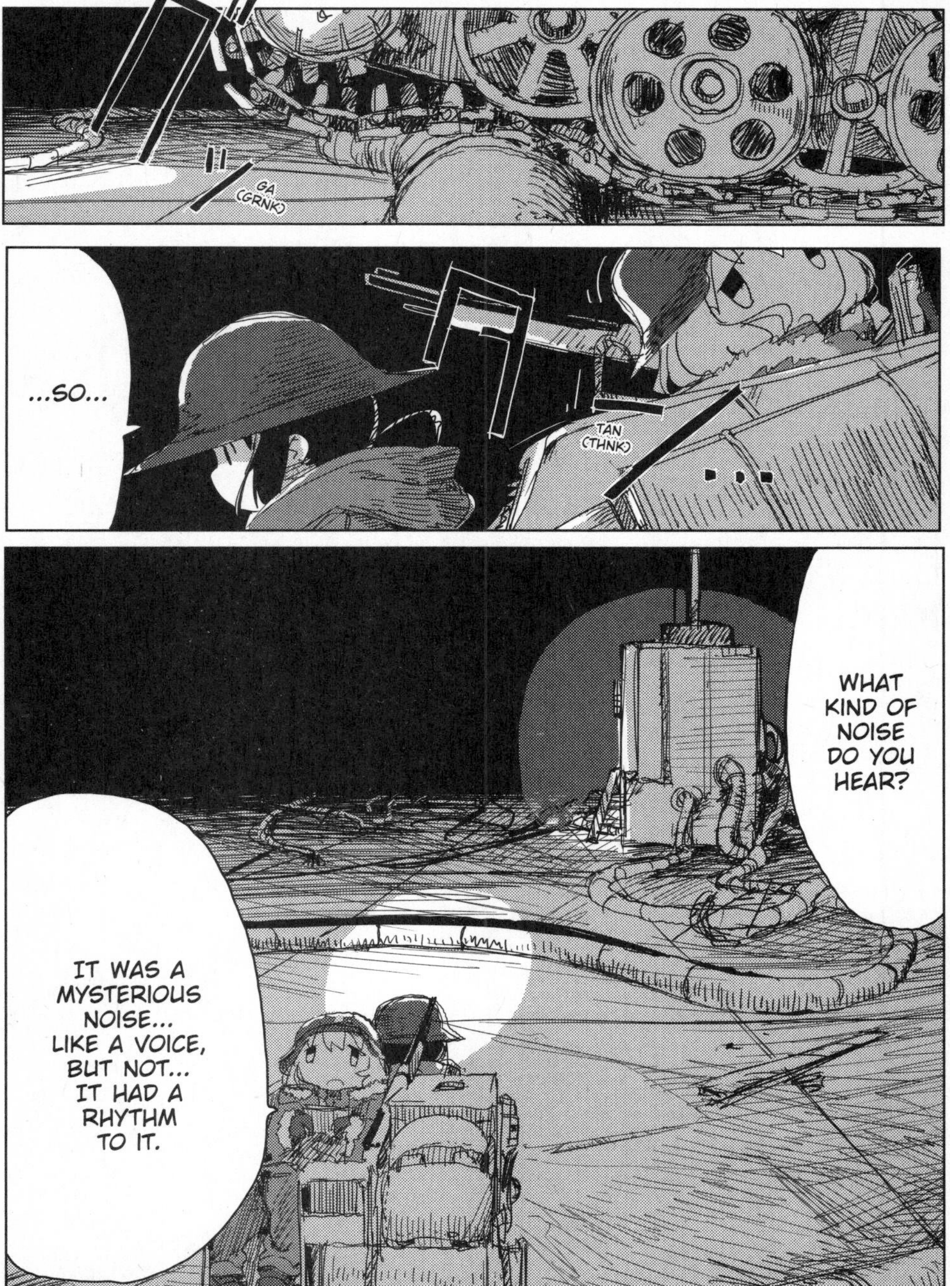
GA (GRNK)
TAN (THNK)
...SO...
WHAT KIND OF NOISE DO YOU HEAR?
IT WAS A MYSTERIOUS NOISE... LIKE A VOICE, BUT NOT... IT HAD A RHYTHM TO IT.
TOTOTOTOTO

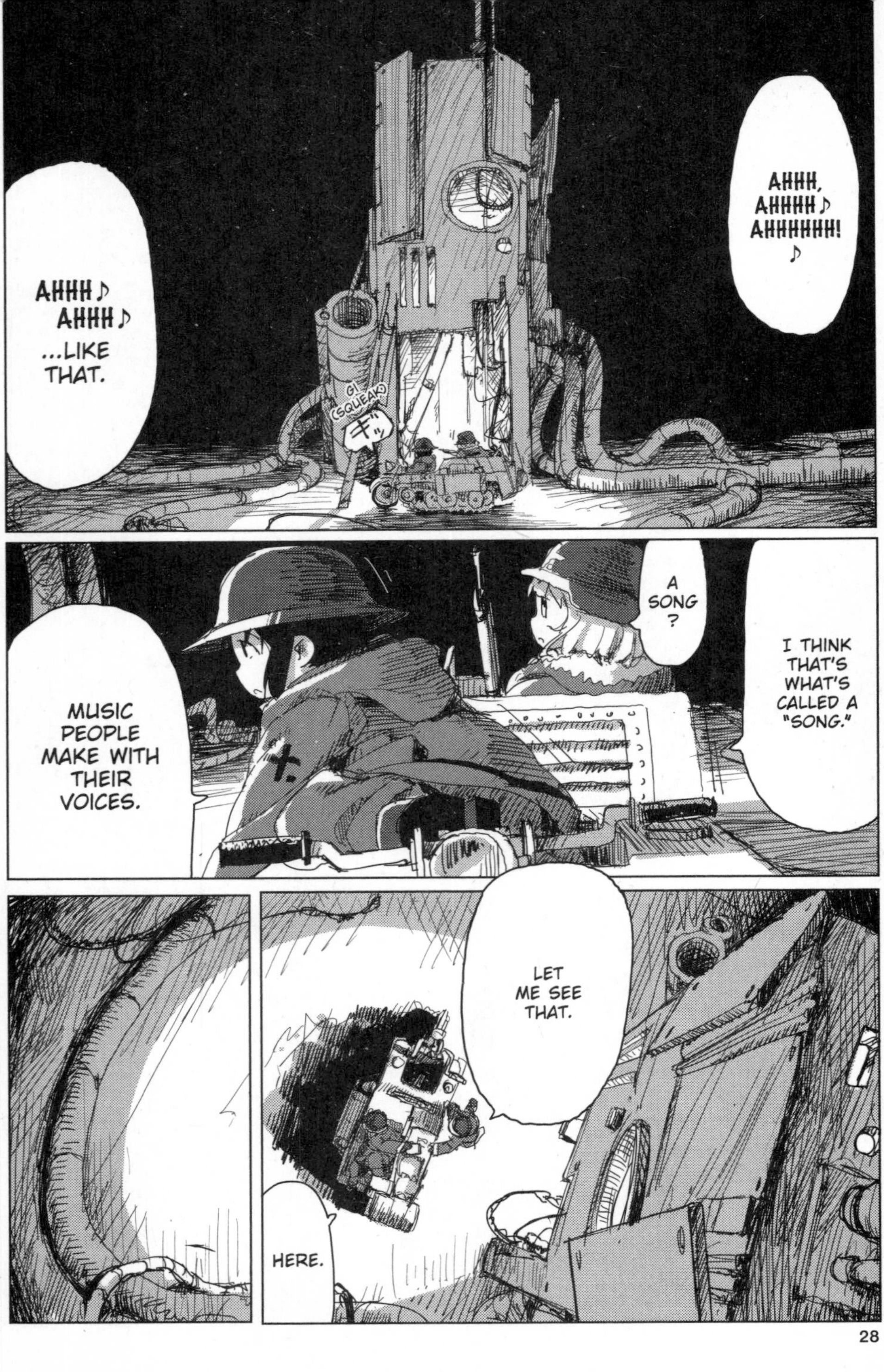
AHHH, AHHHH♪ AHHHHHH! ♪
AHHH♪ AHHH♪ ...LIKE THAT.
GI (SQUEAK)
ギッ
I THINK THAT'S WHAT'S CALLED A "SONG."
A SONG ?
MUSIC PEOPLE MAKE WITH THEIR VOICES.
LET ME SEE THAT.
HERE.

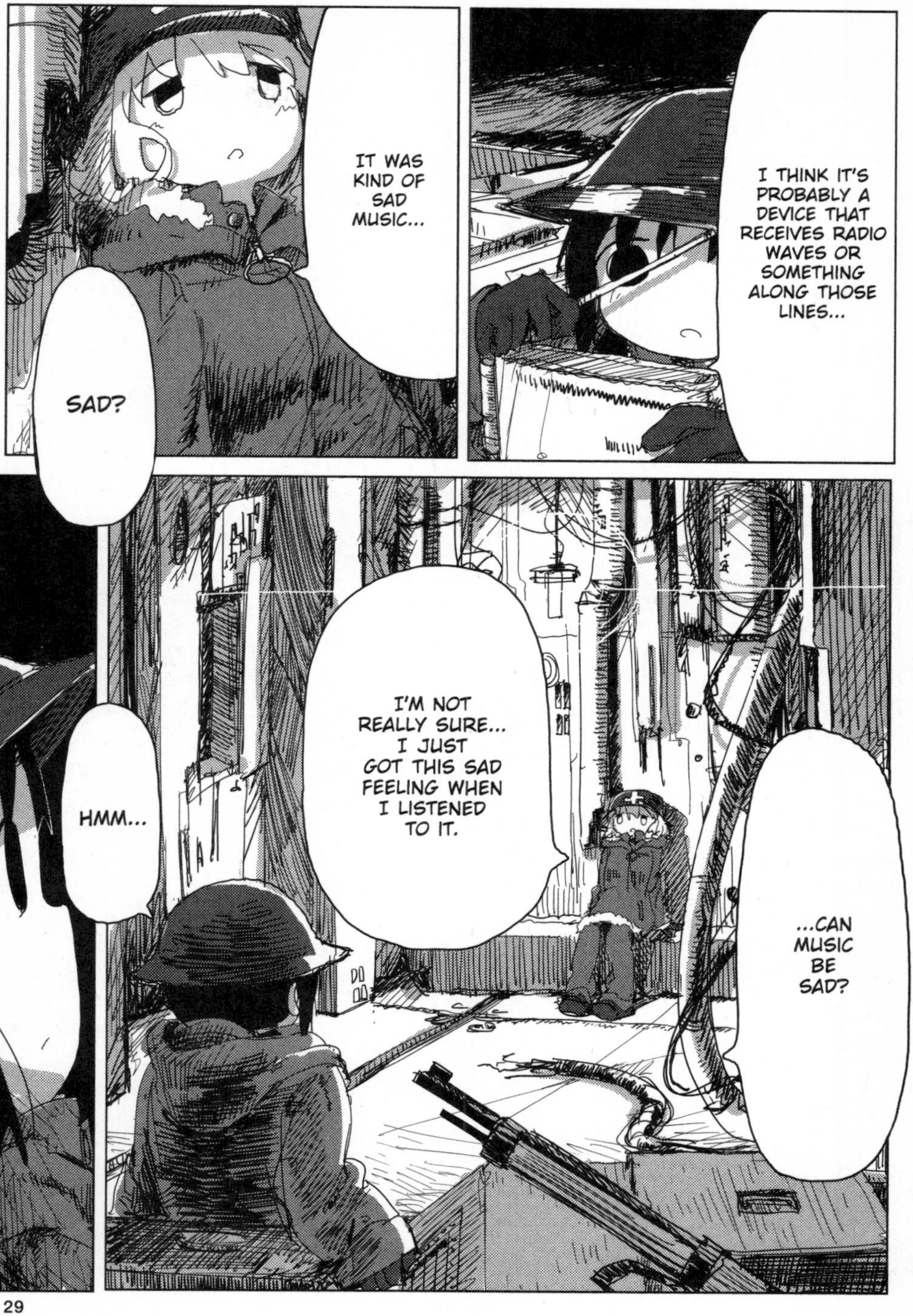

I THINK IT'S PROBABLY A DEVICE THAT RECEIVES RADIO WAVES OR SOMETHING ALONG THOSE LINES...
IT WAS KIND OF SAD MUSIC...
SAD?
...CAN MUSIC BE SAD?
I'M NOT REALLY SURE... I JUST GOT THIS SAD FEELING WHEN I LISTENED TO IT.
HMM...

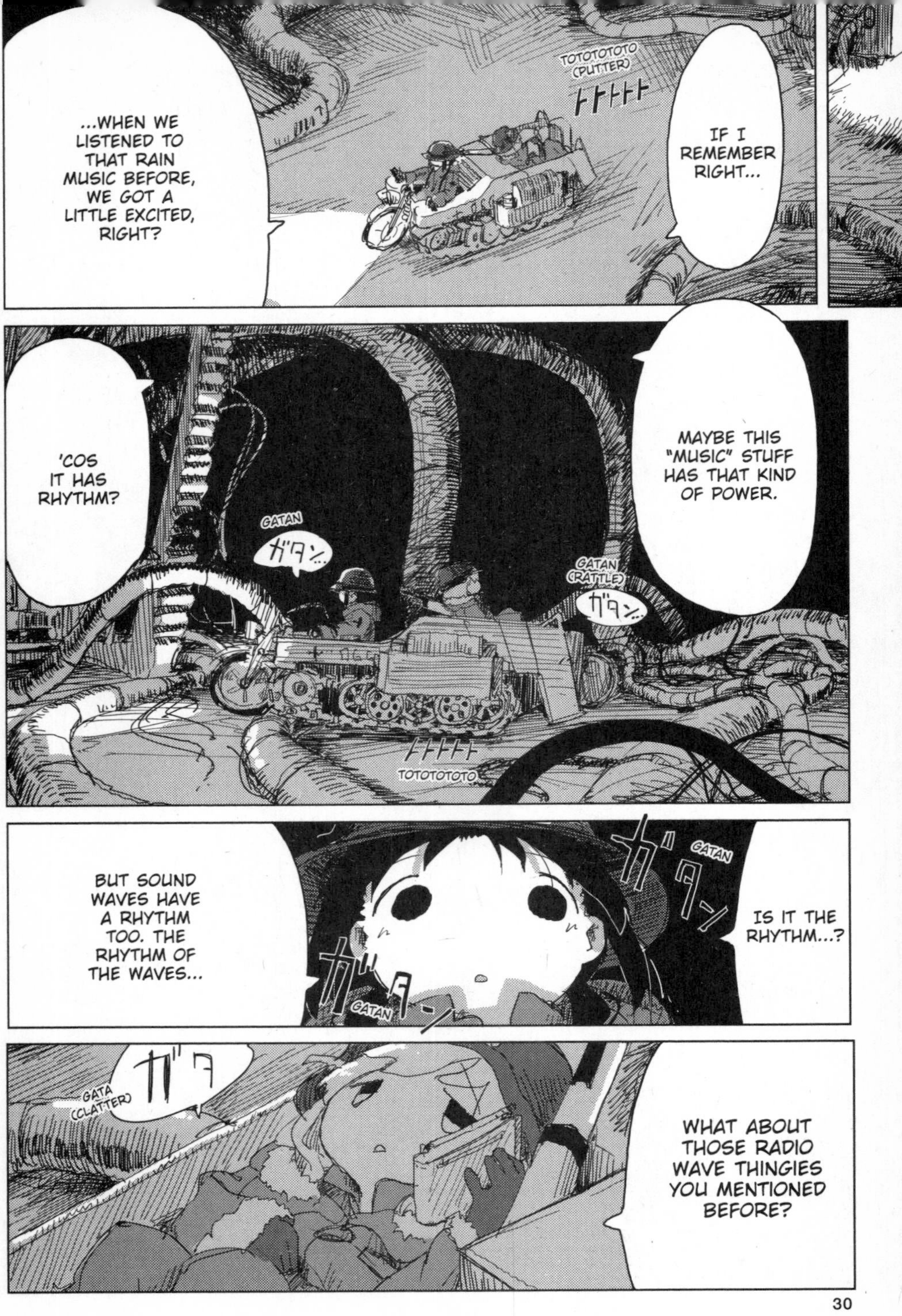
IF I REMEMBER RIGHT...
TOTOTOTOTO (PUTTER)
トトトトト
...WHEN WE LISTENED TO THAT RAIN MUSIC BEFORE, WE GOT A LITTLE EXCITED, RIGHT?
MAYBE THIS "MUSIC" STUFF HAS THAT KIND OF POWER.
GATAN (RATTLE)
ガタン…
GATAN
ガタン…
トトトトト
TOTOTOTOTO
'COS IT HAS RHYTHM?
IS IT THE RHYTHM...?
GATAN
ガタン
GATAN
ガタン
BUT SOUND WAVES HAVE A RHYTHM TOO. THE RHYTHM OF THE WAVES...
WHAT ABOUT THOSE RADIO WAVE THINGIES YOU MENTIONED BEFORE?
GATA (CLATTER)
ガタ

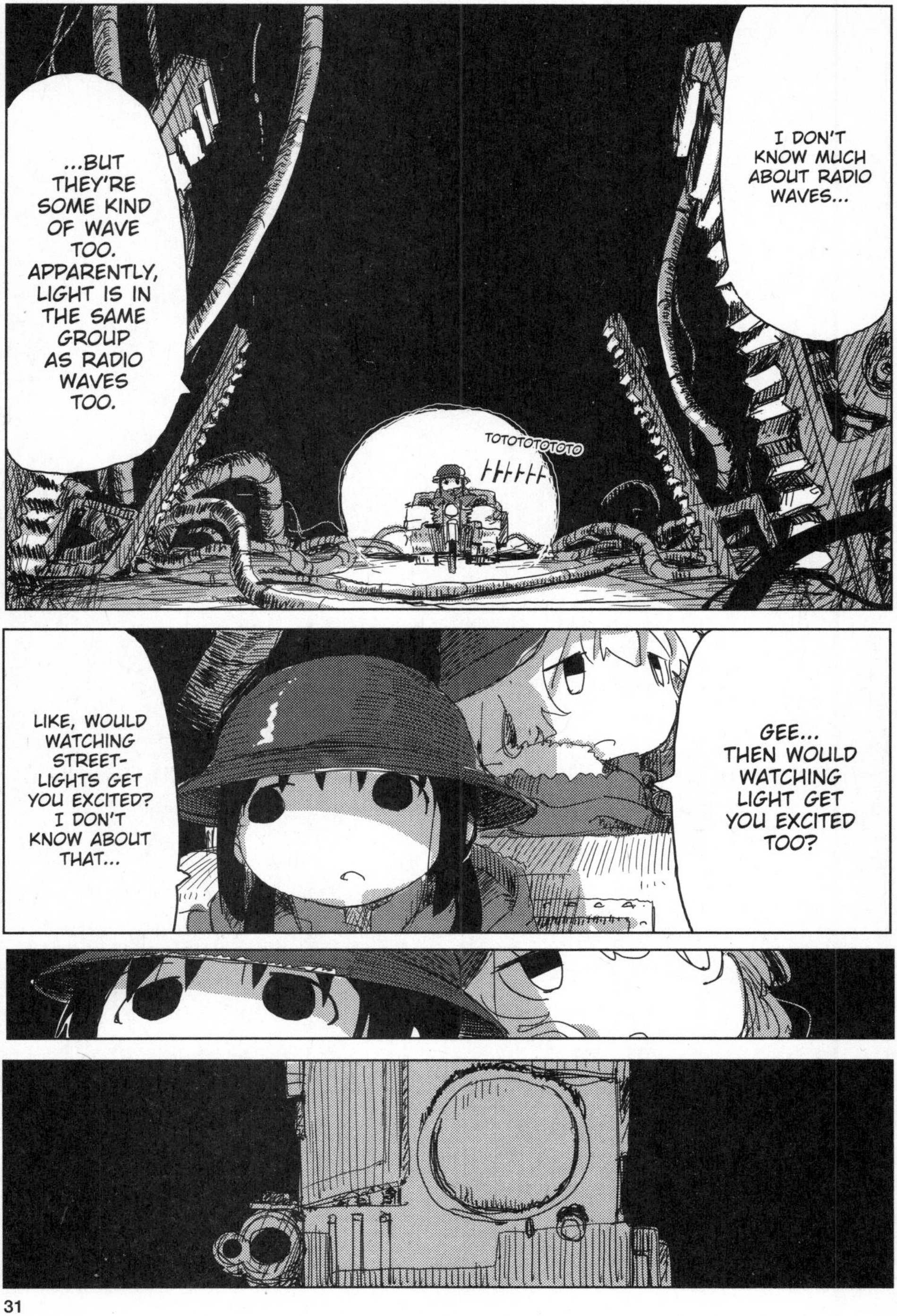
I DON'T KNOW MUCH ABOUT RADIO WAVES...
...BUT THEY'RE SOME KIND OF WAVE TOO. APPARENTLY, LIGHT IS IN THE SAME GROUP AS RADIO WAVES TOO.
TOTOTOTOTOTO
GEE... THEN WOULD WATCHING LIGHT GET YOU EXCITED TOO?
LIKE, WOULD WATCHING STREET-LIGHTS GET YOU EXCITED? I DON'T KNOW ABOUT THAT...

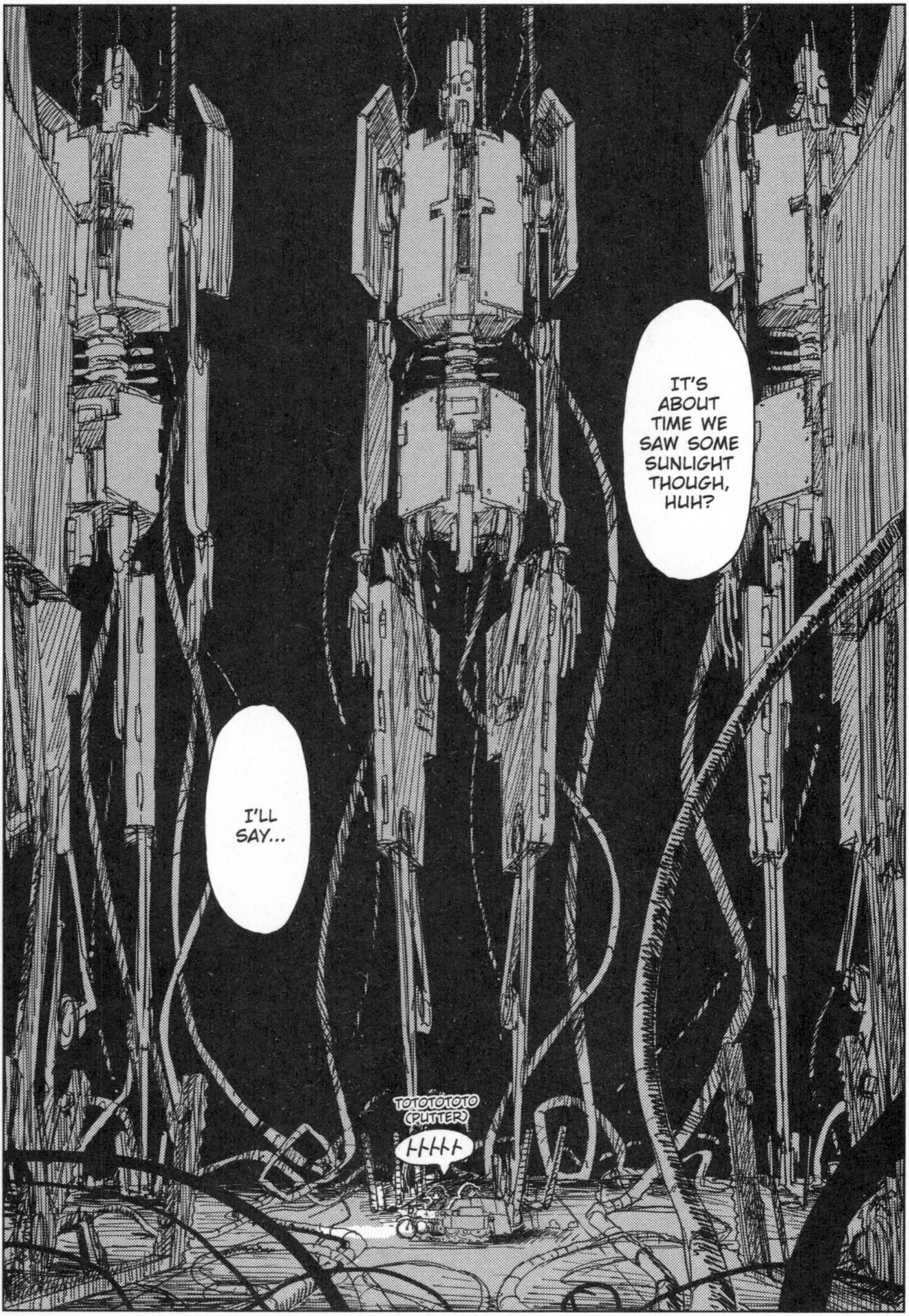
IT'S ABOUT TIME WE SAW SOME SUNLIGHT THOUGH, HUH?
I'LL SAY...
TOTOTOTOTO (PUTTER)
トトトトト

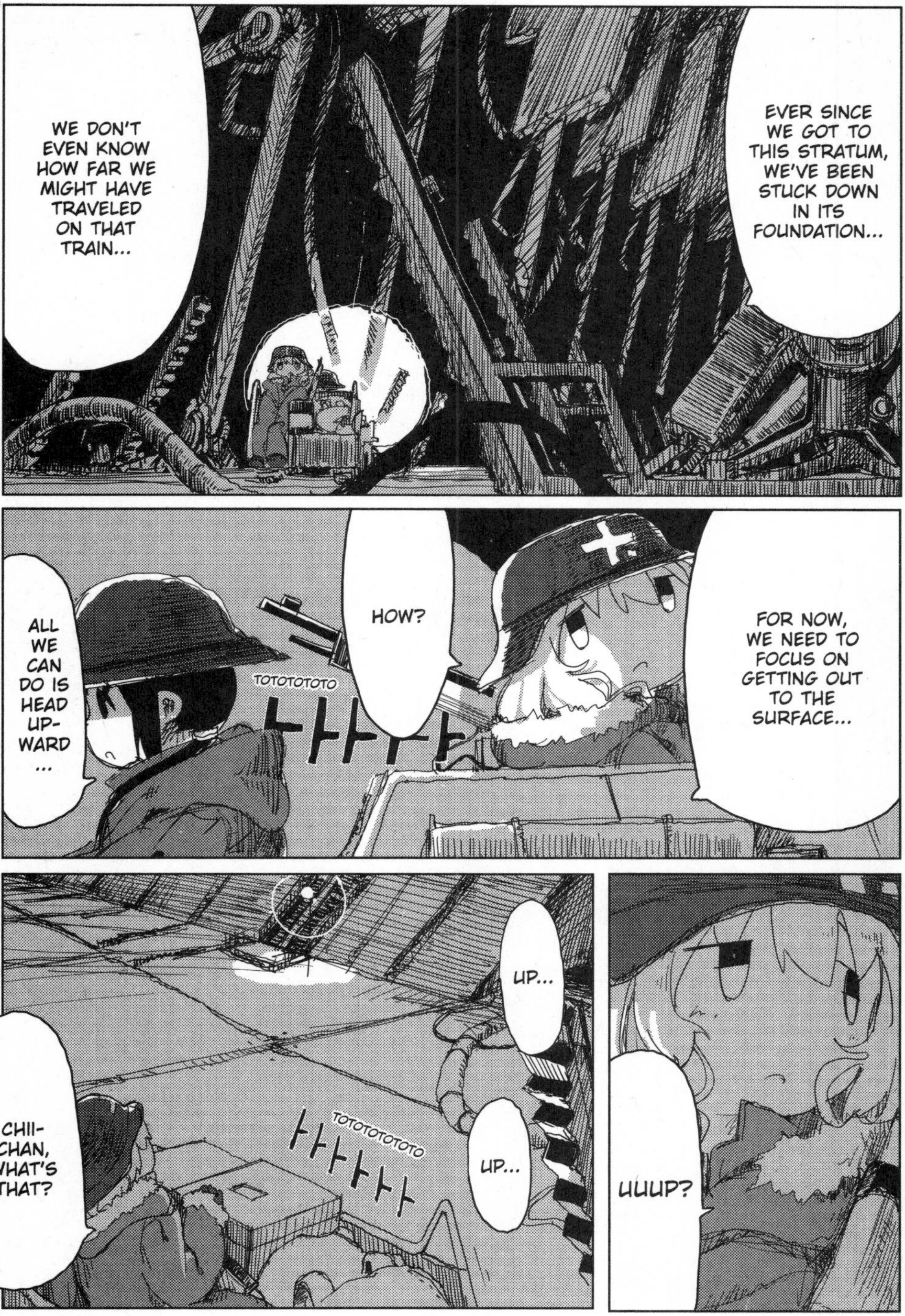
EVER SINCE WE GOT TO THIS STRATUM, WE'VE BEEN STUCK DOWN IN ITS FOUNDATION...
WE DON'T EVEN KNOW HOW FAR WE MIGHT HAVE TRAVELED ON THAT TRAIN...
FOR NOW, WE NEED TO FOCUS ON GETTING OUT TO THE SURFACE...
HOW?
TOTOTOTOTO
ALL WE CAN DO IS HEAD UP-WARD...
UUUP?
UP...
UP...
TOTOTOTOTOTO
CHII-CHAN, WHAT'S THAT?

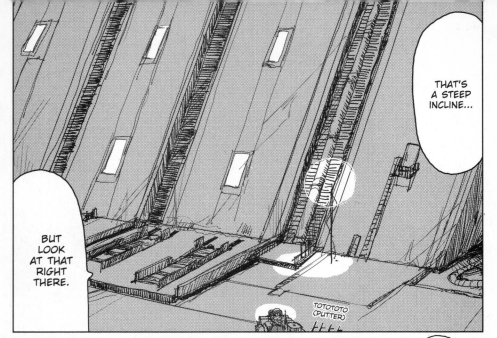

THAT'S A STEEP INCLINE...
BUT LOOK AT THAT RIGHT THERE.
TOTOTOTO (PUTTER)
DOESN'T IT LOOK LIKE A LIFT TO YOU?
WILL IT EVEN WORK ...?
THERE'S A SWITCH-LOOKING THINGIE HERE...
GATTA (CLUNK)
MAYBE THIS?

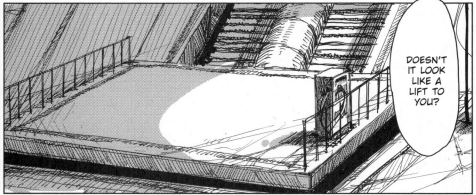

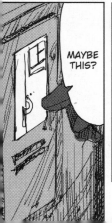

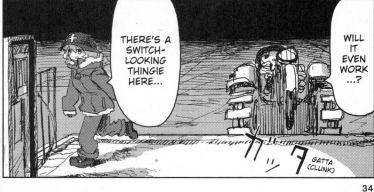

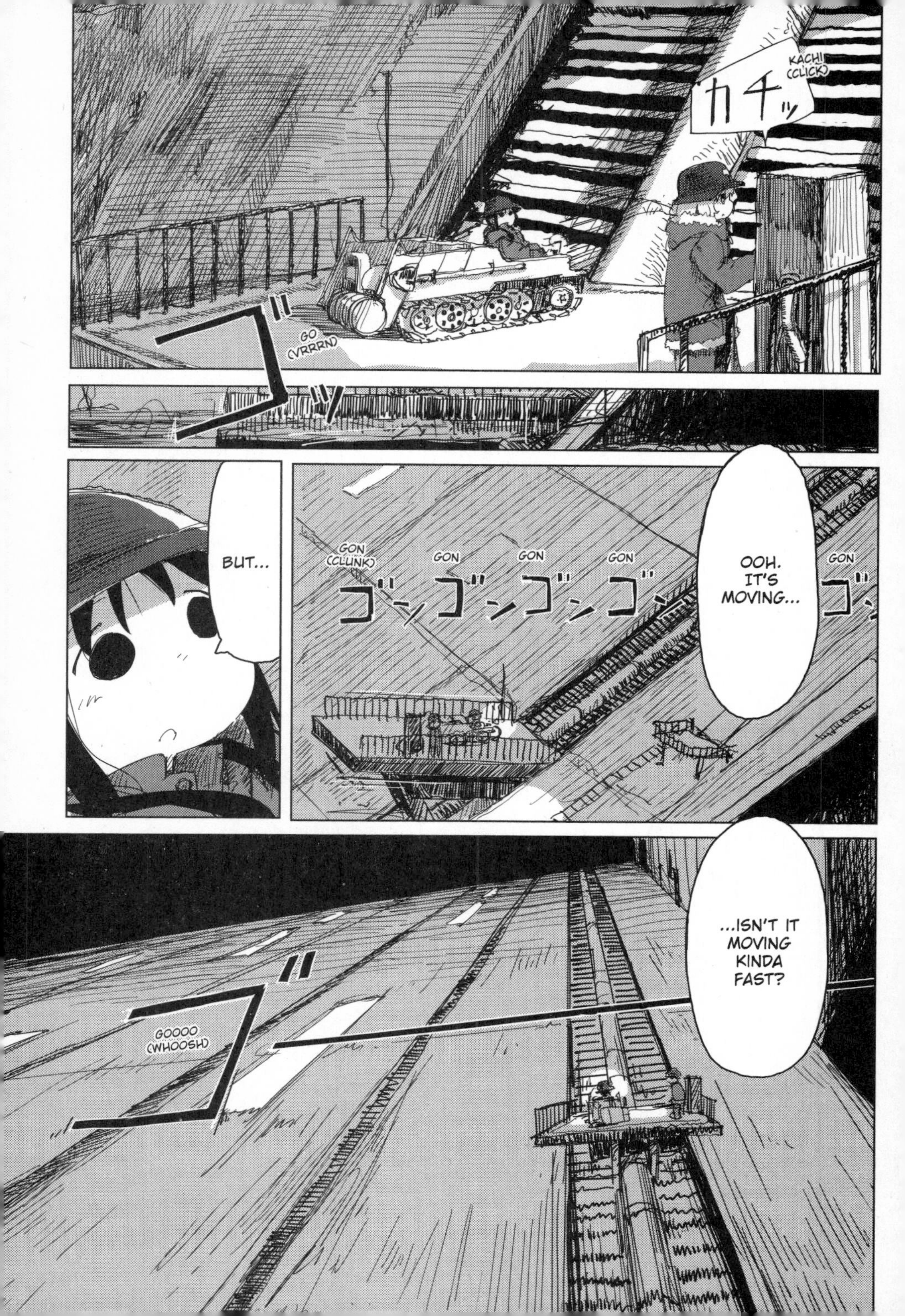
KACHI (CLICK)
カチッ
GO (VRRRN)
GON
OOH. IT'S MOVING...
GON
GON
GON
GON (CLUNK)
BUT...
...ISN'T IT MOVING KINDA FAST?
GOOOO (WHOOSH)

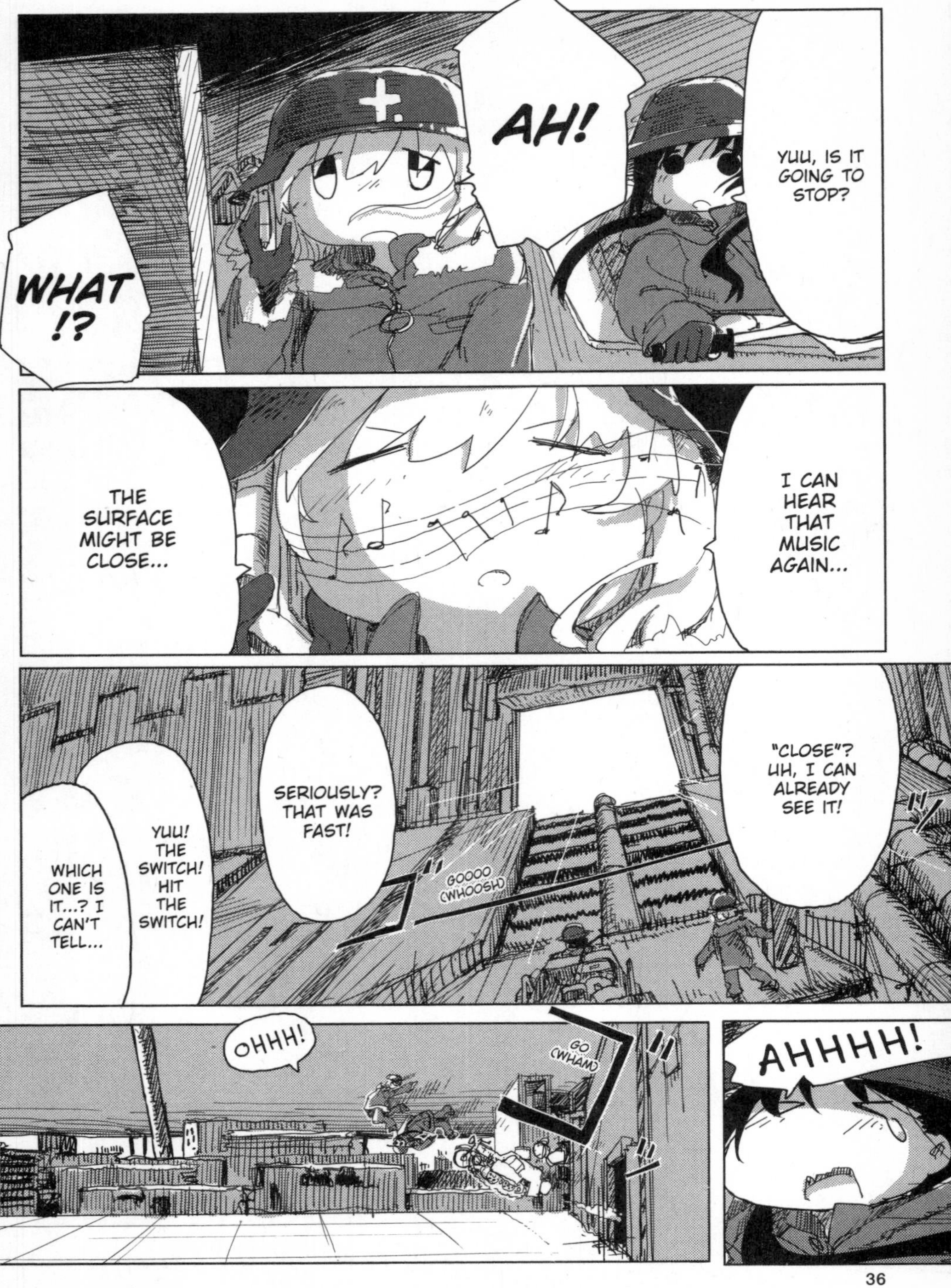
YUU, IS IT GOING TO STOP?
AH!
WHAT!?
I CAN HEAR THAT MUSIC AGAIN...
THE SURFACE MIGHT BE CLOSE...
"CLOSE"? UH, I CAN ALREADY SEE IT!
SERIOUSLY? THAT WAS FAST!
GOOOO (WHOOSH)
YUU! THE SWITCH! HIT THE SWITCH!
WHICH ONE IS IT...? I CAN'T TELL...
AHHHH!
GO (WHAM)
OHHH!

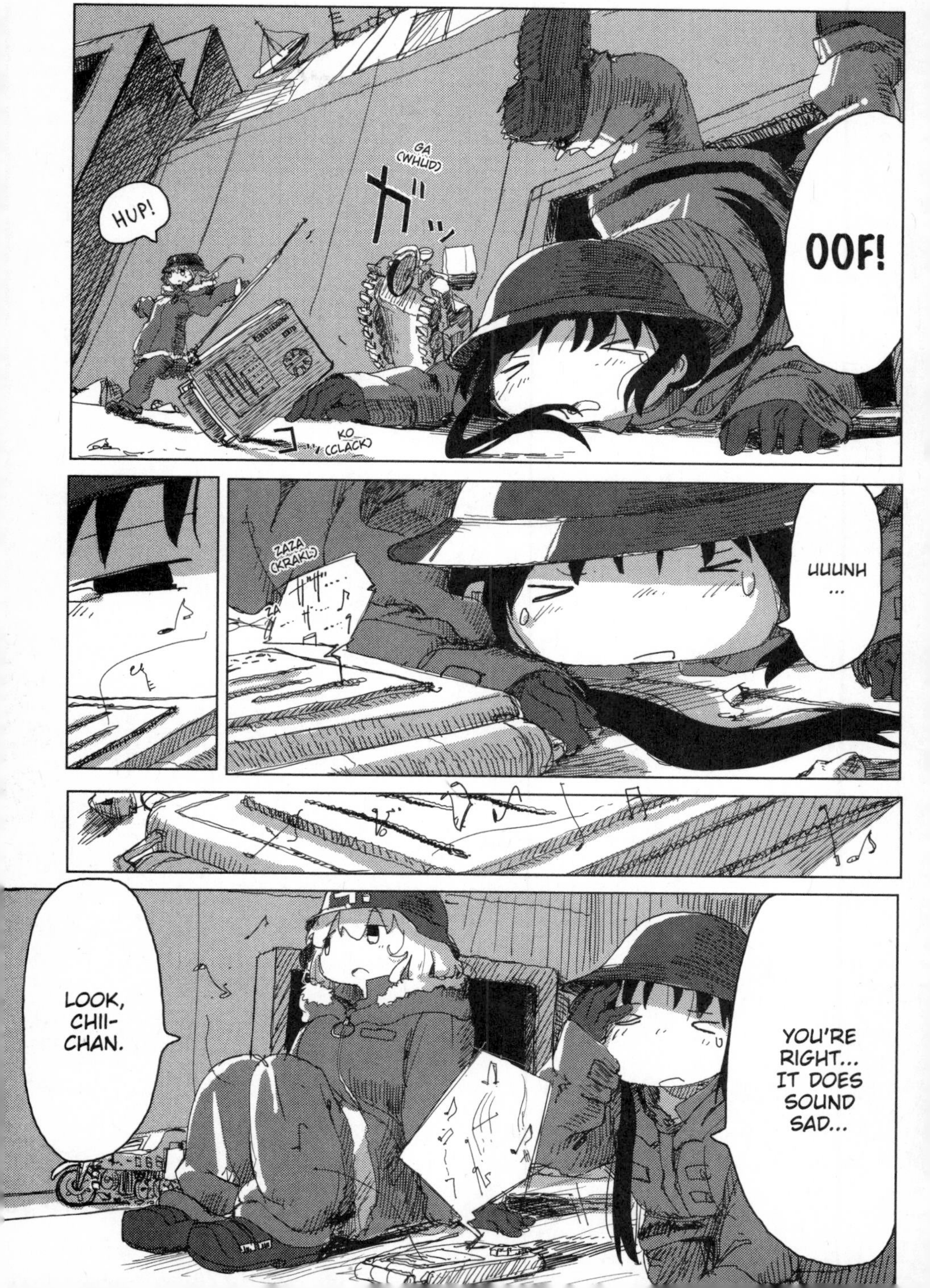
OOF!
GA (WHUD)
ガッ
HUP!
KO (CLACK)
UUUNH ...
ZAZA (KRAKL)
ZA
YOU'RE RIGHT... IT DOES SOUND SAD...
LOOK, CHII-CHAN.

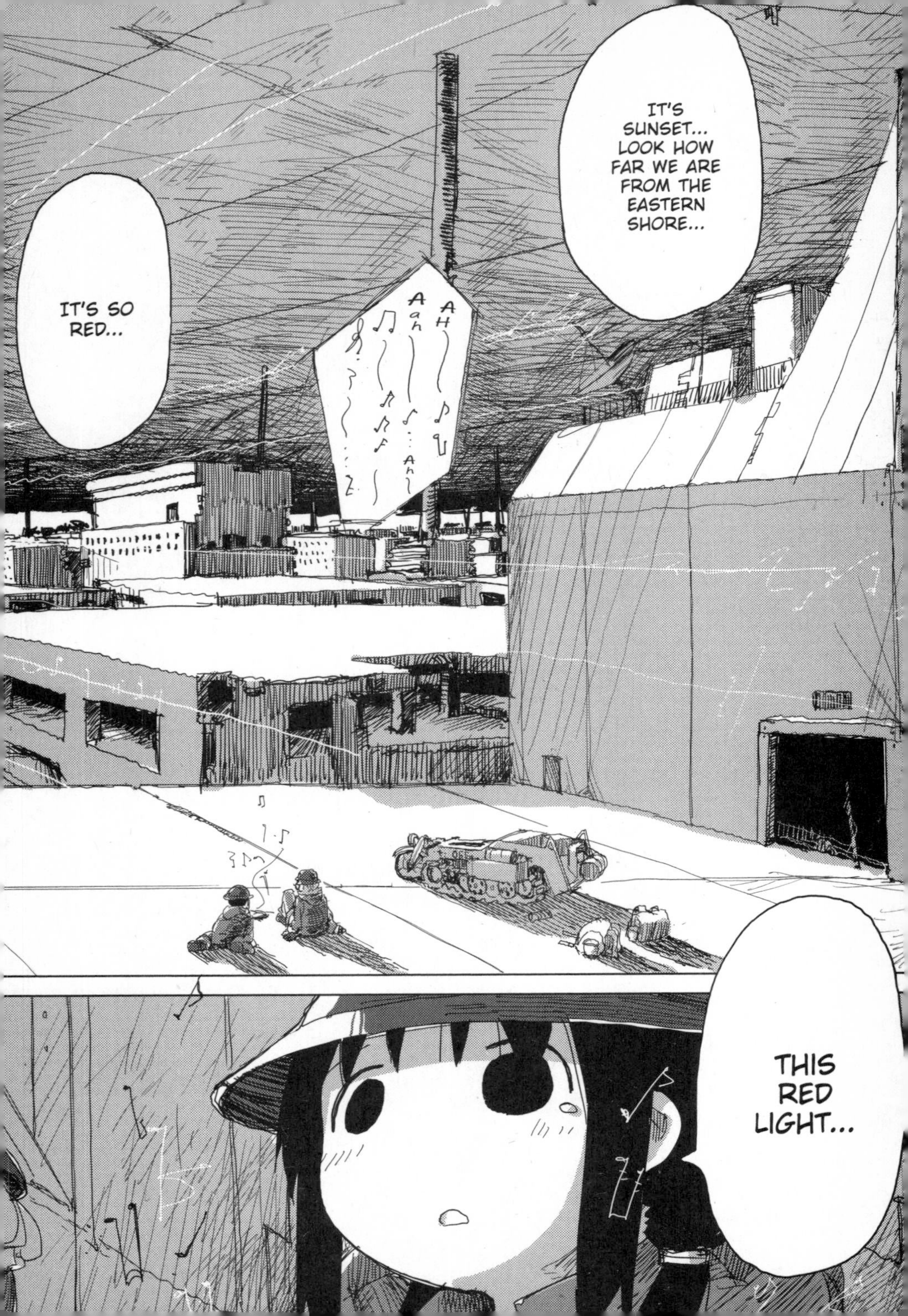
IT'S SUNSET... LOOK HOW FAR WE ARE FROM THE EASTERN SHORE...
IT'S SO RED...
THIS RED LIGHT...

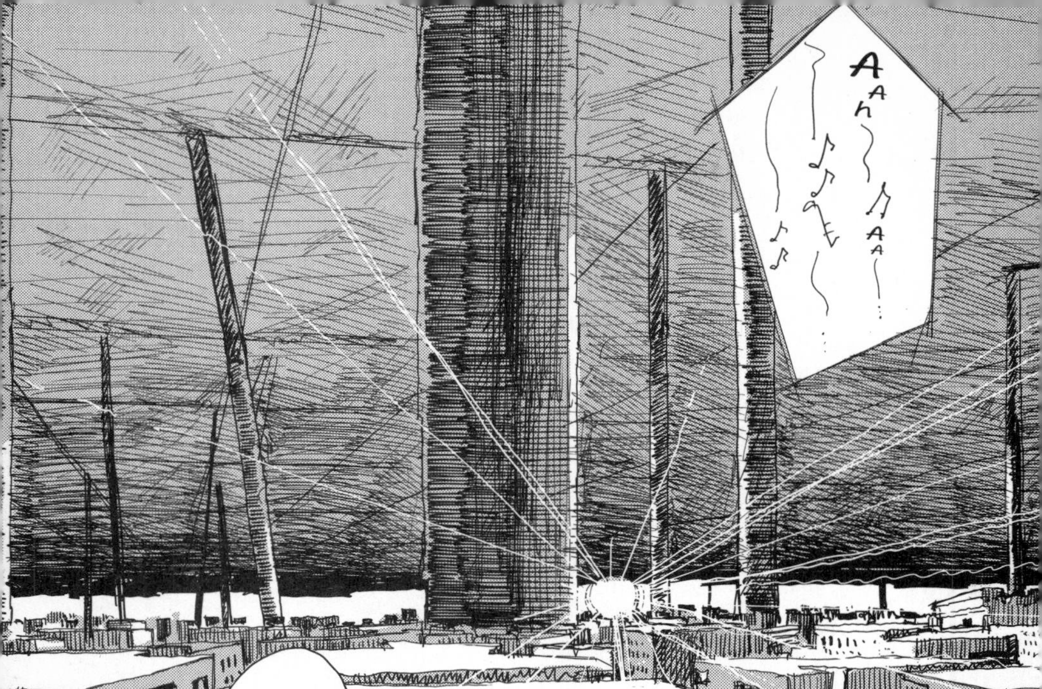
AAh~ ♪ AAA—…
IT SURE IS...
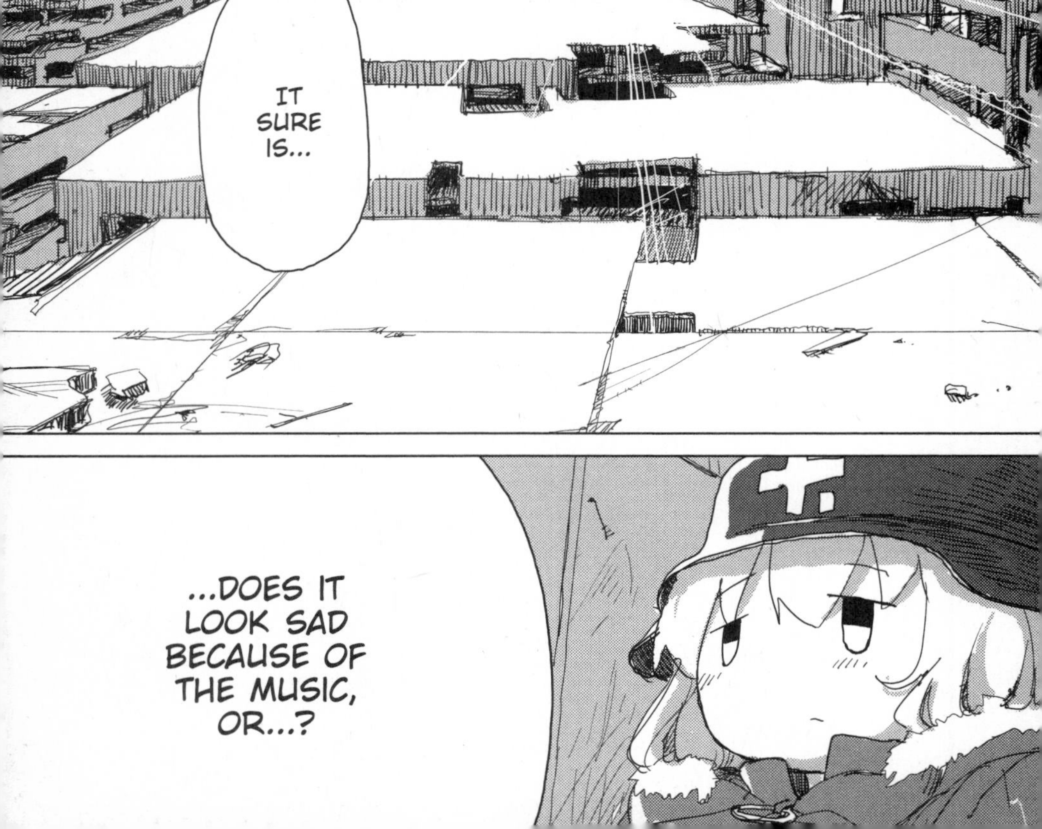
...DOES IT LOOK SAD BECAUSE OF THE MUSIC, OR...?

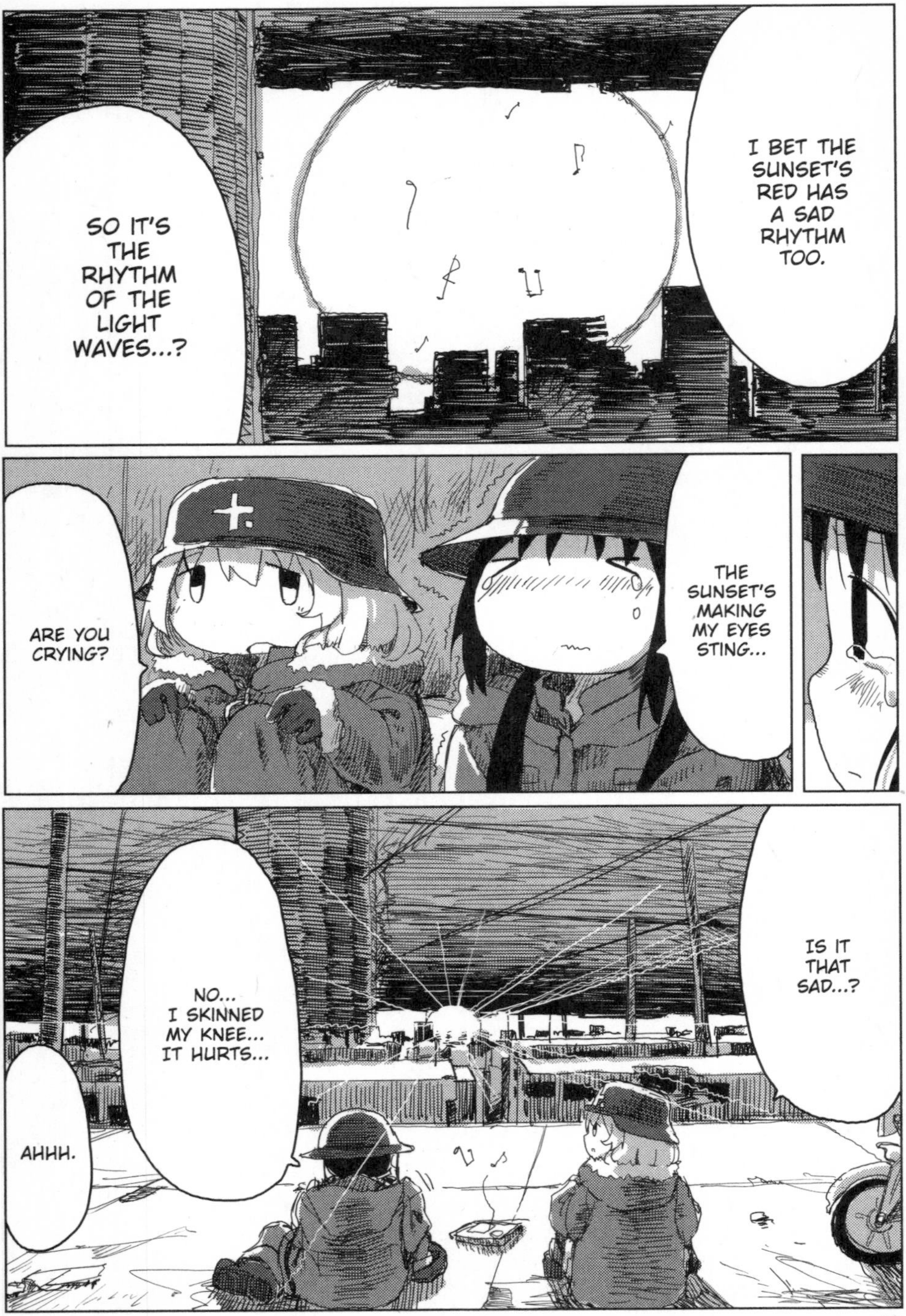
I BET THE SUNSET'S RED HAS A SAD RHYTHM TOO.
SO IT'S THE RHYTHM OF THE LIGHT WAVES...?
THE SUNSET'S MAKING MY EYES STING...
ARE YOU CRYING?
IS IT THAT SAD...?
NO... I SKINNED MY KNEE... IT HURTS...
AHHH.

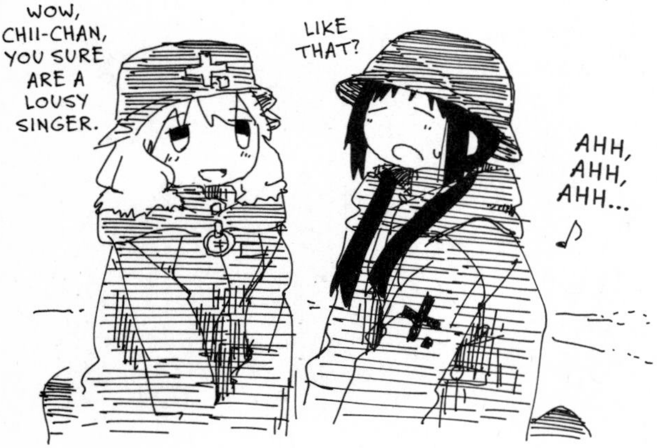
AHH, AHH, AHH... ♪
WOW, CHII-CHAN, YOU SURE ARE A LOUSY SINGER.
LIKE THAT?

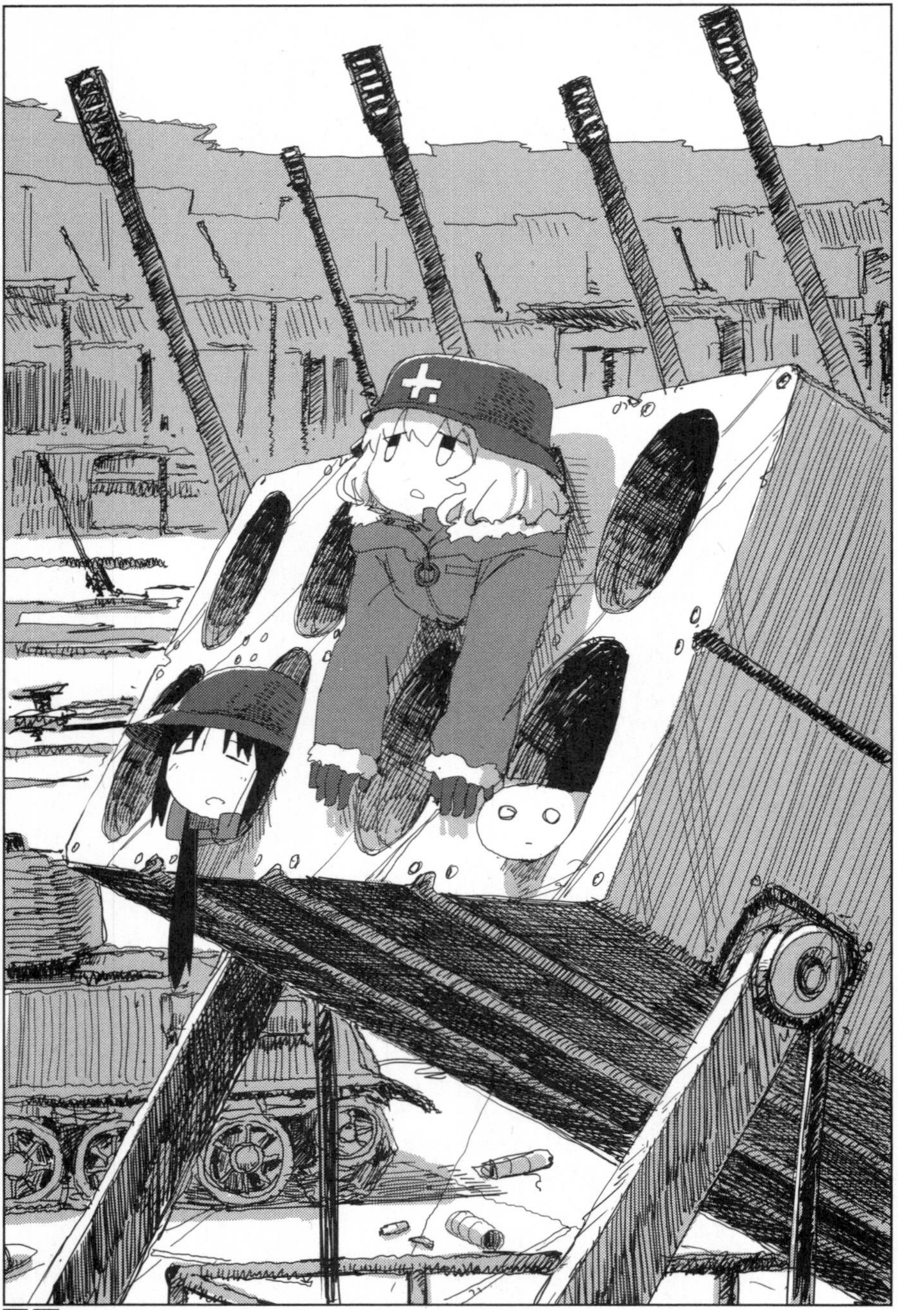

27 CAPTURE

...A NICE VIEW...
...AND NICE MUSIC.
AS FOR THE WEATHER...
NNNN (HUMMM)
NN
...DUNNO HOW THAT IS, BUT STILL...
SHORI (SLICE)
SHORI

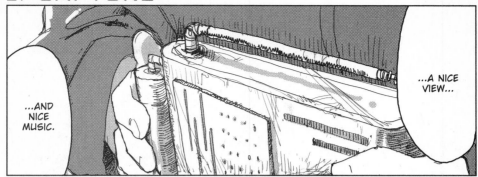

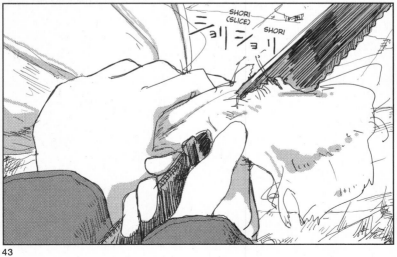

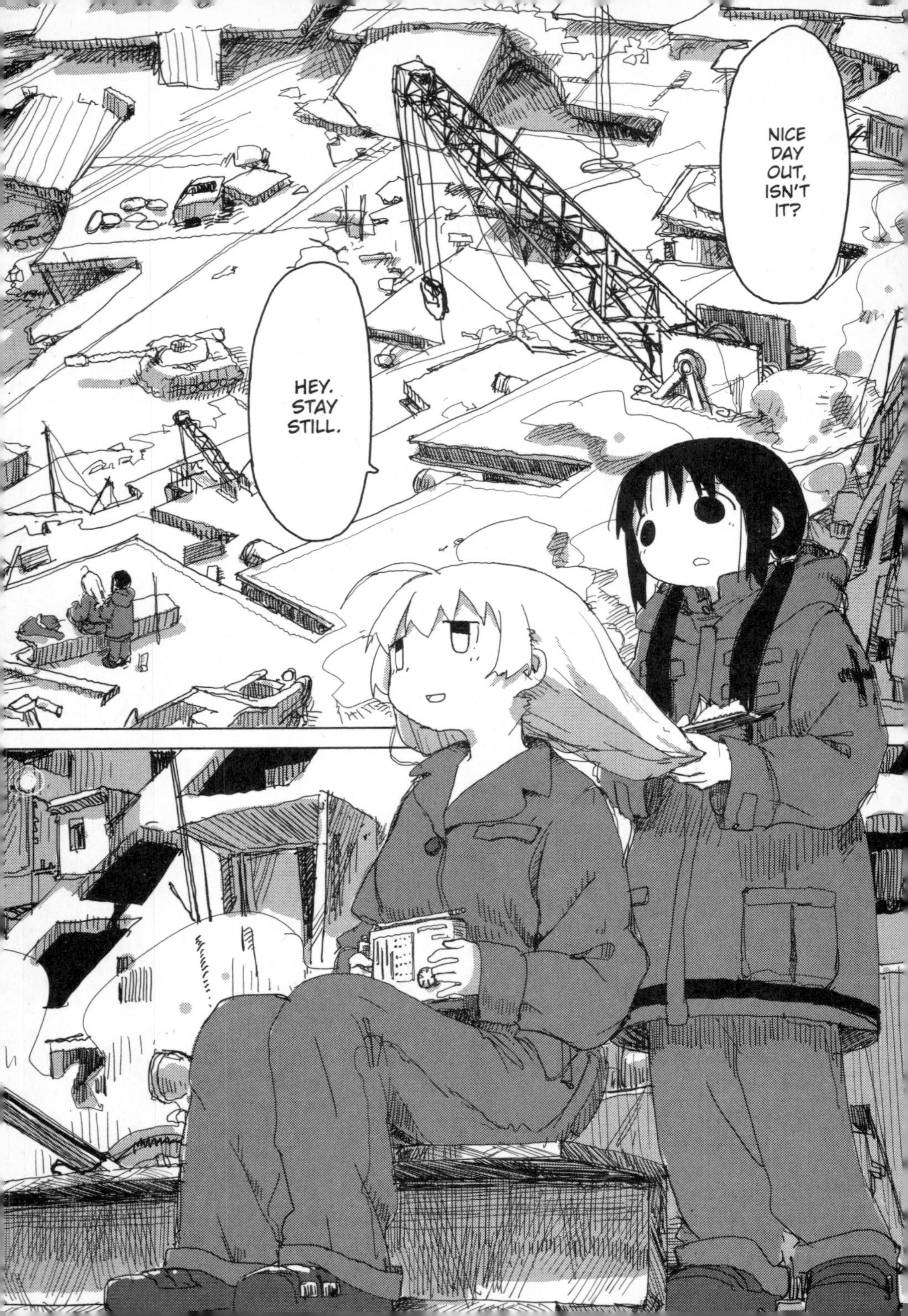
NICE DAY OUT, ISN'T IT?
HEY. STAY STILL.

...LOOK AT THAT BIG HOLE. I WONDER HOW IT GOT THERE?

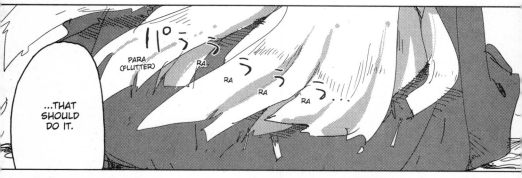

...THAT SHOULD DO IT.

PARA (FLUTTER)
RA
RA
RA
RA...

THE ENDS OF OUR HAIR HAD GOTTEN PRETTY UNEVEN THERE...

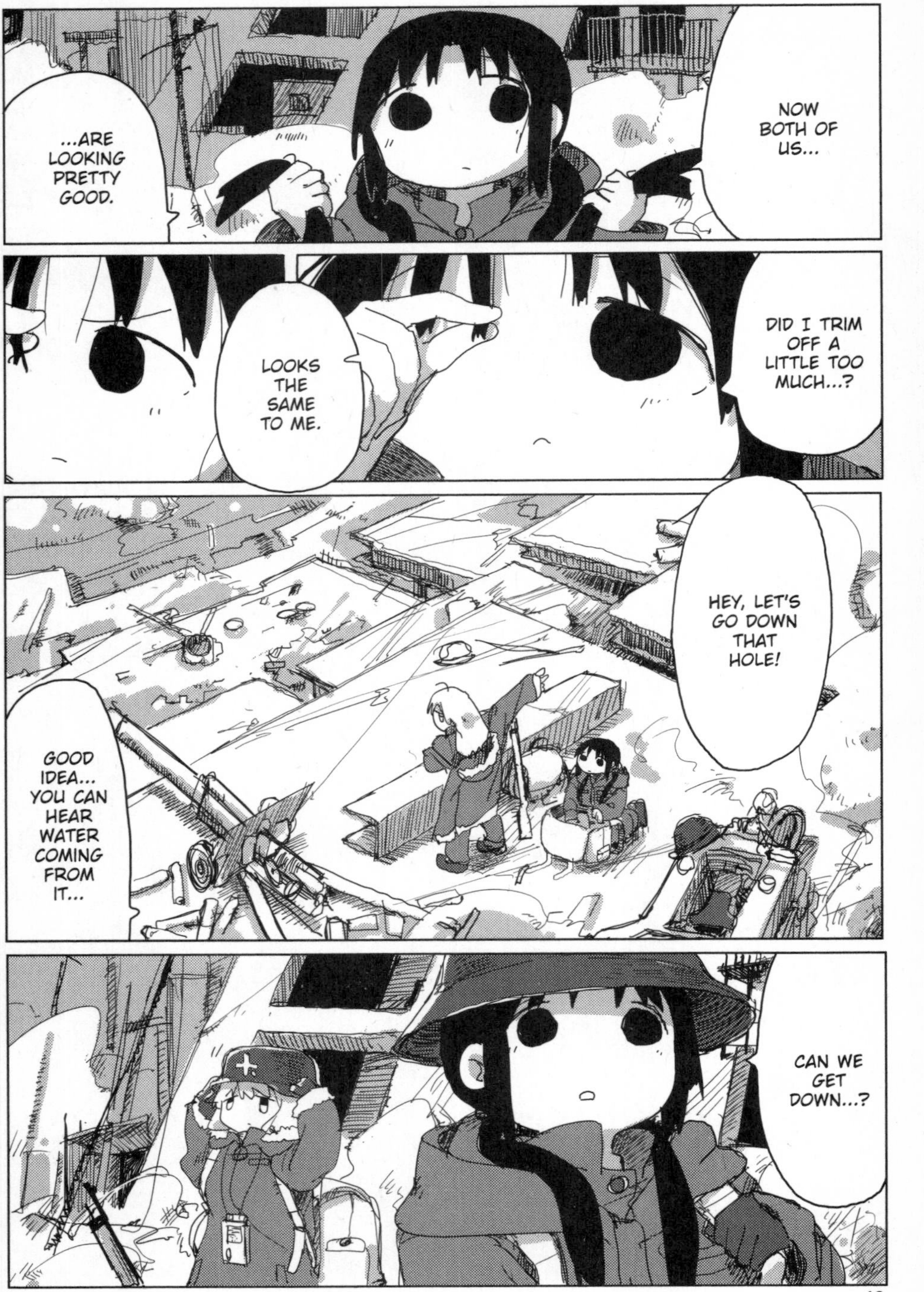
NOW BOTH OF US...
...ARE LOOKING PRETTY GOOD.
DID I TRIM OFF A LITTLE TOO MUCH...?
LOOKS THE SAME TO ME.
HEY, LET'S GO DOWN THAT HOLE!
GOOD IDEA... YOU CAN HEAR WATER COMING FROM IT...
CAN WE GET DOWN...?

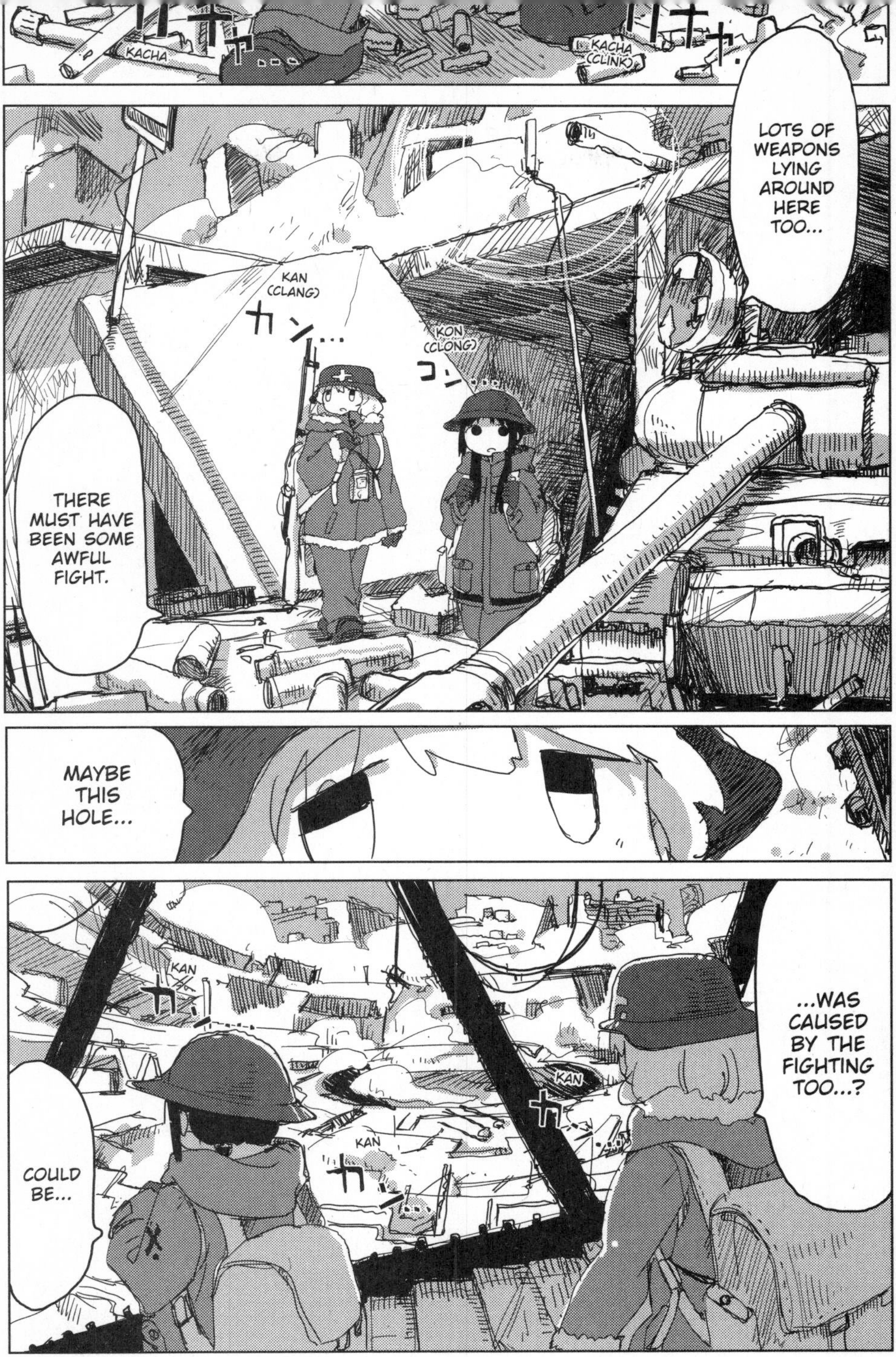

KACHA (CLINK)
KACHA
LOTS OF WEAPONS LYING AROUND HERE TOO...
KAN (CLANG)
KON (CLONG)
THERE MUST HAVE BEEN SOME AWFUL FIGHT.
MAYBE THIS HOLE...
...WAS CAUSED BY THE FIGHTING TOO...?
KAN
KAN
KAN
COULD BE...

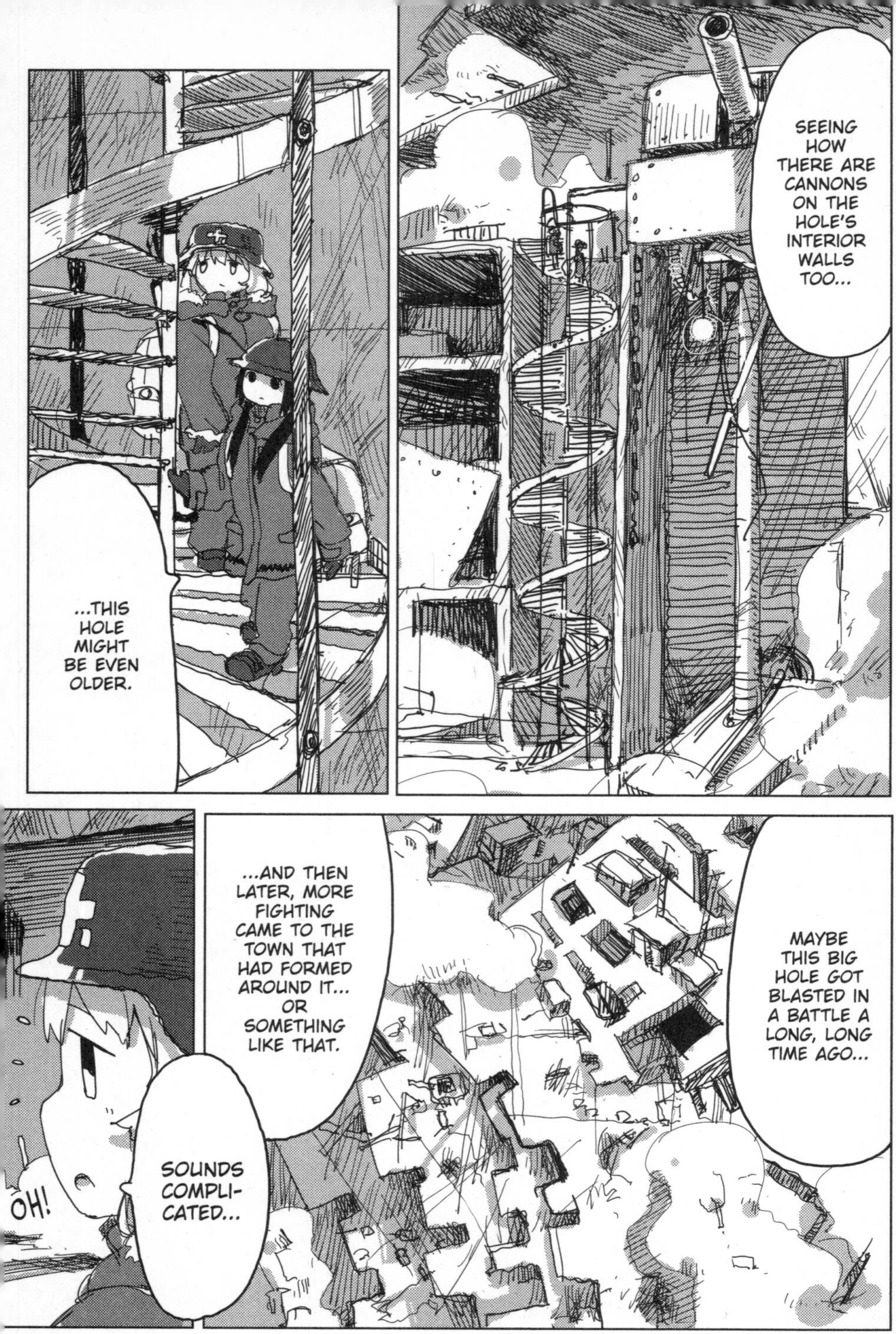
SEEING HOW THERE ARE CANNONS ON THE HOLE'S INTERIOR WALLS TOO...
...THIS HOLE MIGHT BE EVEN OLDER.
MAYBE THIS BIG HOLE GOT BLASTED IN A BATTLE A LONG, LONG TIME AGO...
...AND THEN LATER, MORE FIGHTING CAME TO THE TOWN THAT HAD FORMED AROUND IT... OR SOMETHING LIKE THAT.
OH!
SOUNDS COMPLI-CATED...

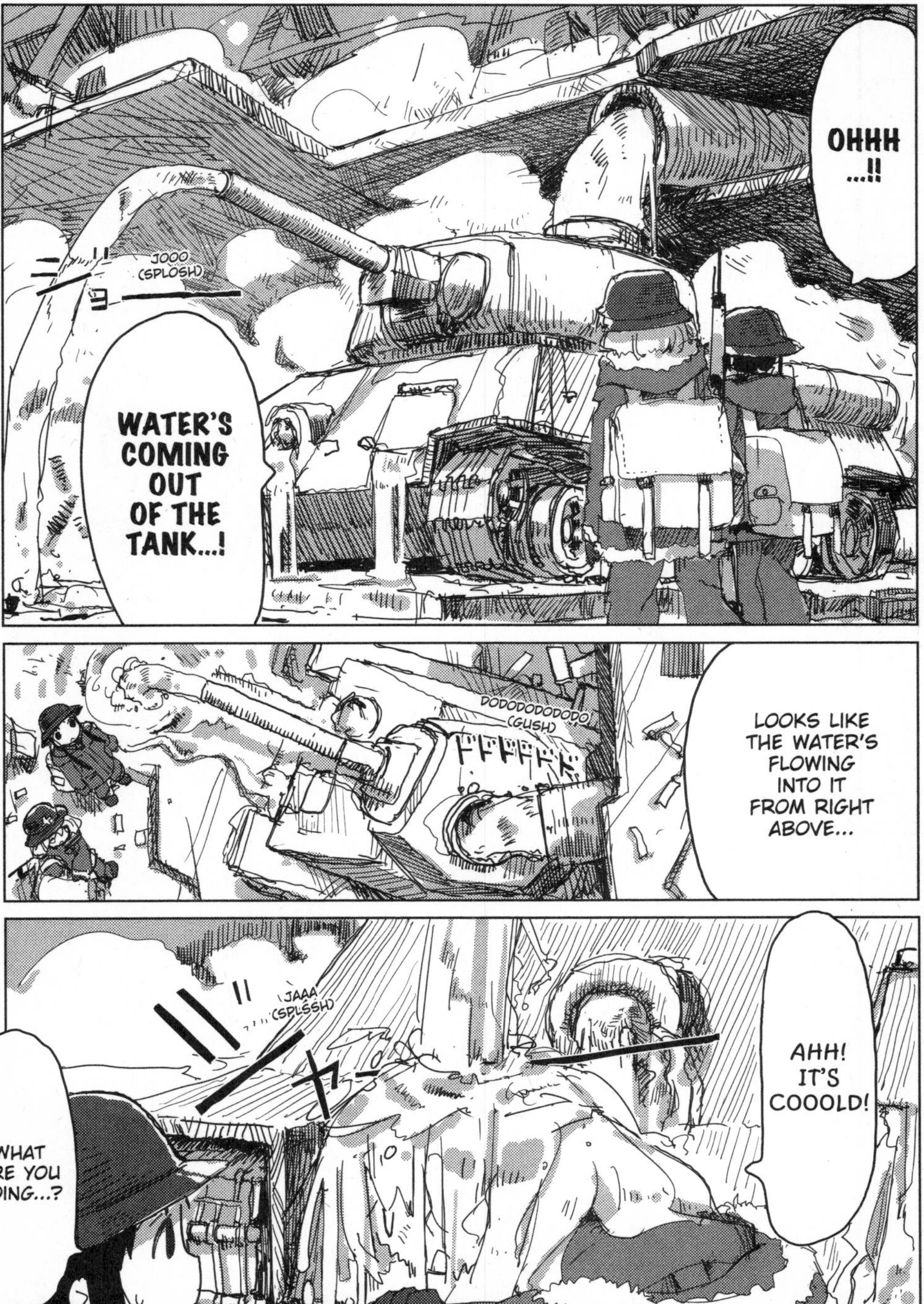
OHHH ...!!
JOOO (SPLOSH)
WATER'S COMING OUT OF THE TANK...!
LOOKS LIKE THE WATER'S FLOWING INTO IT FROM RIGHT ABOVE...
DODODODODODO (GUSH)
AHH! IT'S COOOLD!
JAAA (SPLSSH)
WHAT ARE YOU DOING...?

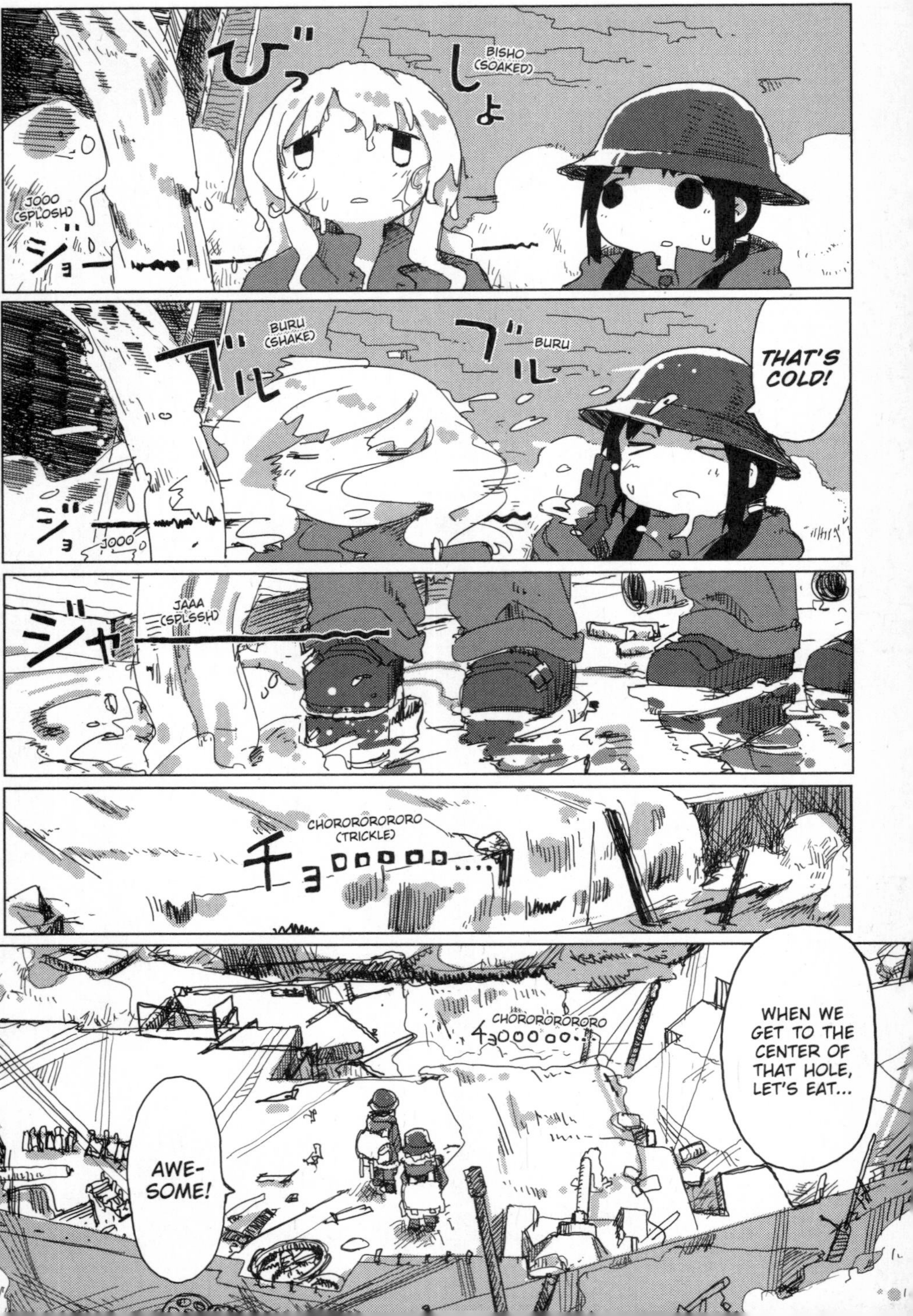

ぴっしょ
BISHO (SOAKED)
JOOO (SPLOSH)
ジョー
THAT'S COLD!
ブル
BURU
BURU (SHAKE)
ブル
ジョ
JOOO
JAAA (SPLSSH)
ジャー
CHORORORORORO (TRICKLE)
WHEN WE GET TO THE CENTER OF THAT HOLE, LET'S EAT...
CHORORORORORO
AWE-SOME!

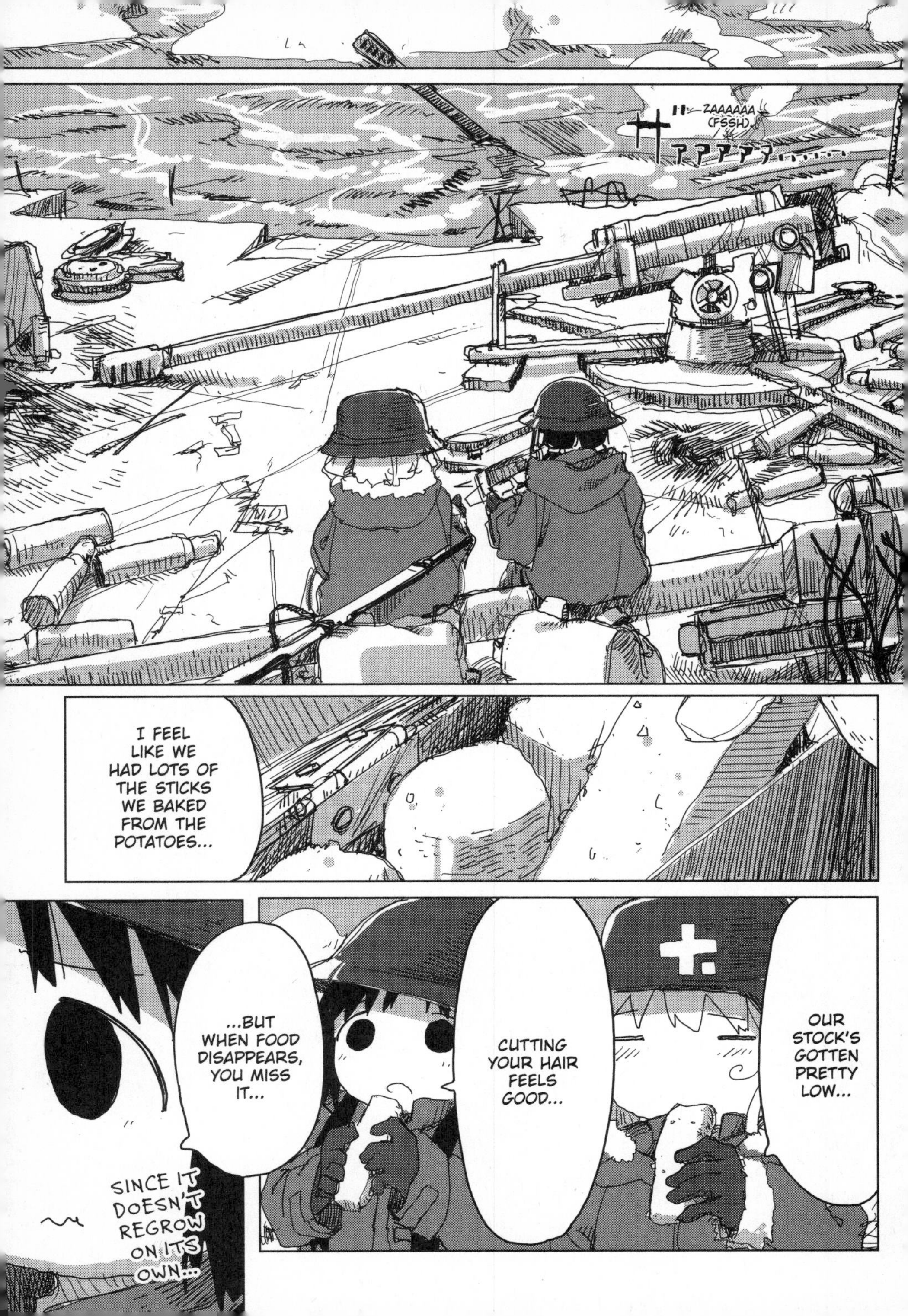
ZAAAAAA (FSSH)
I FEEL LIKE WE HAD LOTS OF THE STICKS WE BAKED FROM THE POTATOES...
OUR STOCK'S GOTTEN PRETTY LOW...
CUTTING YOUR HAIR FEELS GOOD...
...BUT WHEN FOOD DISAPPEARS, YOU MISS IT...
SINCE IT DOESN'T REGROW ON ITS OWN...

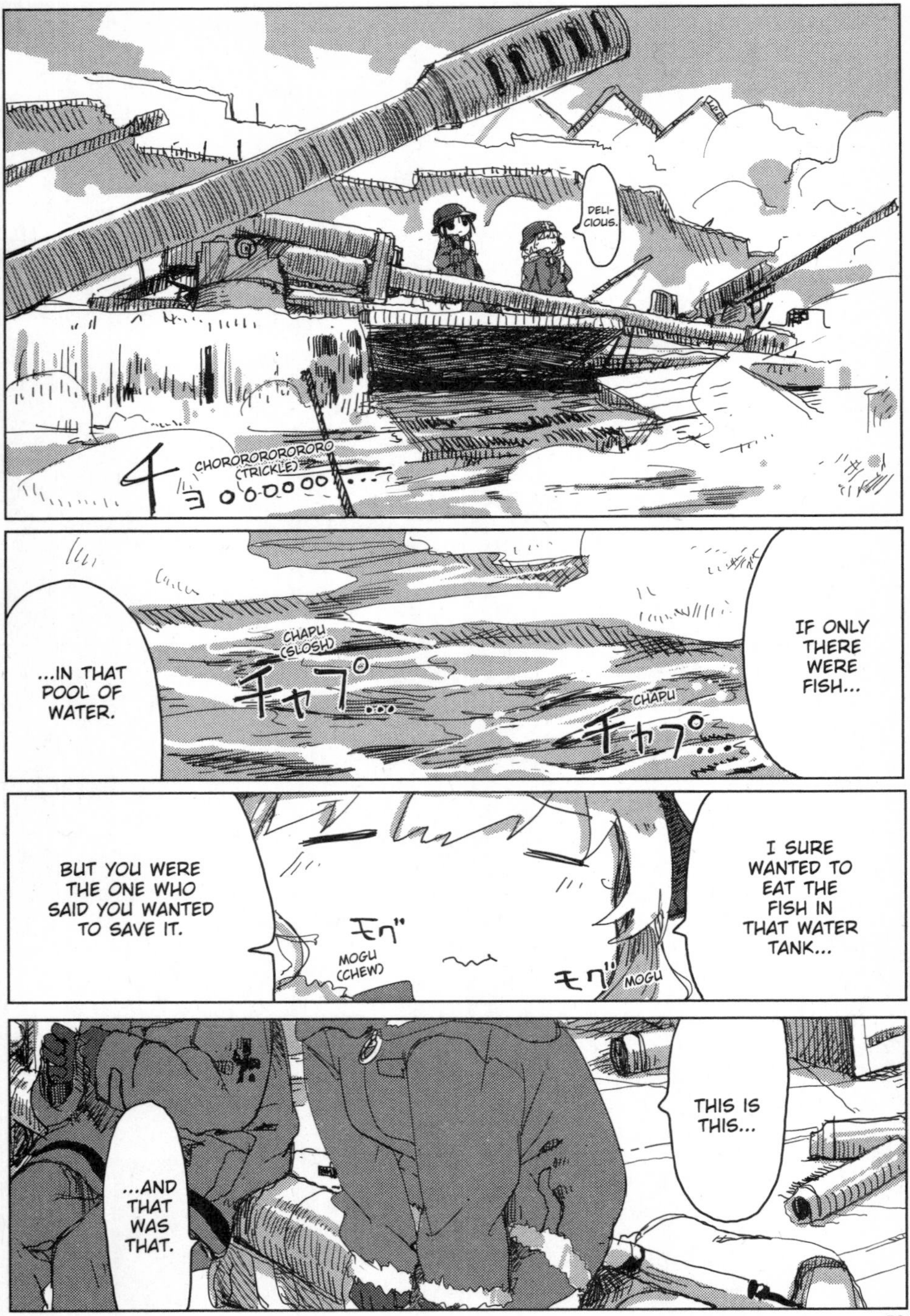
DELI-CIOUS.
CHORORORORORO (TRICKLE)
IF ONLY THERE WERE FISH...
CHAPU (SLOSH)
チャプ...
CHAPU
チャプ...
...IN THAT POOL OF WATER.
I SURE WANTED TO EAT THE FISH IN THAT WATER TANK...
モグ
MOGU
モグ
MOGU (CHEW)
BUT YOU WERE THE ONE WHO SAID YOU WANTED TO SAVE IT.
THIS IS THIS...
...AND THAT WAS THAT.

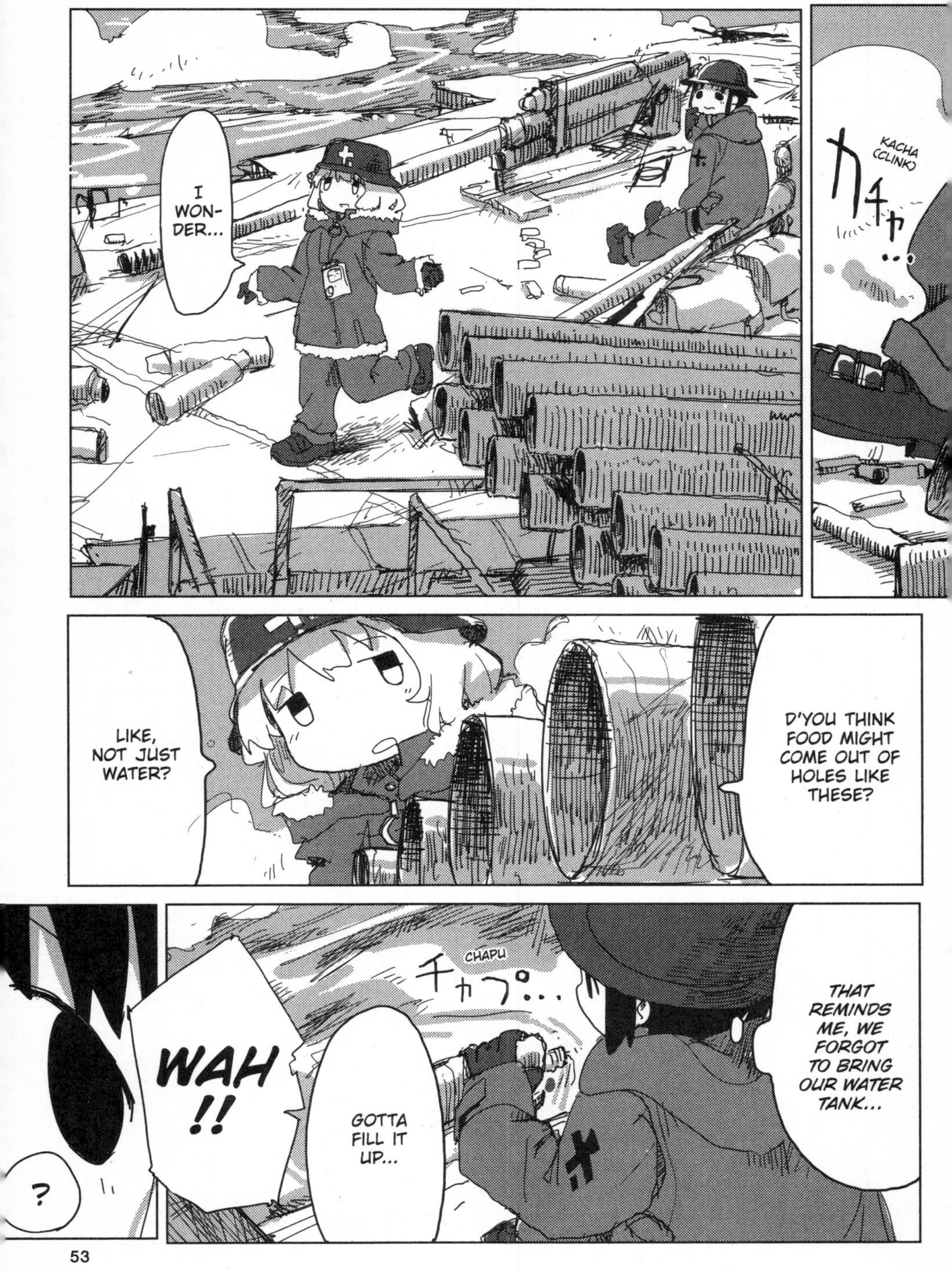
KACHA (CLINK)
カチャ…
I WONDER…
D'YOU THINK FOOD MIGHT COME OUT OF HOLES LIKE THESE?
LIKE, NOT JUST WATER?
THAT REMINDS ME, WE FORGOT TO BRING OUR WATER TANK…
CHAPU
チャプ…
GOTTA FILL IT UP…
WAH !!
?

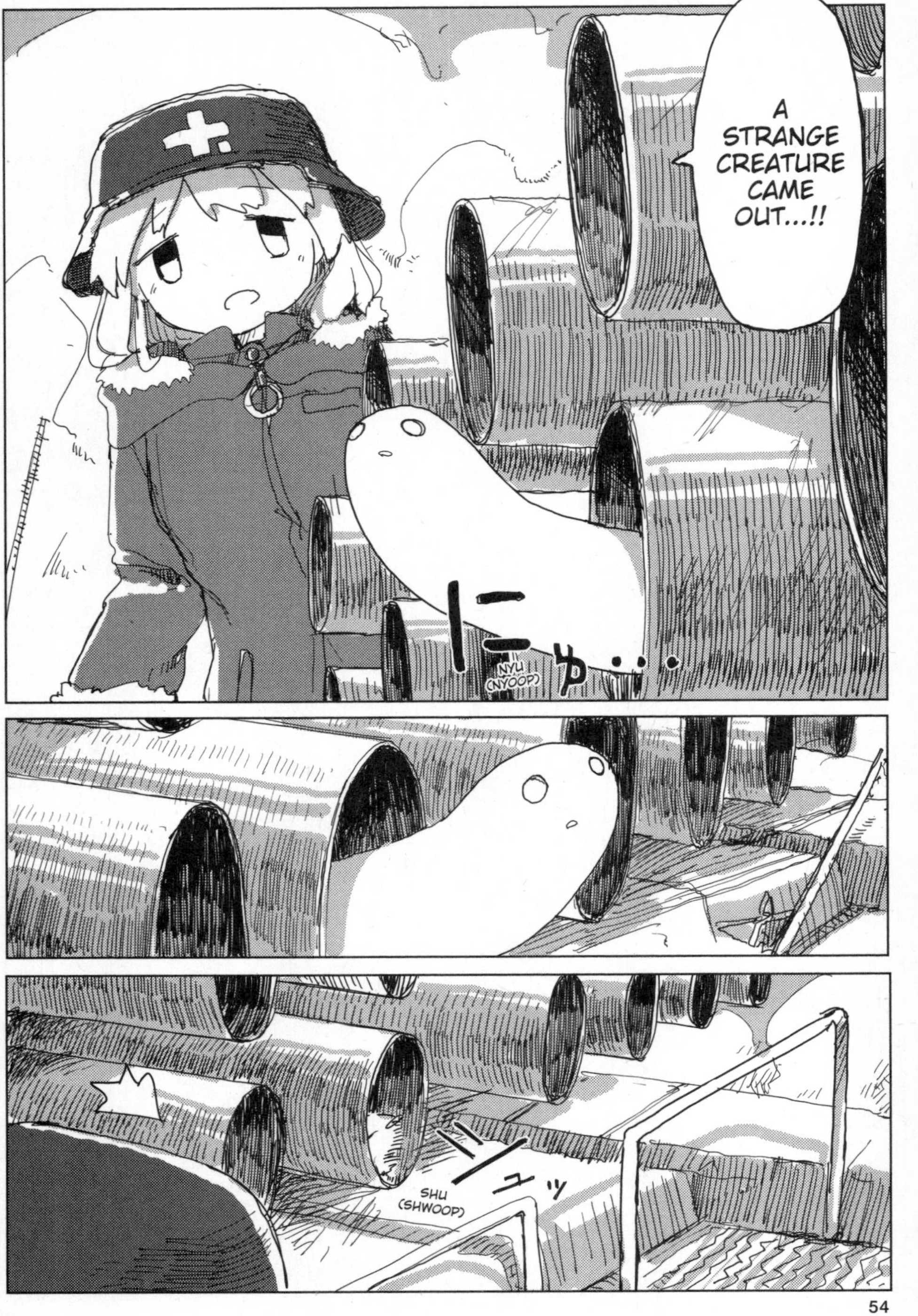
A STRANGE CREATURE CAME OUT...!!
にーゅ…
NYU (NYOOP)
シュッ
SHU (SHWOOP)

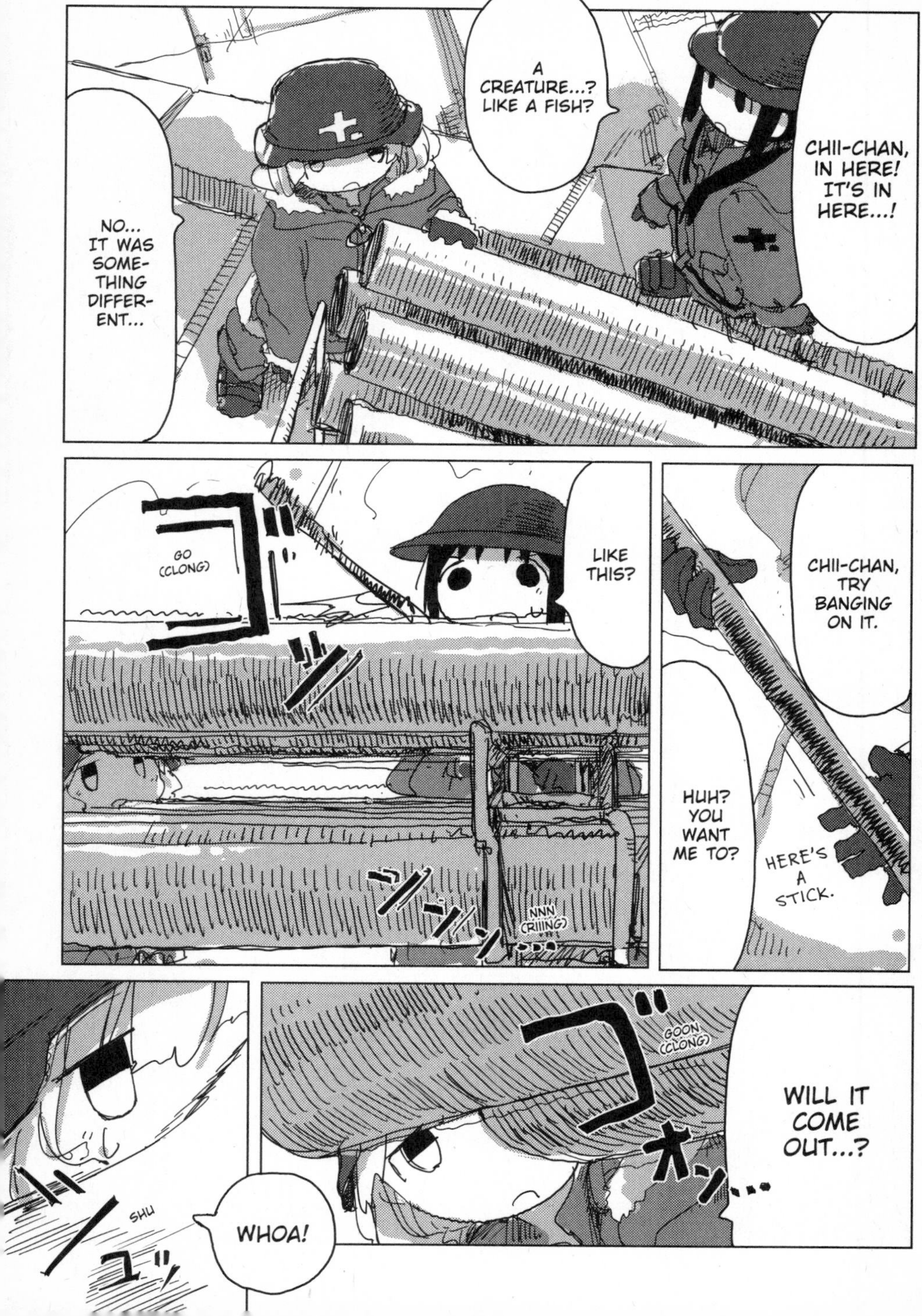
CHII-CHAN, IN HERE! IT'S IN HERE...!
A CREATURE...? LIKE A FISH?
NO... IT WAS SOME-THING DIFFER-ENT...
CHII-CHAN, TRY BANGING ON IT.
HUH? YOU WANT ME TO?
HERE'S A STICK.
LIKE THIS?
GO (CLONG)
NNN (RIIING)
WILL IT COME OUT...?
GOON (CLONG)
WHOA!
SHU

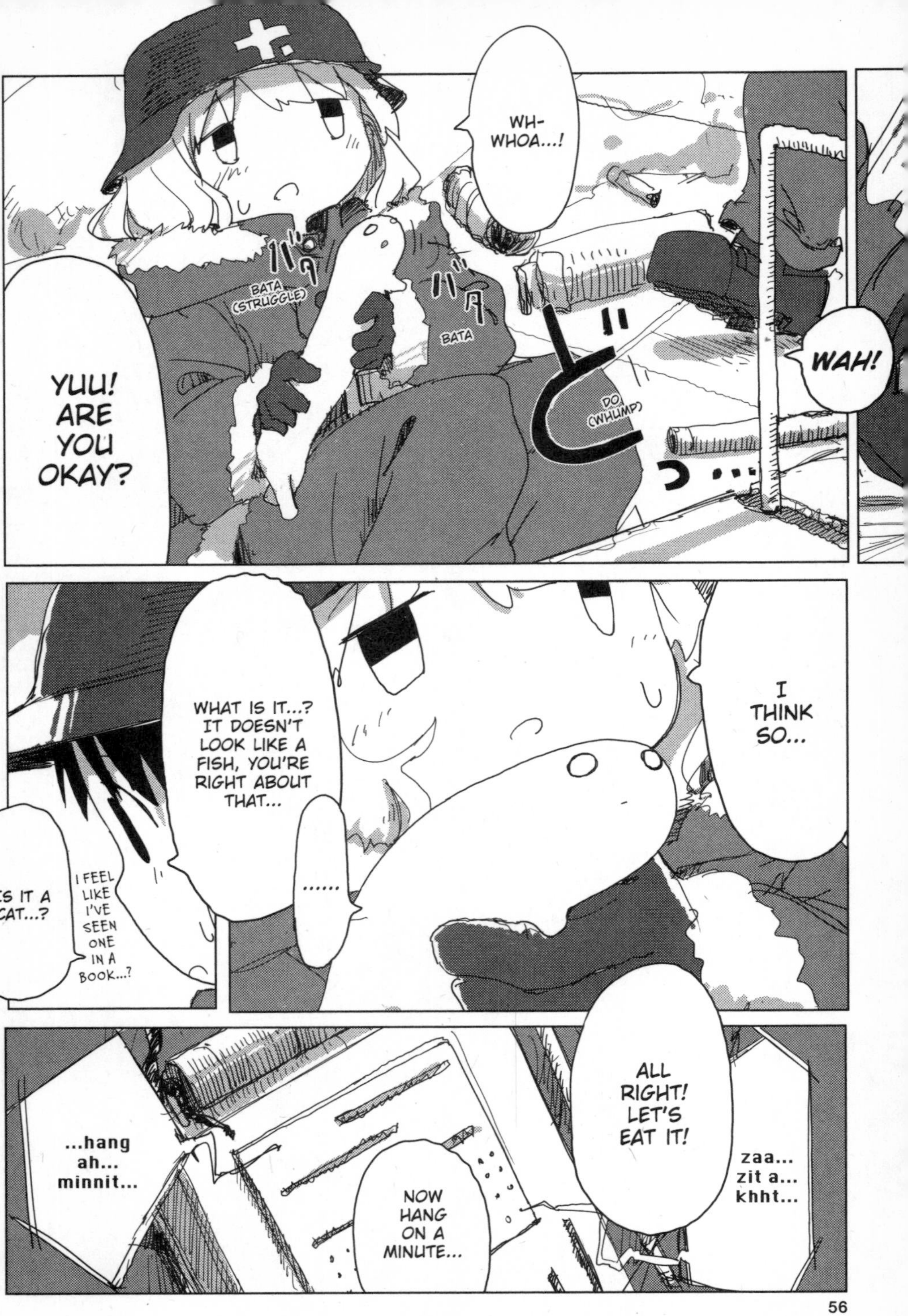
WAH!
WH-WHOA...!
BATA (STRUGGLE)
BATA
DO (WHUMP)
YUU! ARE YOU OKAY?
I THINK SO...
WHAT IS IT...? IT DOESN'T LOOK LIKE A FISH, YOU'RE RIGHT ABOUT THAT...
......
I FEEL LIKE I'VE SEEN ONE IN A BOOK...?
IS IT A CAT...?
ALL RIGHT! LET'S EAT IT!
zaa... zit a... khht...
NOW HANG ON A MINUTE...
...hang ah... minnit...

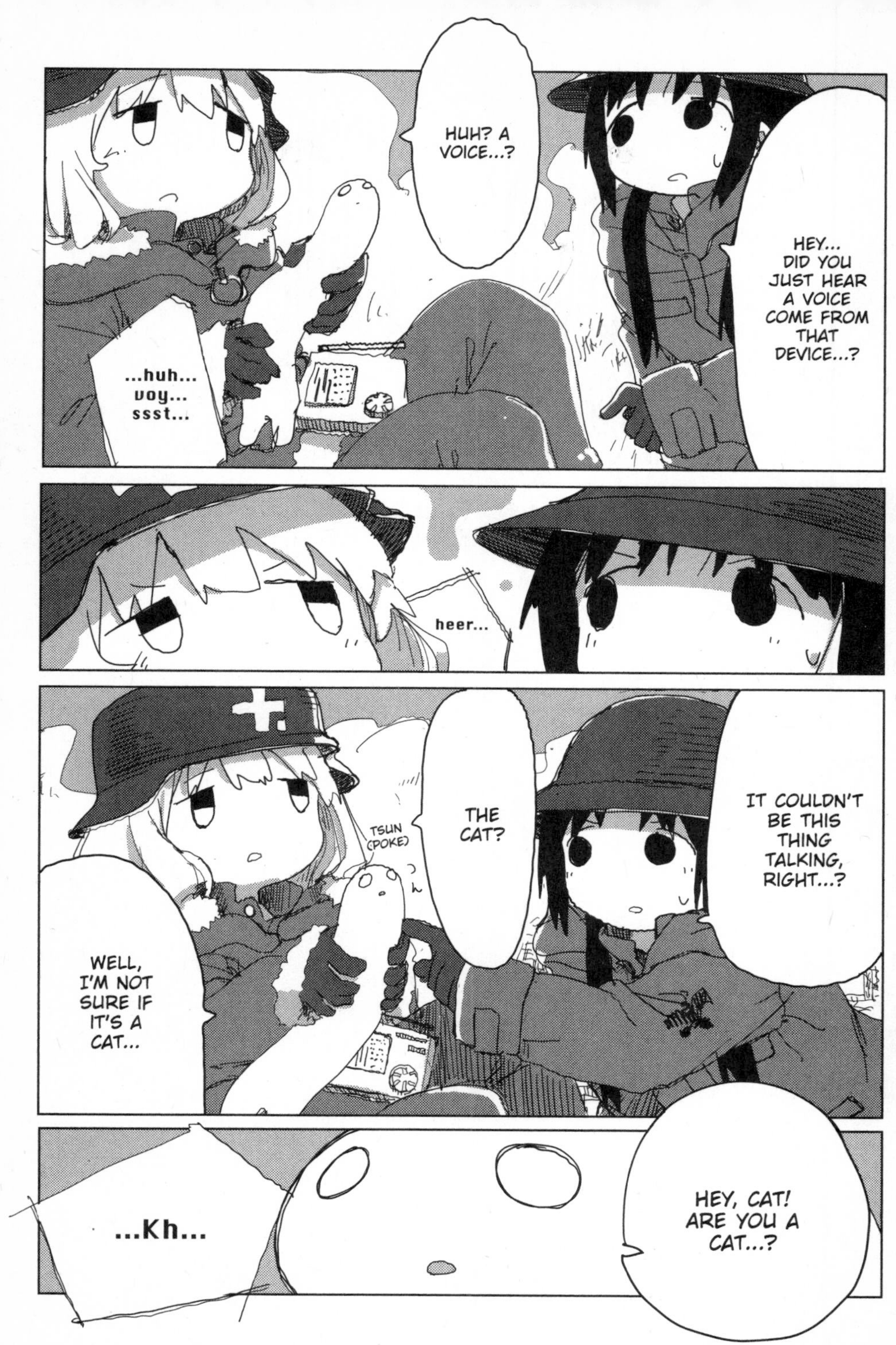
HEY... DID YOU JUST HEAR A VOICE COME FROM THAT DEVICE...?
HUH? A VOICE...?
...huh... voy... ssst...
heer...
IT COULDN'T BE THIS THING TALKING, RIGHT...?
THE CAT?
TSUN (POKE)
WELL, I'M NOT SURE IF IT'S A CAT...
HEY, CAT! ARE YOU A CAT...?
...Kh...

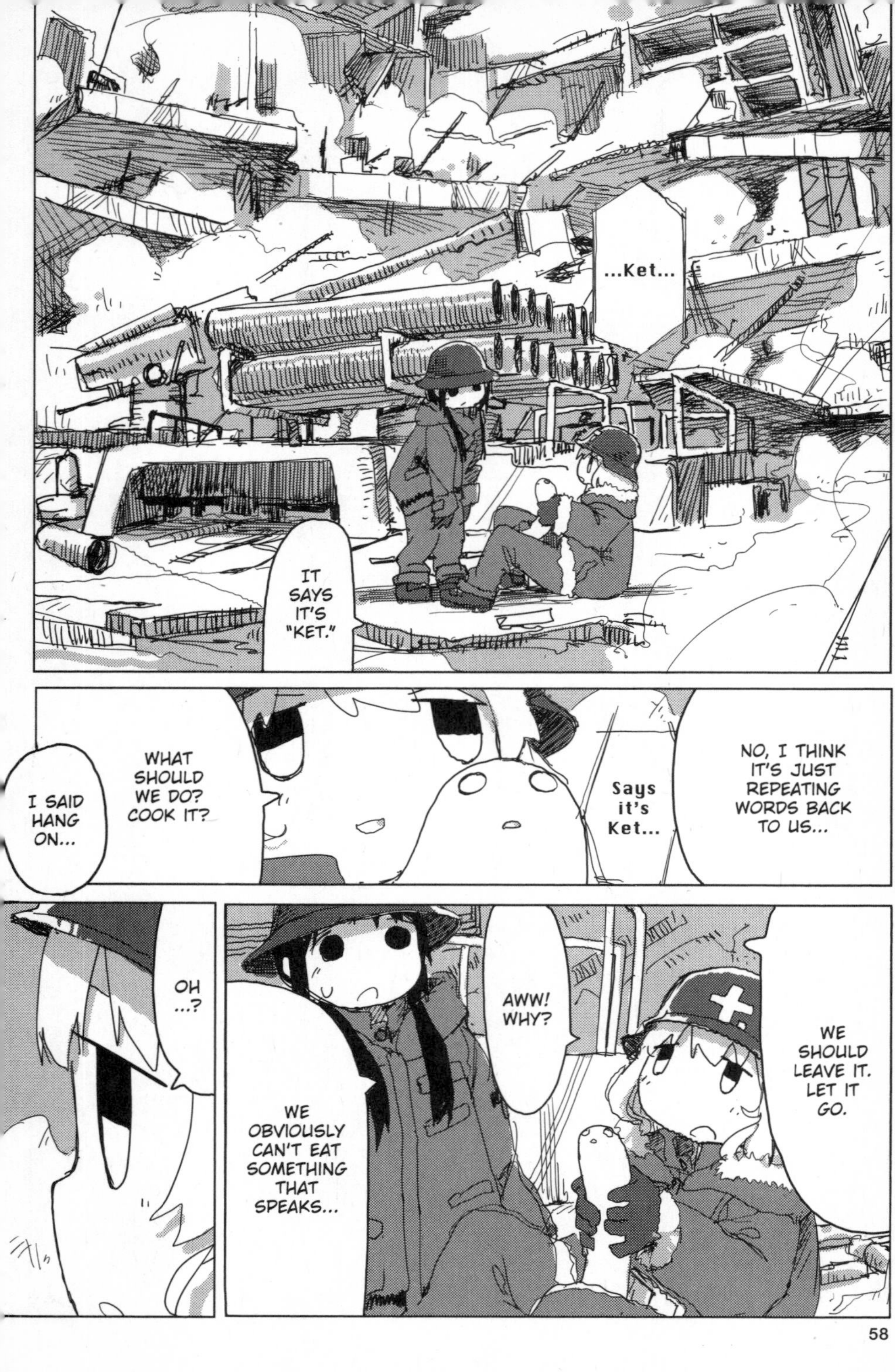
...Ket...
IT SAYS IT'S "KET."
NO, I THINK IT'S JUST REPEATING WORDS BACK TO US...
Says it's Ket...
WHAT SHOULD WE DO? COOK IT?
I SAID HANG ON...
WE SHOULD LEAVE IT. LET IT GO.
AWW! WHY?
WE OBVIOUSLY CAN'T EAT SOMETHING THAT SPEAKS...
OH ...?

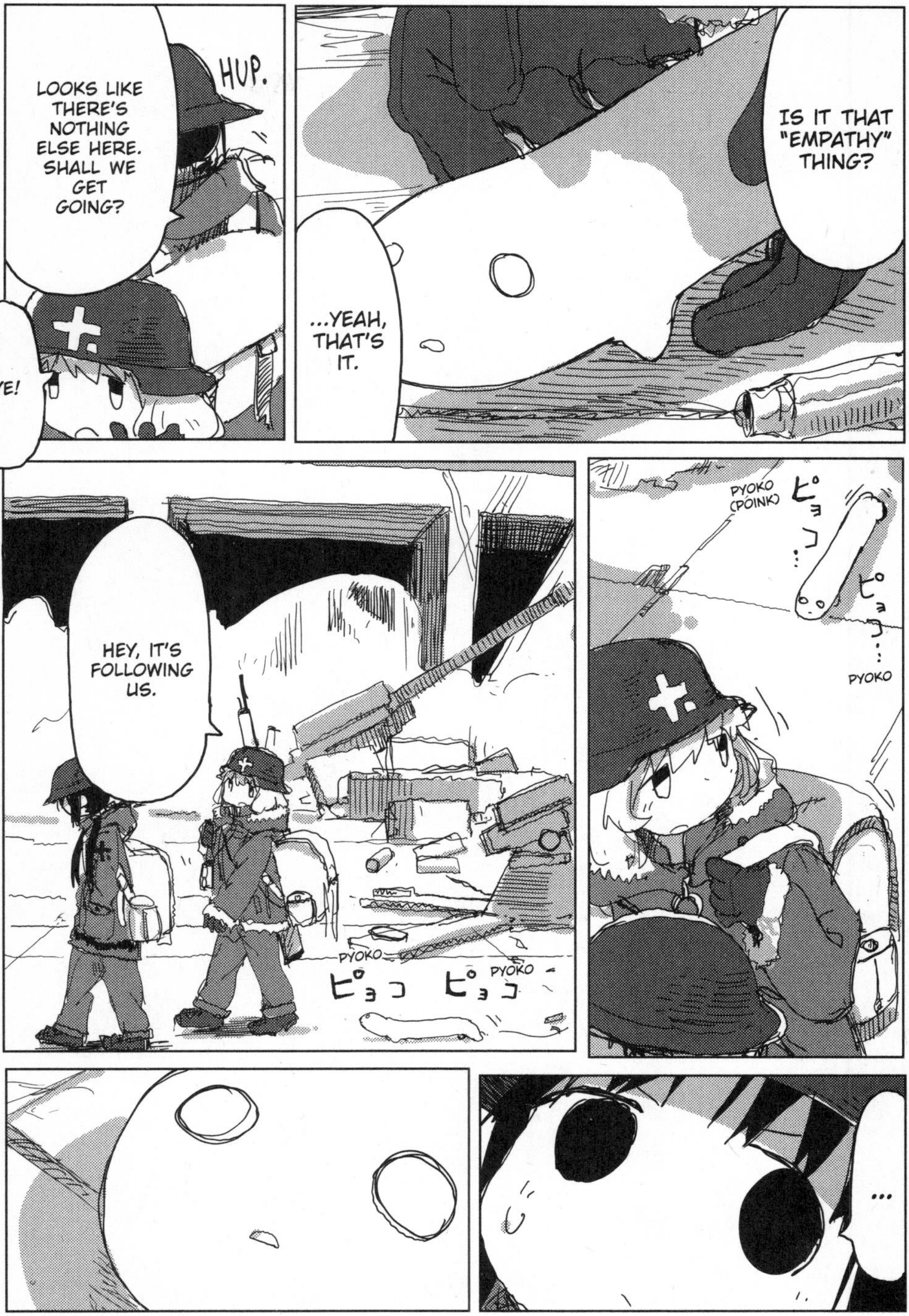
IS IT THAT "EMPATHY" THING?
...YEAH, THAT'S IT.
HUP.
LOOKS LIKE THERE'S NOTHING ELSE HERE. SHALL WE GET GOING?
BYE!
PYOKO (POINK)
ピョコ…
ピョコ…
PYOKO
HEY, IT'S FOLLOWING US.
PYOKO
ピョコ
PYOKO
ピョコ
...

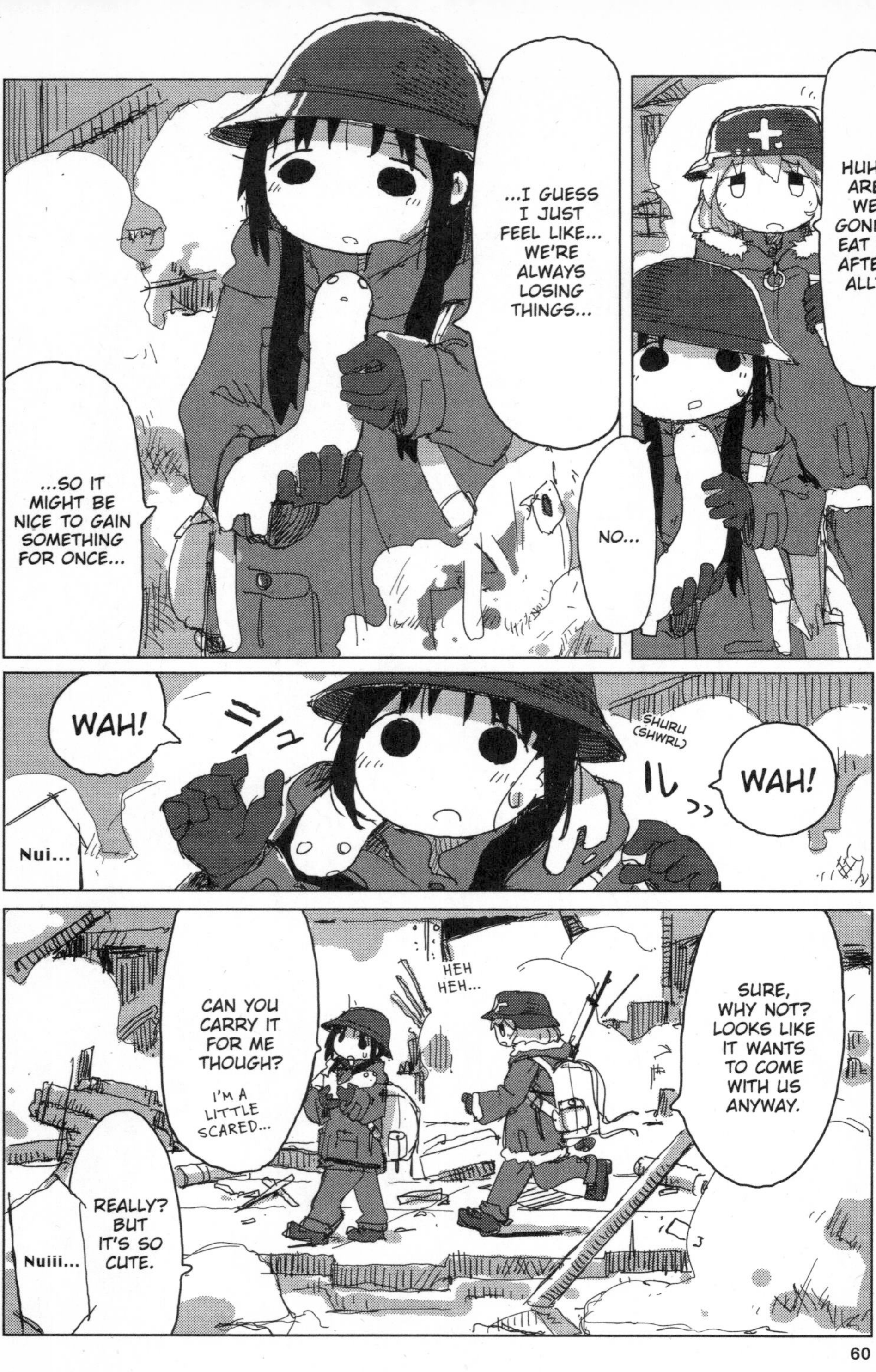
HUH? ARE WE GONNA EAT IT AFTER ALL?
NO...
...I GUESS I JUST FEEL LIKE... WE'RE ALWAYS LOSING THINGS...
...SO IT MIGHT BE NICE TO GAIN SOMETHING FOR ONCE...
SHURU (SHWRL)
WAH!
WAH!
Nui...
SURE, WHY NOT? LOOKS LIKE IT WANTS TO COME WITH US ANYWAY.
HEH HEH...
CAN YOU CARRY IT FOR ME THOUGH?
I'M A LITTLE SCARED...
REALLY? BUT IT'S SO CUTE.
Nuiii...

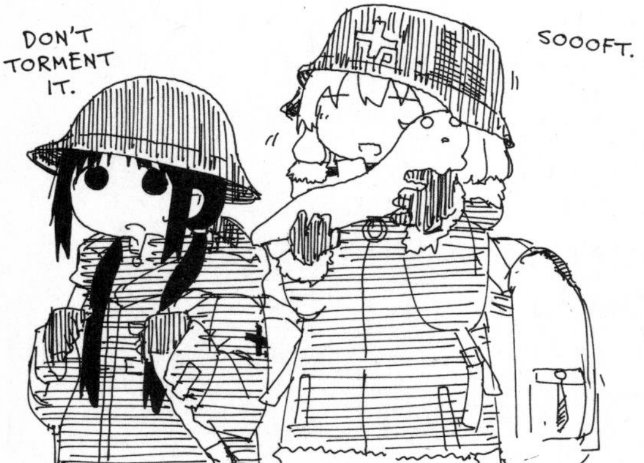
SOOOFT.
DON'T TORMENT IT.

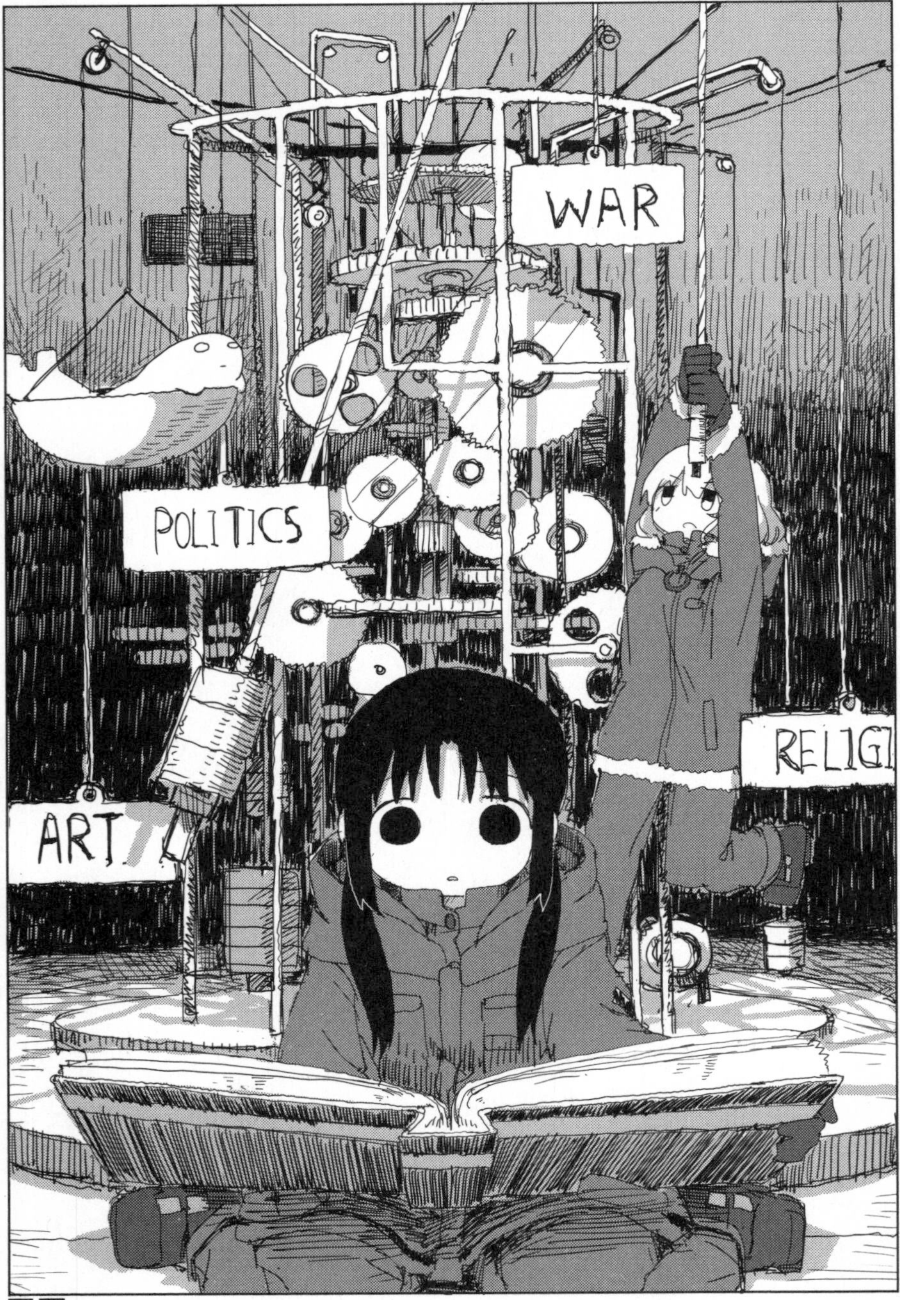
WAR
POLITICS
RELIGI
ART

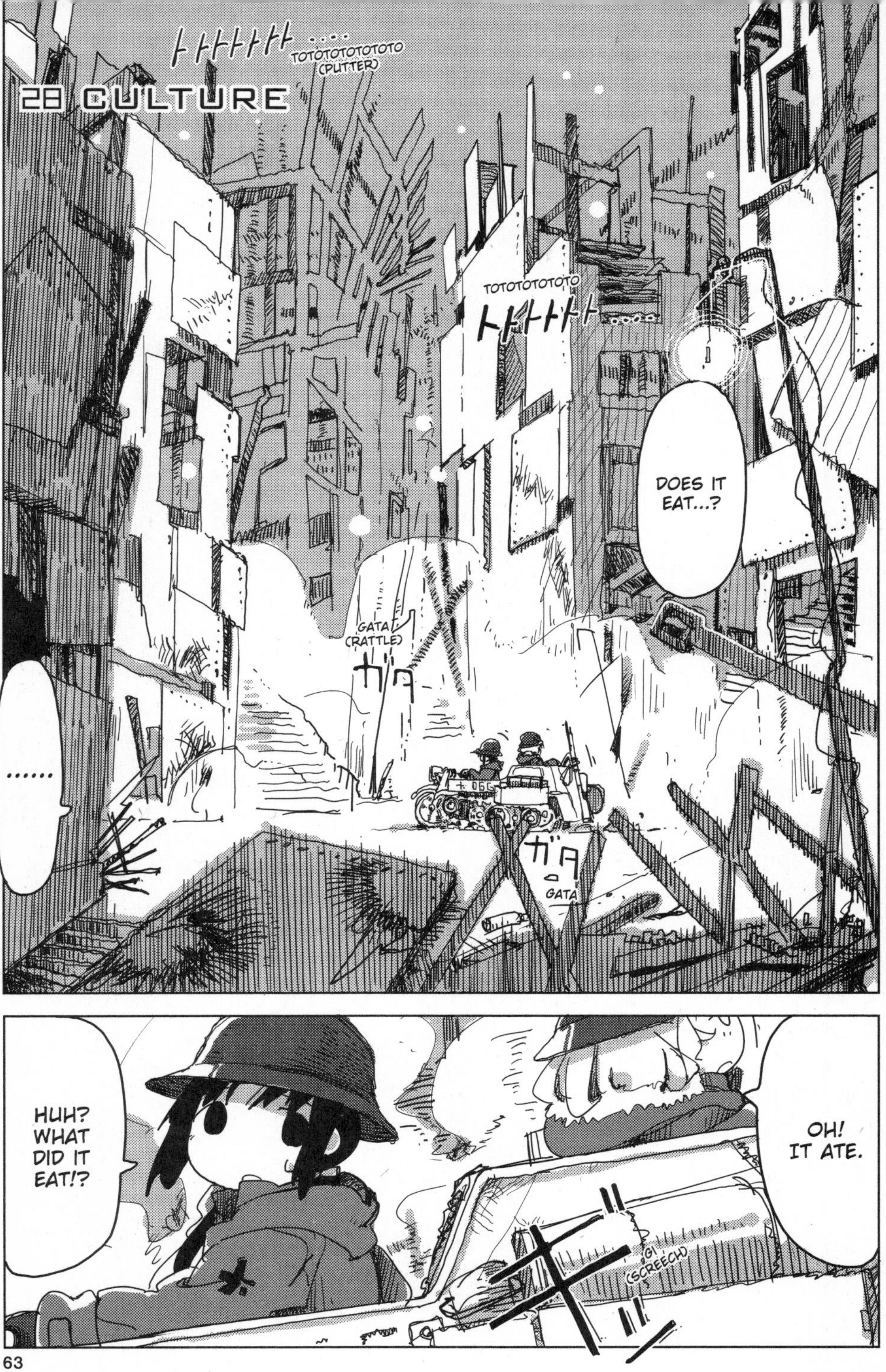
トトトトトト
TOTOTOTOTOTOTO (PUTTER)
28 CULTURE
TOTOTOTOTOTO
トトトトトト
DOES IT EAT...?
......
GATA (RATTLE)
ガタ
ガタ
GATA
OH! IT ATE.
GI (SCREECH)
HUH? WHAT DID IT EAT!?

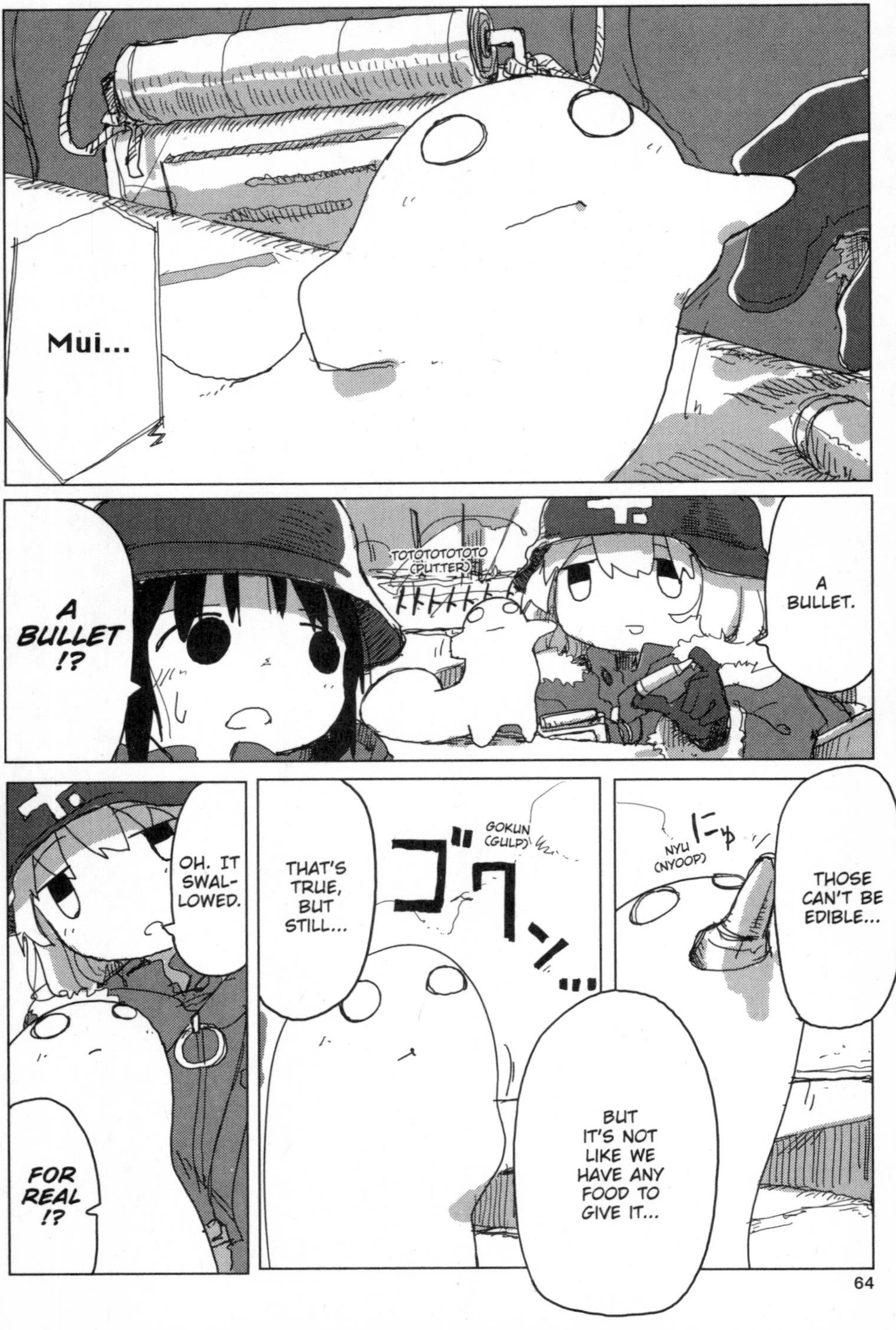
Mui...
A BULLET.
TOTOTOTOTOTO (PUTTER)
A BULLET !?
NYU (NYOOP)
にゅ
THOSE CAN'T BE EDIBLE...
GOKUN (GULP)
ゴクン…
THAT'S TRUE, BUT STILL...
BUT IT'S NOT LIKE WE HAVE ANY FOOD TO GIVE IT...
OH. IT SWALLOWED.
FOR REAL !?

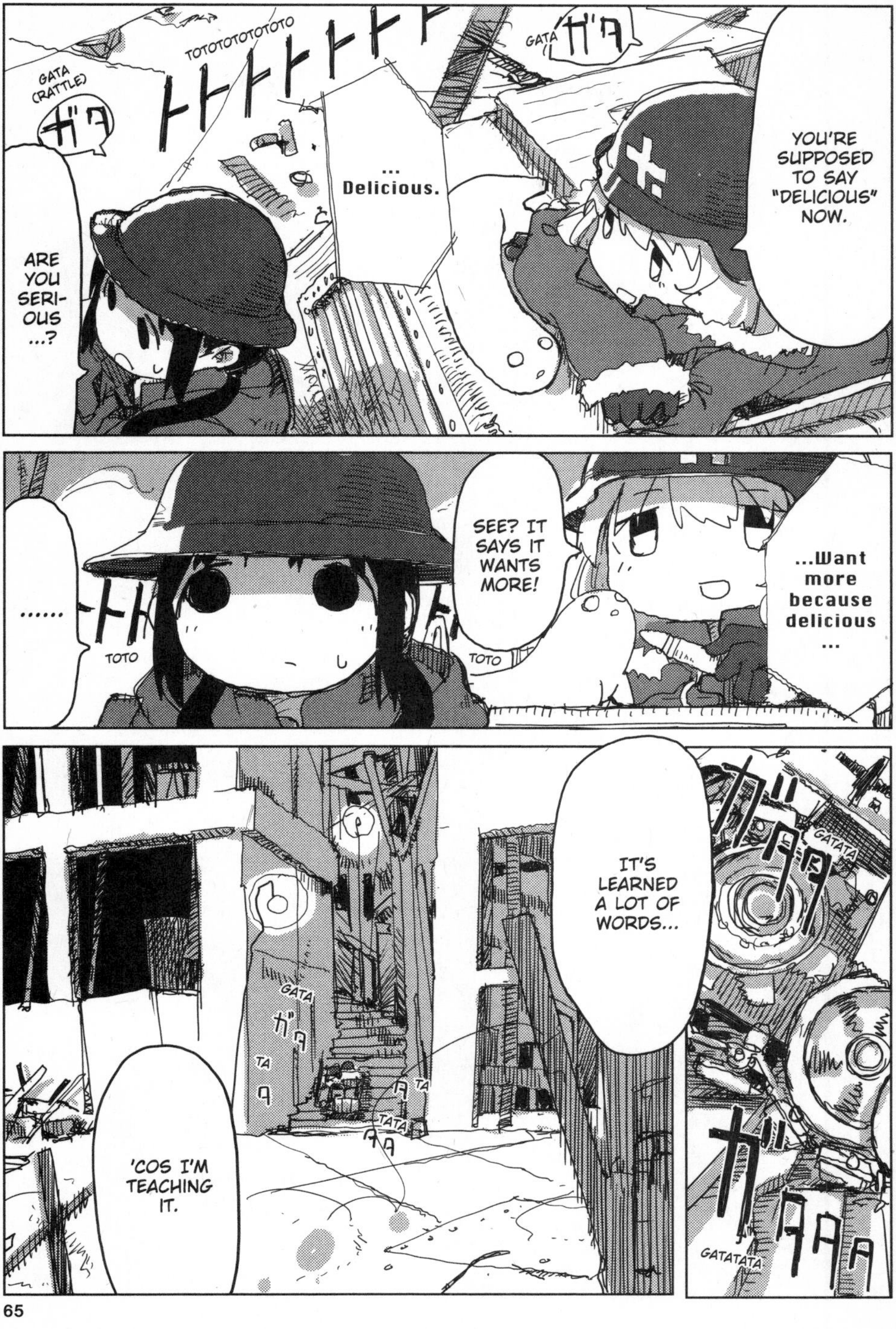
GATA
YOU'RE SUPPOSED TO SAY "DELICIOUS" NOW.
TOTOTOTOTOTOTO
... Delicious.
GATA (RATTLE)
ARE YOU SERI-OUS ...?
...Want more because delicious ...
SEE? IT SAYS IT WANTS MORE!
TOTO
TOTO
......
GATATA
GATATATA
IT'S LEARNED A LOT OF WORDS...
GATA
TA
TA
TATA
'COS I'M TEACHING IT.

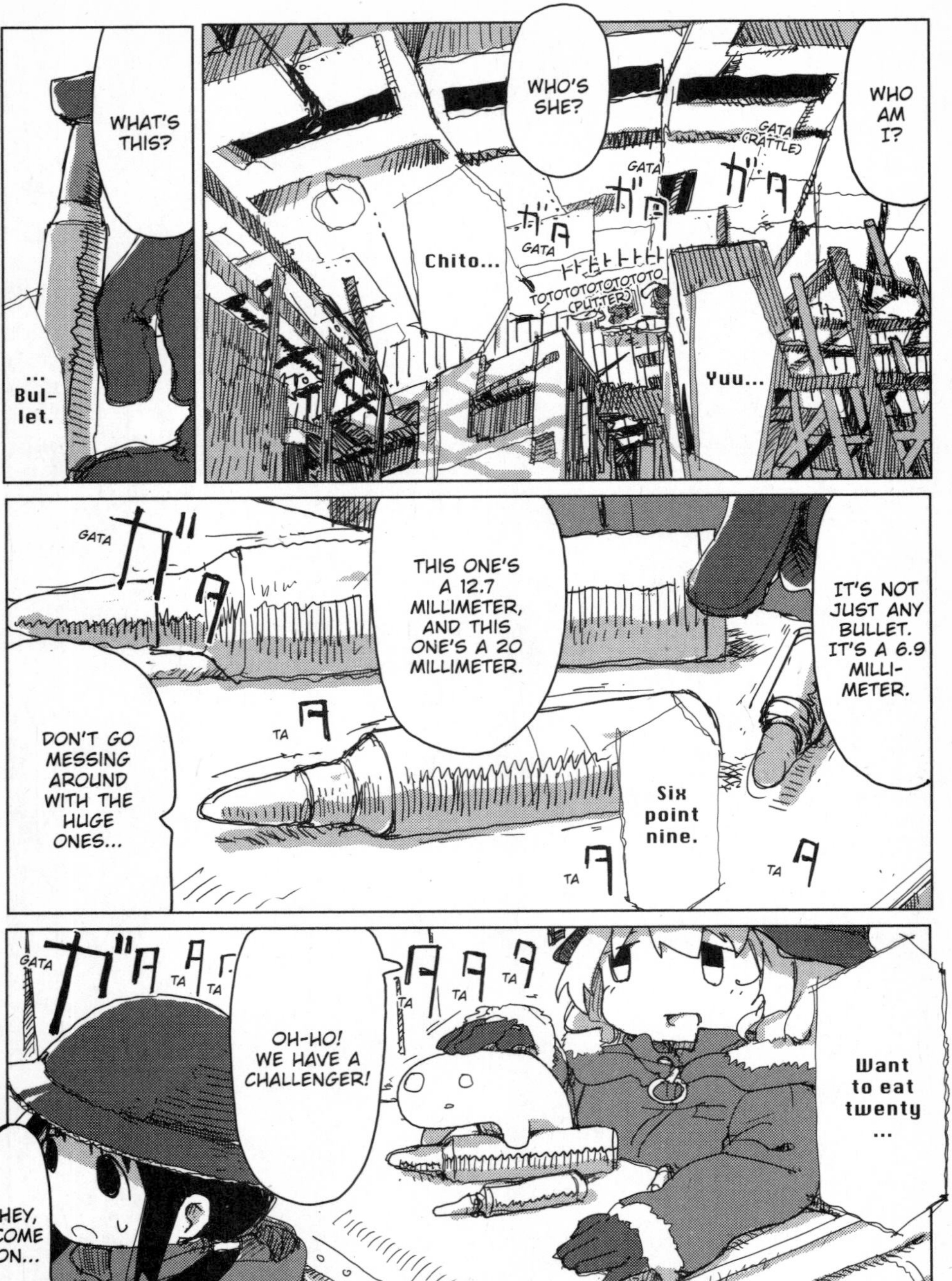
WHO AM I?
GATA (RATTLE)
GATA
GATA
WHO'S SHE?
TOTOTOTOTOTOTOTO (PUTTER)
Chito...
Yuu...
WHAT'S THIS?
... Bul-let.
IT'S NOT JUST ANY BULLET. IT'S A 6.9 MILLI-METER.
THIS ONE'S A 12.7 MILLIMETER, AND THIS ONE'S A 20 MILLIMETER.
GATA
Six point nine.
TA
TA
TA
DON'T GO MESSING AROUND WITH THE HUGE ONES...
Want to eat twenty ...
TA
TA
TA
OH-HO! WE HAVE A CHALLENGER!
GATA
TA
TA
HEY, COME ON...

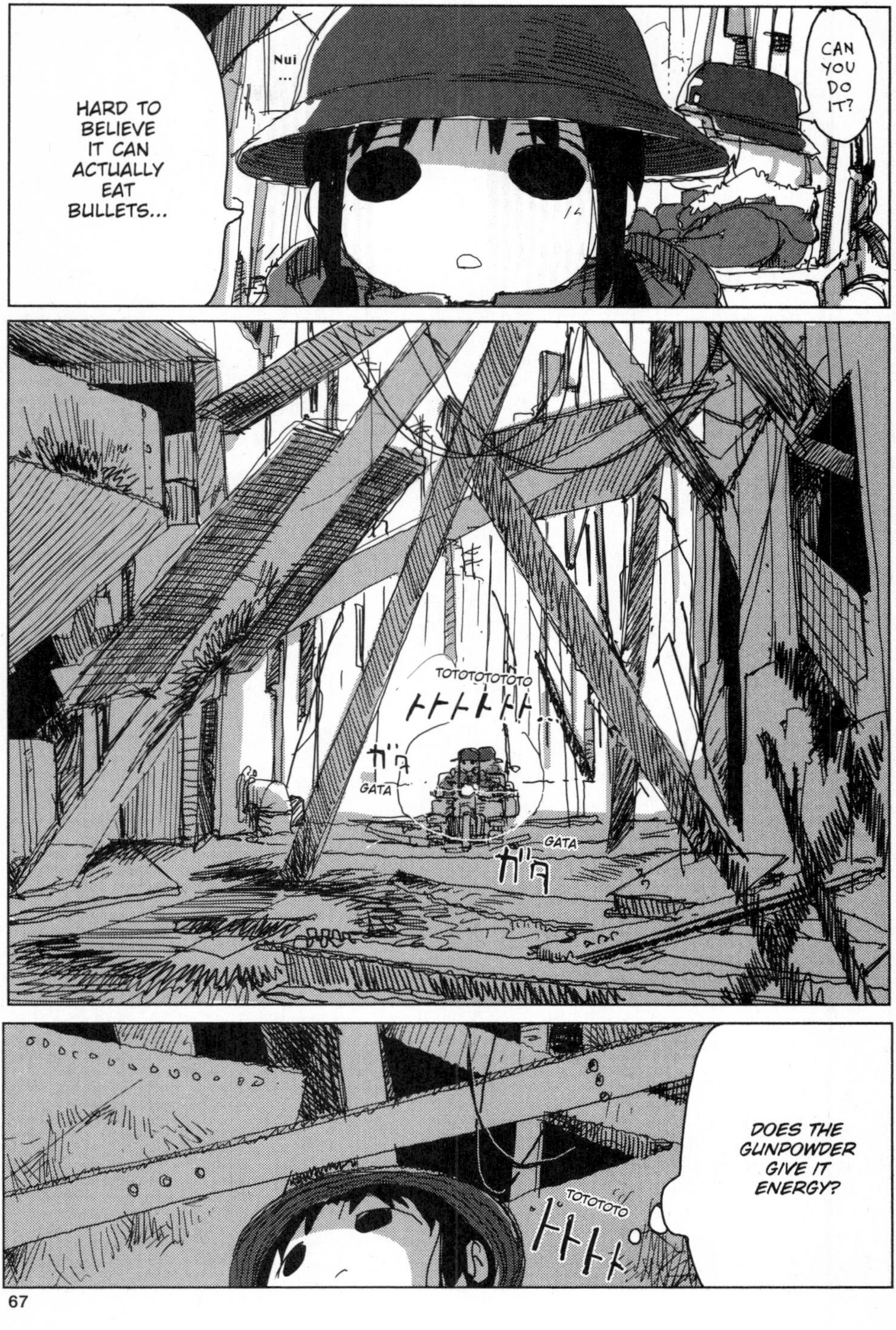
CAN YOU DO IT?
Nui ...
HARD TO BELIEVE IT CAN ACTUALLY EAT BULLETS...
TOTOTOTOTOTO
トトトトトトト…
ガタ
GATA
GATA
ガタ
DOES THE GUNPOWDER GIVE IT ENERGY?
TOTOTOTO
トトト

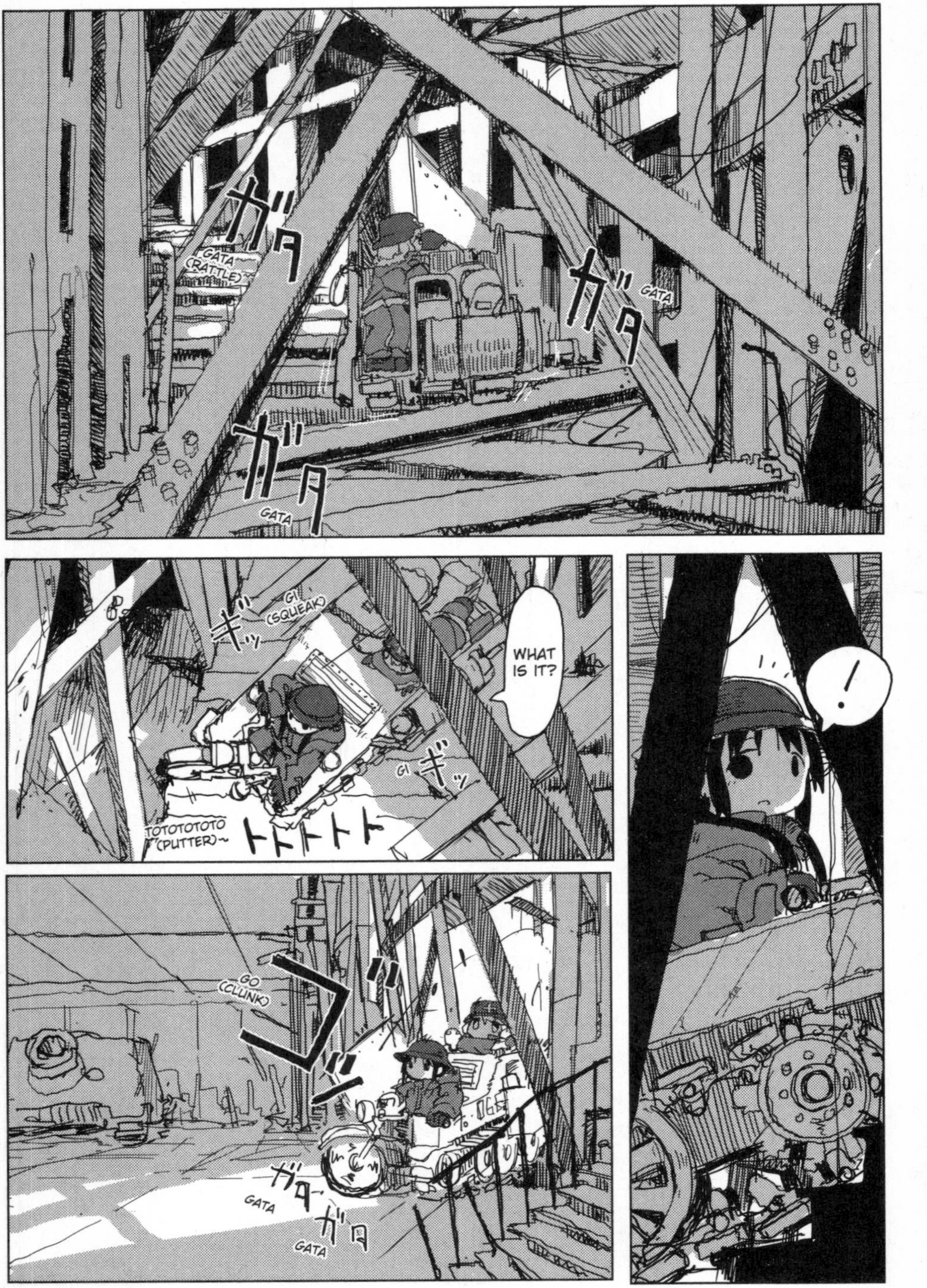
ガタ
GATA
ガタ
GATA (RATTLE)
ガタ
GATA
!
WHAT IS IT?
GI (SQUEAK)
ギッ
GI
ギッ
トトトトト
TOTOTOTOTO (PUTTER)~
ゴッ
GO (CLINK)
ガタ
GATA
ガタ
GATA

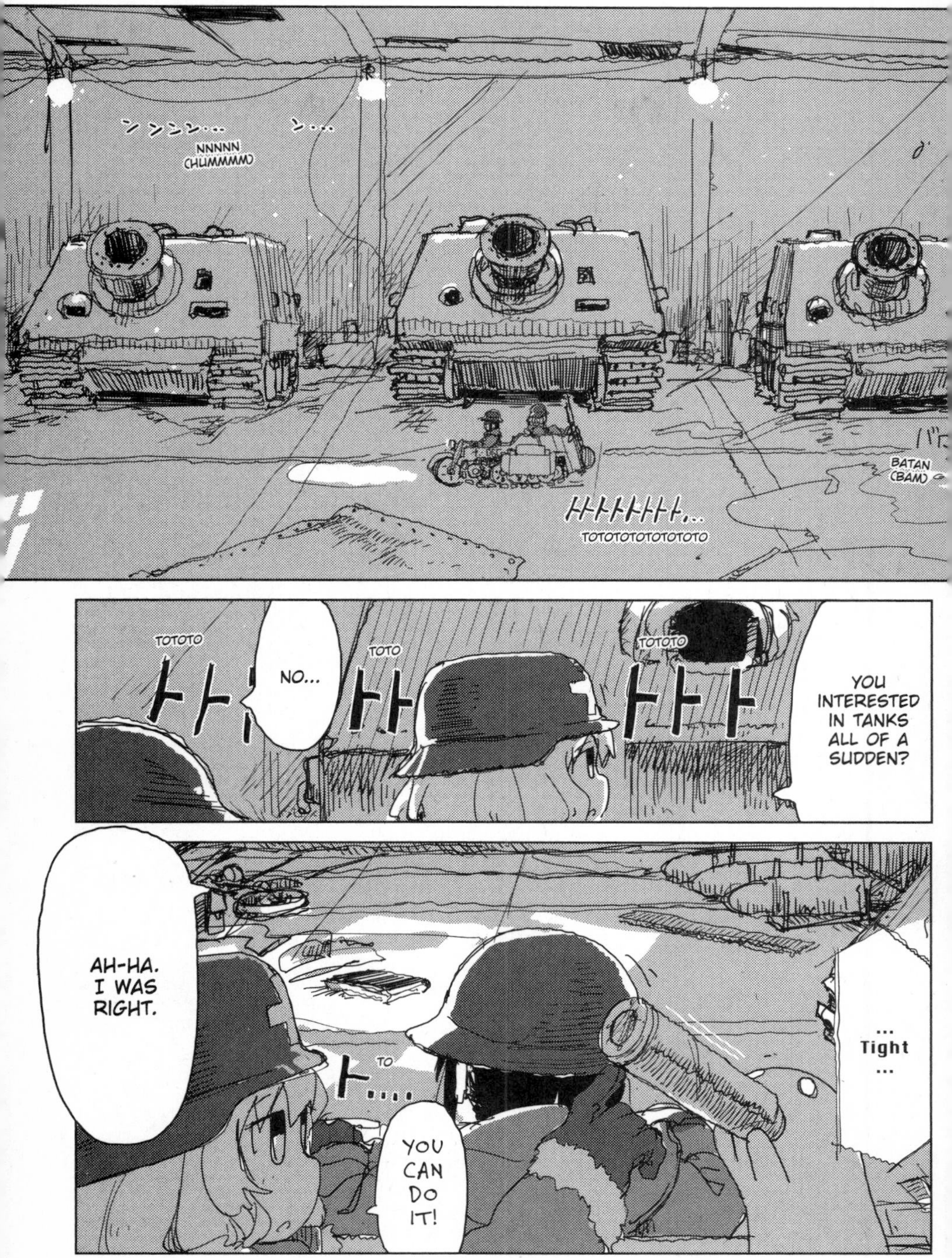
BATAN (BAM)
NNNNN (CHUMMMM)
TOTOTOTOTOTOTOTO
YOU INTERESTED IN TANKS ALL OF A SUDDEN?
TOTOTO
TOTO
NO...
TOTOTO
... Tight ...
TO
AH-HA. I WAS RIGHT.
YOU CAN DO IT!

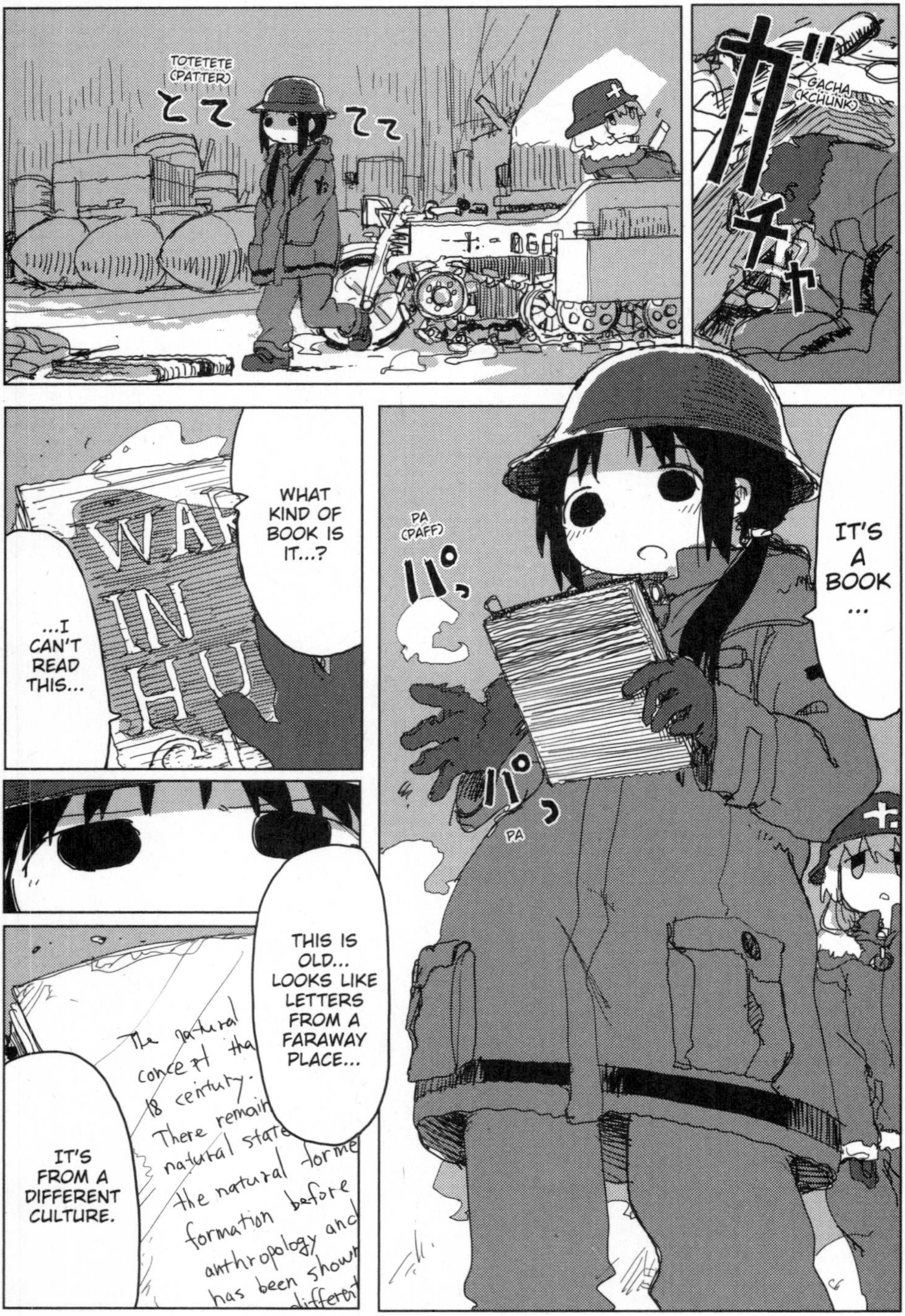
ガチャ
GACHA (KCHUNK)
とててて
TOTETETE (PATTER)
パッ
PA (PAFF)
IT'S A BOOK...
パッ
PA
WHAT KIND OF BOOK IS IT...?
WAR IN HU
...I CAN'T READ THIS...
THIS IS OLD... LOOKS LIKE LETTERS FROM A FARAWAY PLACE...
The natural
concept tha
18 century.
There remain
natural state
the natural forme
formation before
anthropology and
has been shown
IT'S FROM A DIFFERENT CULTURE.

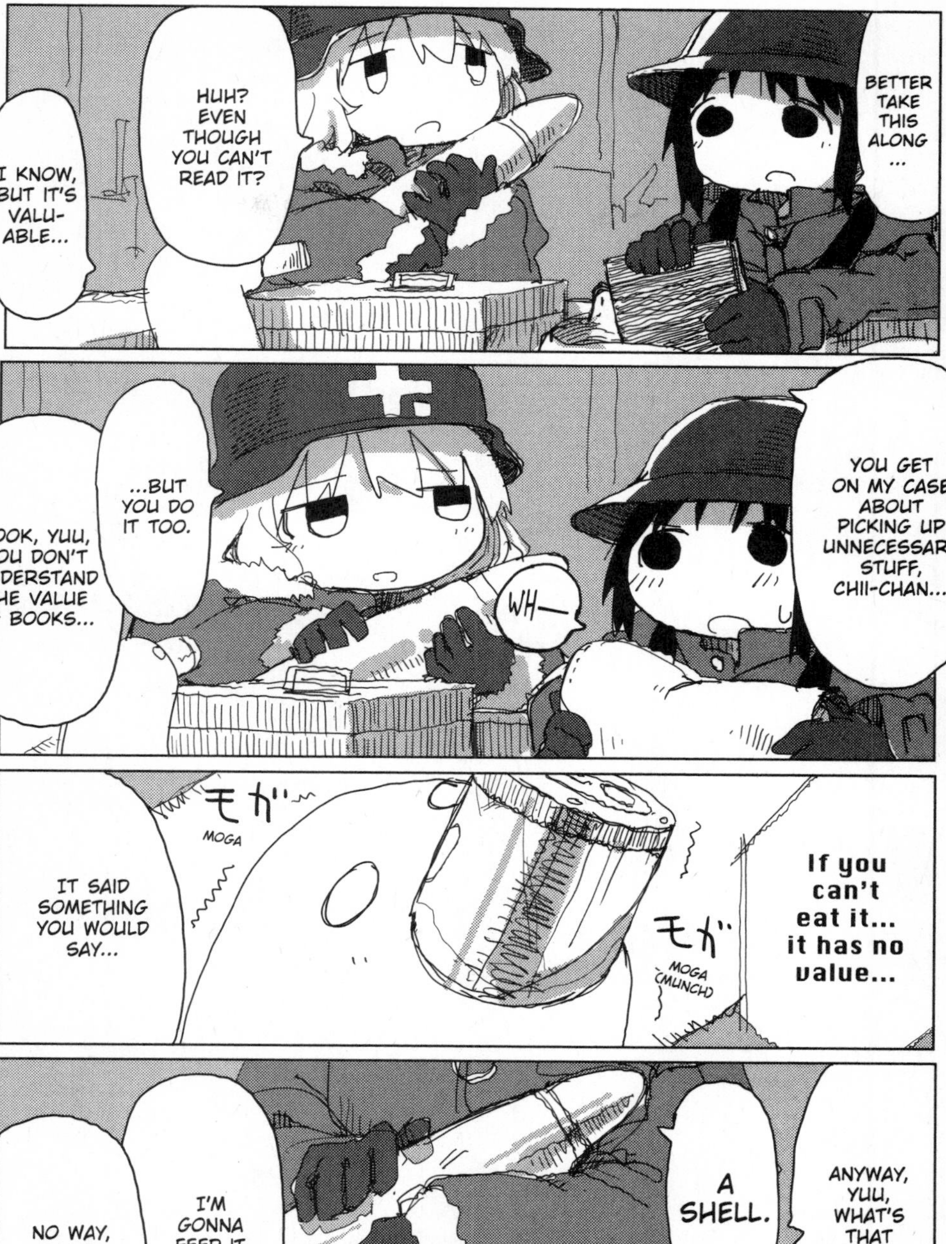
BETTER TAKE THIS ALONG ...
HUH? EVEN THOUGH YOU CAN'T READ IT?
I KNOW, BUT IT'S VALU-ABLE...
YOU GET ON MY CASE ABOUT PICKING UP UNNECESSARY STUFF, CHII-CHAN...
WH—
...BUT YOU DO IT TOO.
LOOK, YUU, YOU DON'T UNDERSTAND THE VALUE OF BOOKS...
If you can't eat it... it has no value...
モガ
MOGA (MUNCH)
モガ
MOGA
IT SAID SOMETHING YOU WOULD SAY...
ANYWAY, YUU, WHAT'S THAT YOU'RE CARRYING?
A SHELL.
I'M GONNA FEED IT TO KET.
NO WAY, THAT'S TOO BIG.
GET RID OF IT.

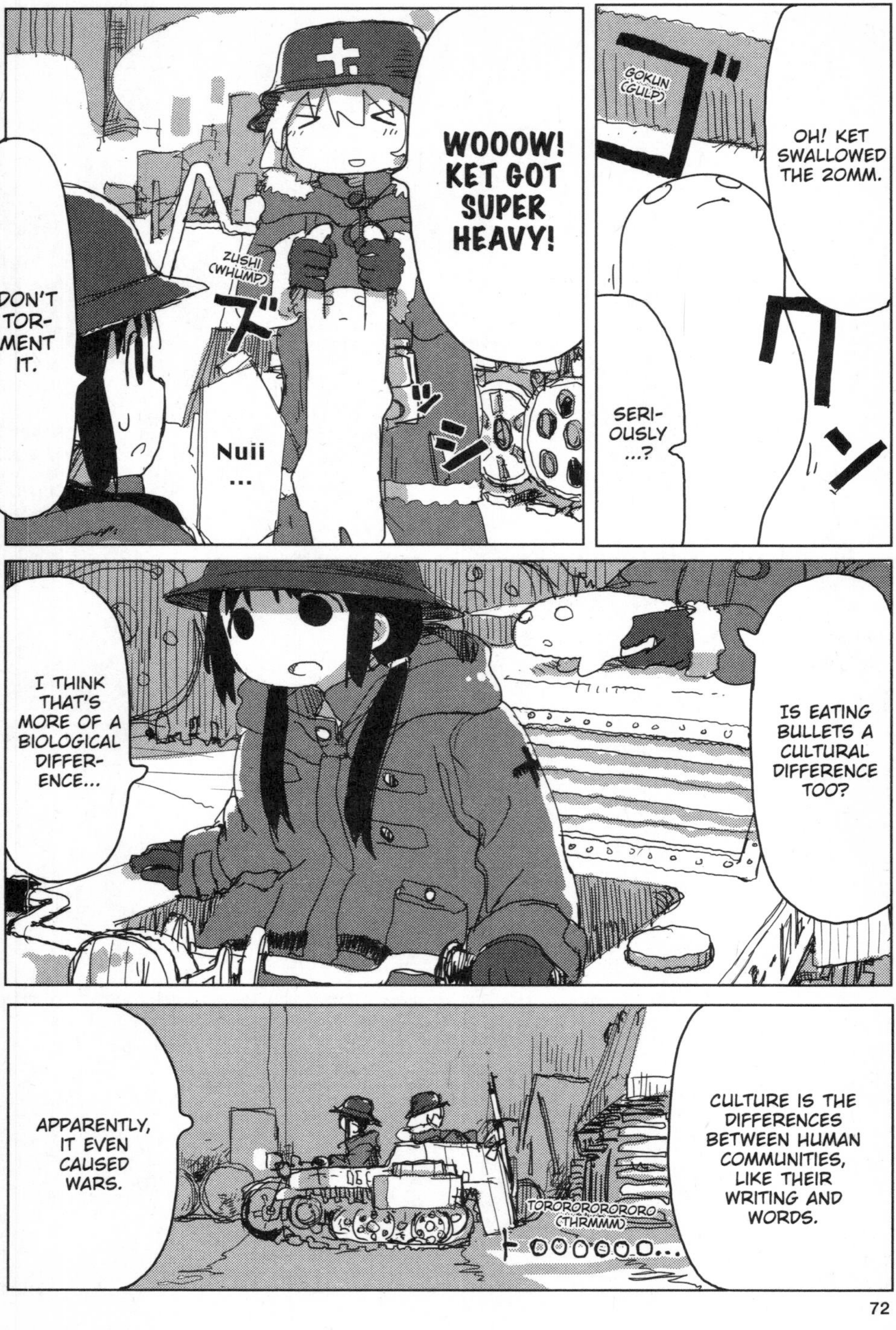
GOKUN (GULP)
OH! KET SWALLOWED THE 20MM.
SERI-OUSLY ...?
WOOOW! KET GOT SUPER HEAVY!
ZUSHI (WHUMP)
Nuii ...
DON'T TOR-MENT IT.
IS EATING BULLETS A CULTURAL DIFFERENCE TOO?
I THINK THAT'S MORE OF A BIOLOGICAL DIFFER-ENCE...
CULTURE IS THE DIFFERENCES BETWEEN HUMAN COMMUNITIES, LIKE THEIR WRITING AND WORDS.
TORORORORORORO (THRMMM)
APPARENTLY, IT EVEN CAUSED WARS.

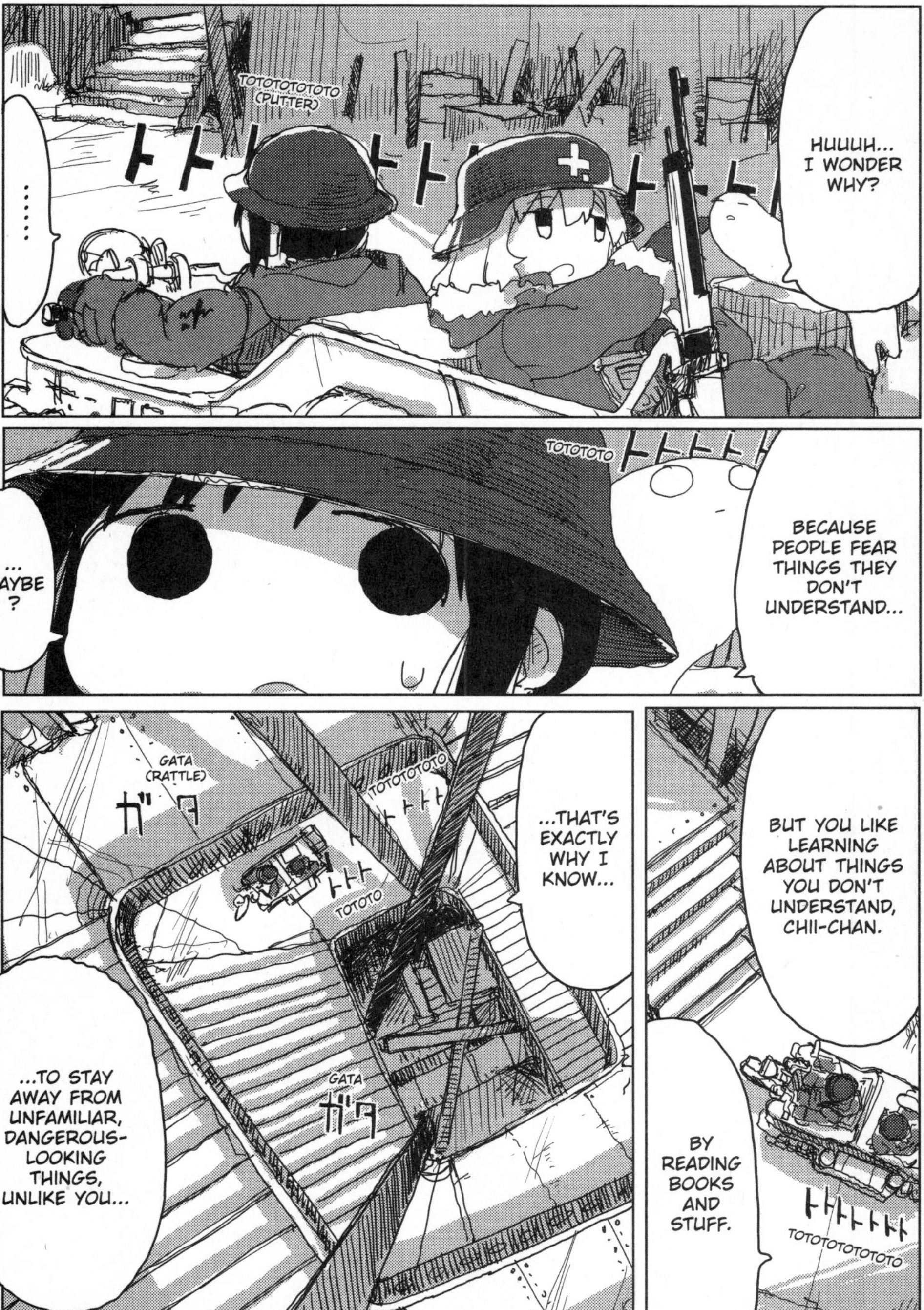
HUUUH... I WONDER WHY?
TOTOTOTOTOTO (PUTTER)
......
BECAUSE PEOPLE FEAR THINGS THEY DON'T UNDERSTAND...
TOTOTOTO
...MAYBE?
BUT YOU LIKE LEARNING ABOUT THINGS YOU DON'T UNDERSTAND, CHII-CHAN.
BY READING BOOKS AND STUFF.
TOTOTOTOTOTO
...THAT'S EXACTLY WHY I KNOW...
GATA (RATTLE)
TOTOTOTOTO
TOTOTO
GATA
...TO STAY AWAY FROM UNFAMILIAR, DANGEROUS-LOOKING THINGS, UNLIKE YOU...

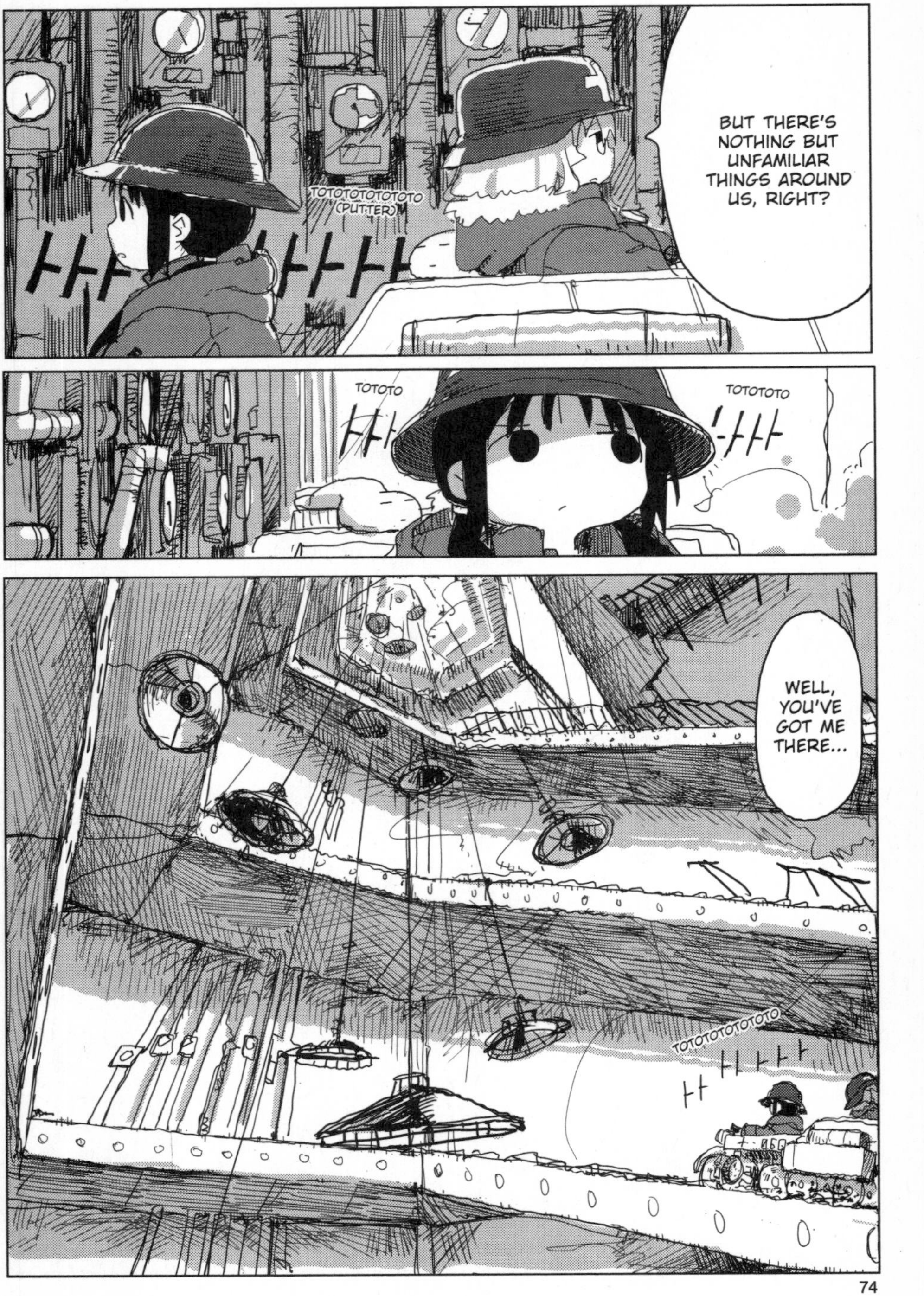
BUT THERE'S NOTHING BUT UNFAMILIAR THINGS AROUND US, RIGHT?
TOTOTOTOTOTOTOTO (PUTTER)
TOTOTOTO
TOTOTO
WELL, YOU'VE GOT ME THERE...
TOTOTOTOTOTOTOTO

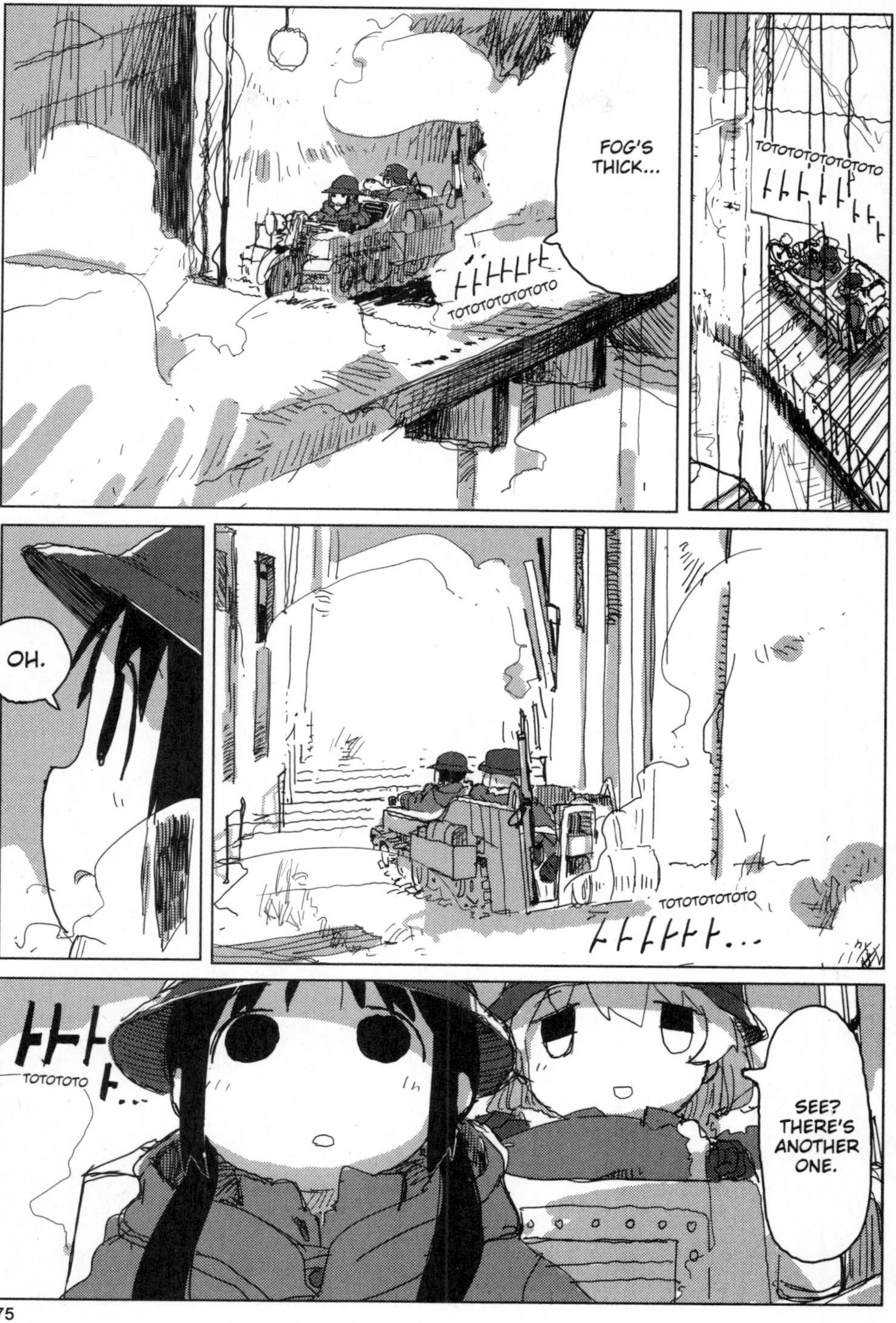
TOTOTOTOTOTOTOTO
FOG'S THICK...
TOTOTOTOTOTOTO
TOTOTOTOTOTO
OH.
SEE? THERE'S ANOTHER ONE.
TOTOTOTO

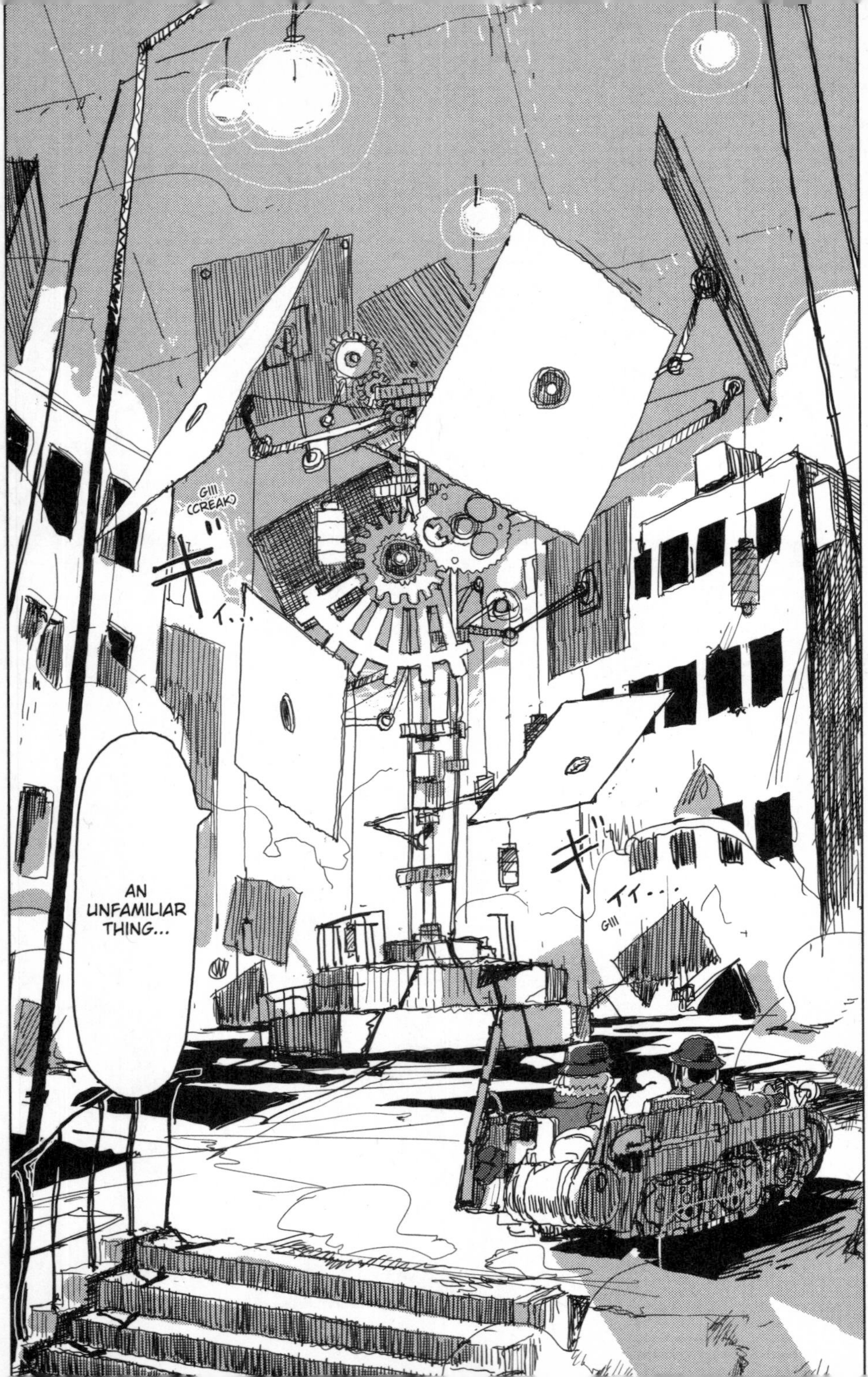
GIII (CREAK)
ギィ...
ギィィ...
GIII
AN UNFAMILIAR THING...

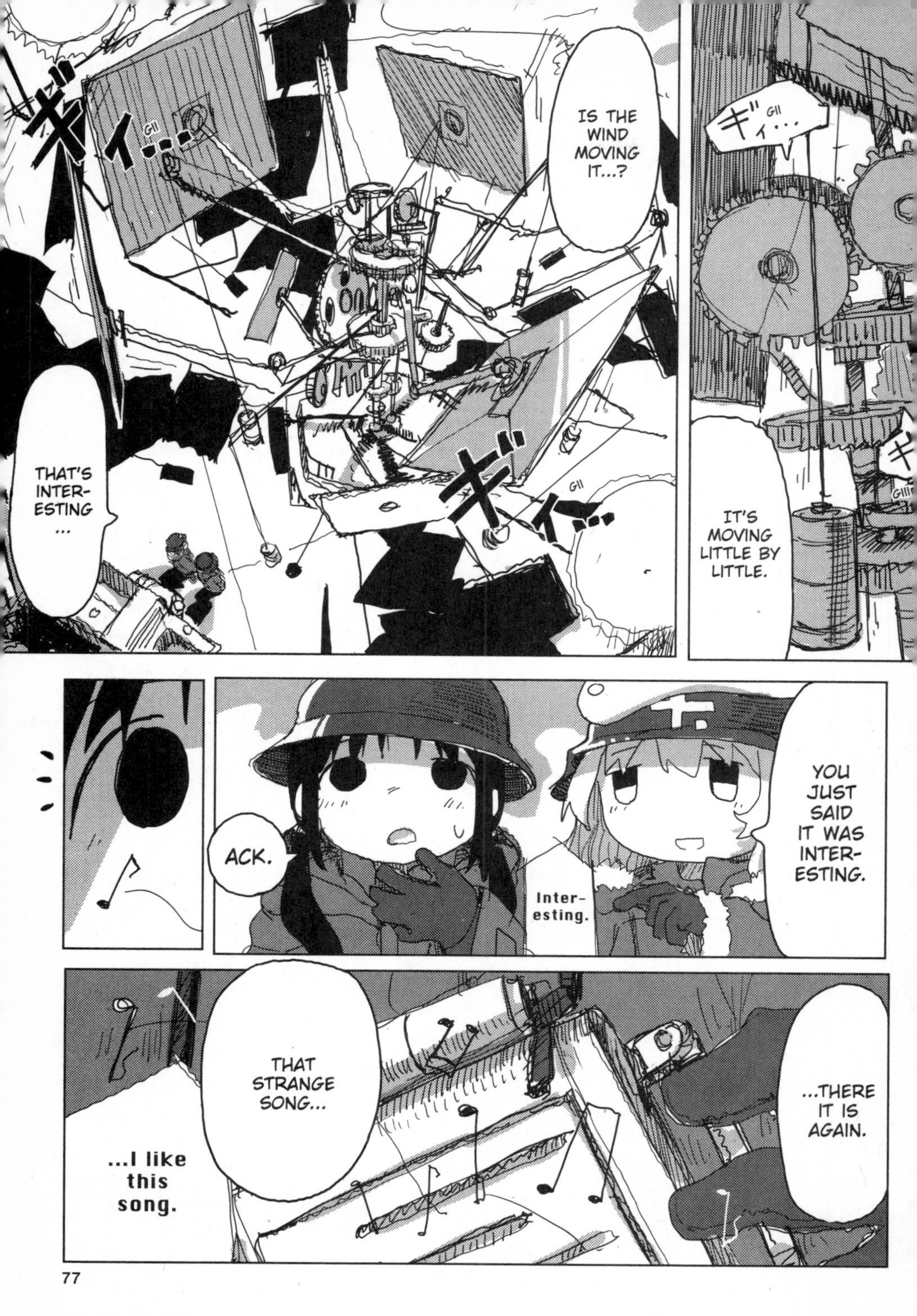
ギィ…
GII
IT'S MOVING LITTLE BY LITTLE.
ギ
GIII
IS THE WIND MOVING IT...?
ギィ…
GII
ギィ…
GII
THAT'S INTER- ESTING ...
YOU JUST SAID IT WAS INTER- ESTING.
Inter- esting.
ACK.
...THERE IT IS AGAIN.
THAT STRANGE SONG...
...I like this song.

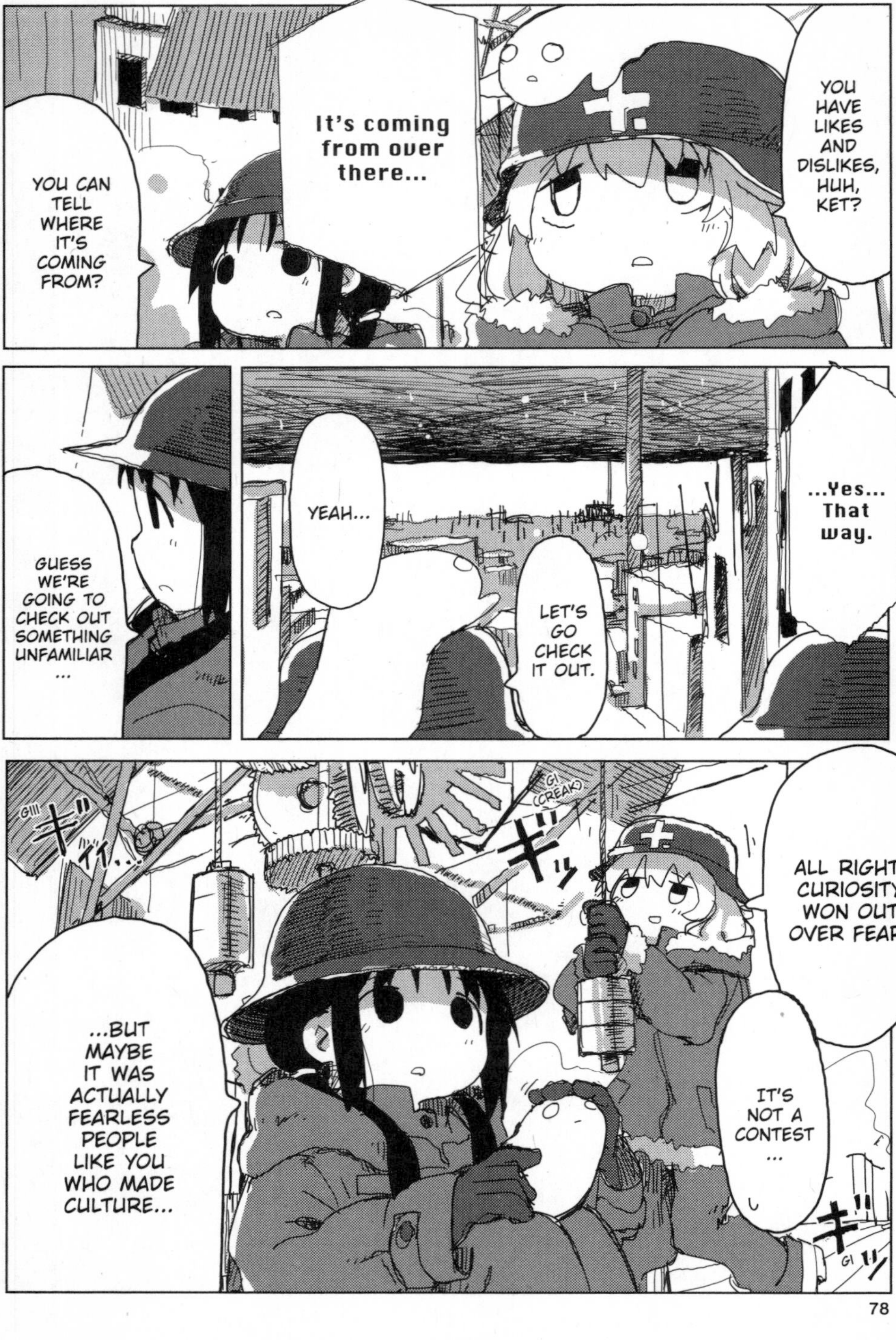
YOU HAVE LIKES AND DISLIKES, HUH, KET?
It's coming from over there...
YOU CAN TELL WHERE IT'S COMING FROM?
...Yes... That way.
YEAH...
LET'S GO CHECK IT OUT.
GUESS WE'RE GOING TO CHECK OUT SOMETHING UNFAMILIAR...
GI (CREAK)
ALL RIGHT! CURIOSITY WON OUT OVER FEAR!
GIII
IT'S NOT A CONTEST...
...BUT MAYBE IT WAS ACTUALLY FEARLESS PEOPLE LIKE YOU WHO MADE CULTURE...
GI

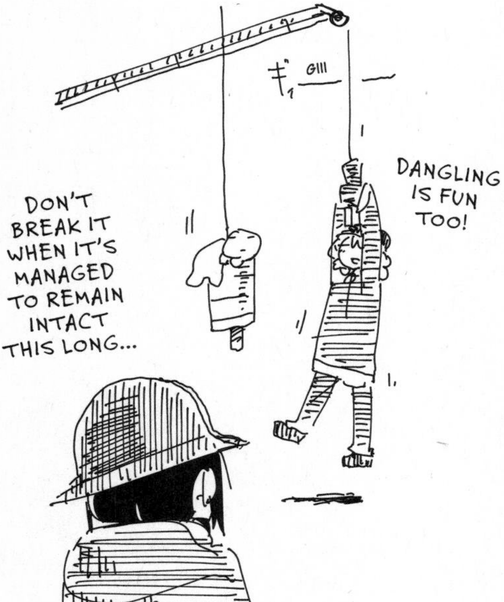
GIII
DANGLING IS FUN TOO!
DON'T BREAK IT WHEN IT'S MANAGED TO REMAIN INTACT THIS LONG...

GIRLS' LAST TOUR

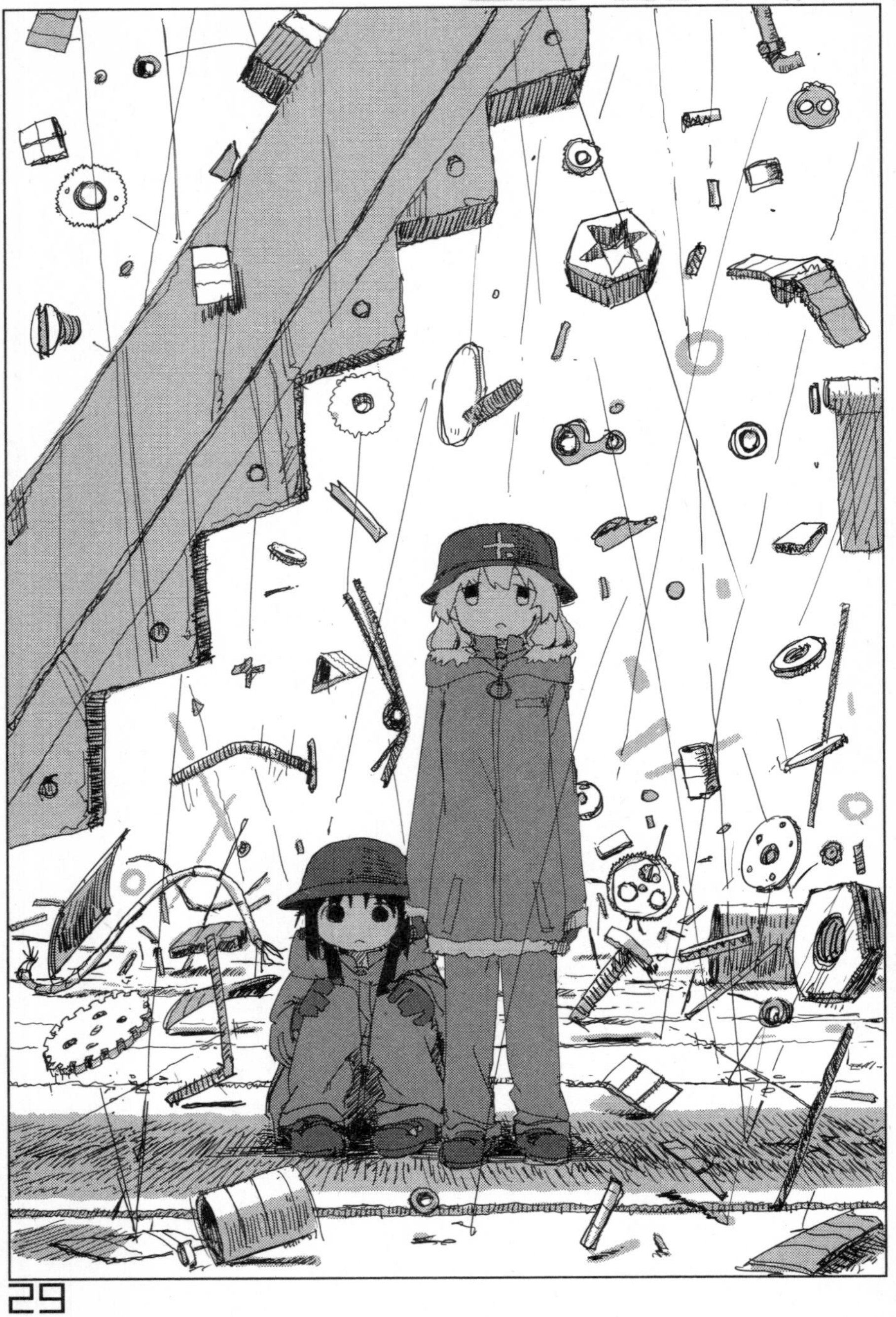

29 DESTRUCTION

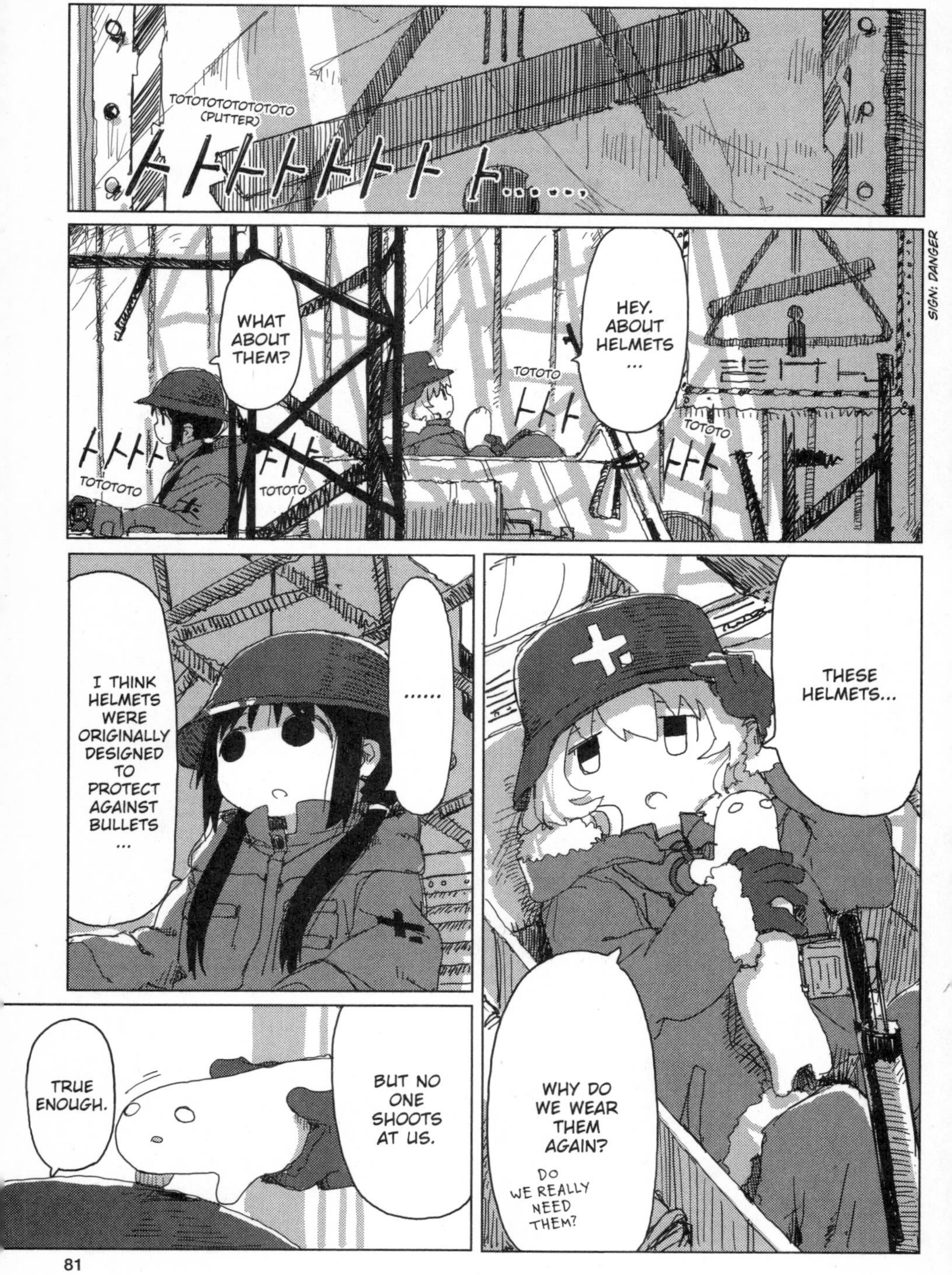
TOTOTOTOTOTOTOTOTO (PUTTER)
トトトトトトトトト……
SIGN: DANGER
HEY. ABOUT HELMETS ...
WHAT ABOUT THEM?
TOTOTO
TOTOTO
TOTOTO
TOTOTOTO
THESE HELMETS...
WHY DO WE WEAR THEM AGAIN?
DO WE REALLY NEED THEM?
......
I THINK HELMETS WERE ORIGINALLY DESIGNED TO PROTECT AGAINST BULLETS ...
BUT NO ONE SHOOTS AT US.
TRUE ENOUGH.

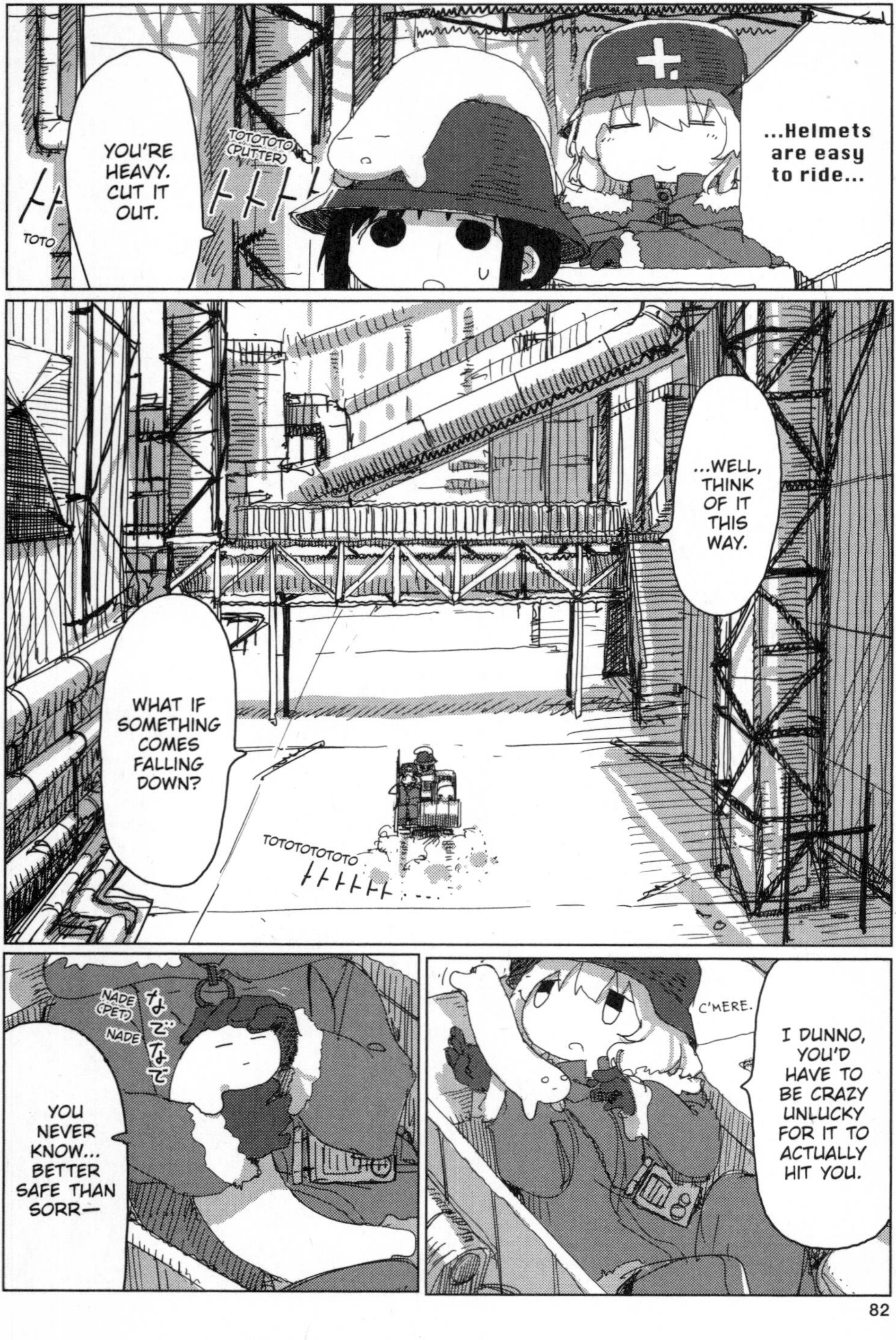
...Helmets are easy to ride...
TOTOTOTO (PUTTER)
YOU'RE HEAVY. CUT IT OUT.
TOTO
...WELL, THINK OF IT THIS WAY.
WHAT IF SOMETHING COMES FALLING DOWN?
TOTOTOTOTOTO
I DUNNO, YOU'D HAVE TO BE CRAZY UNLUCKY FOR IT TO ACTUALLY HIT YOU.
C'MERE.
NADE (PET) NADE
なでなで
YOU NEVER KNOW... BETTER SAFE THAN SORR—

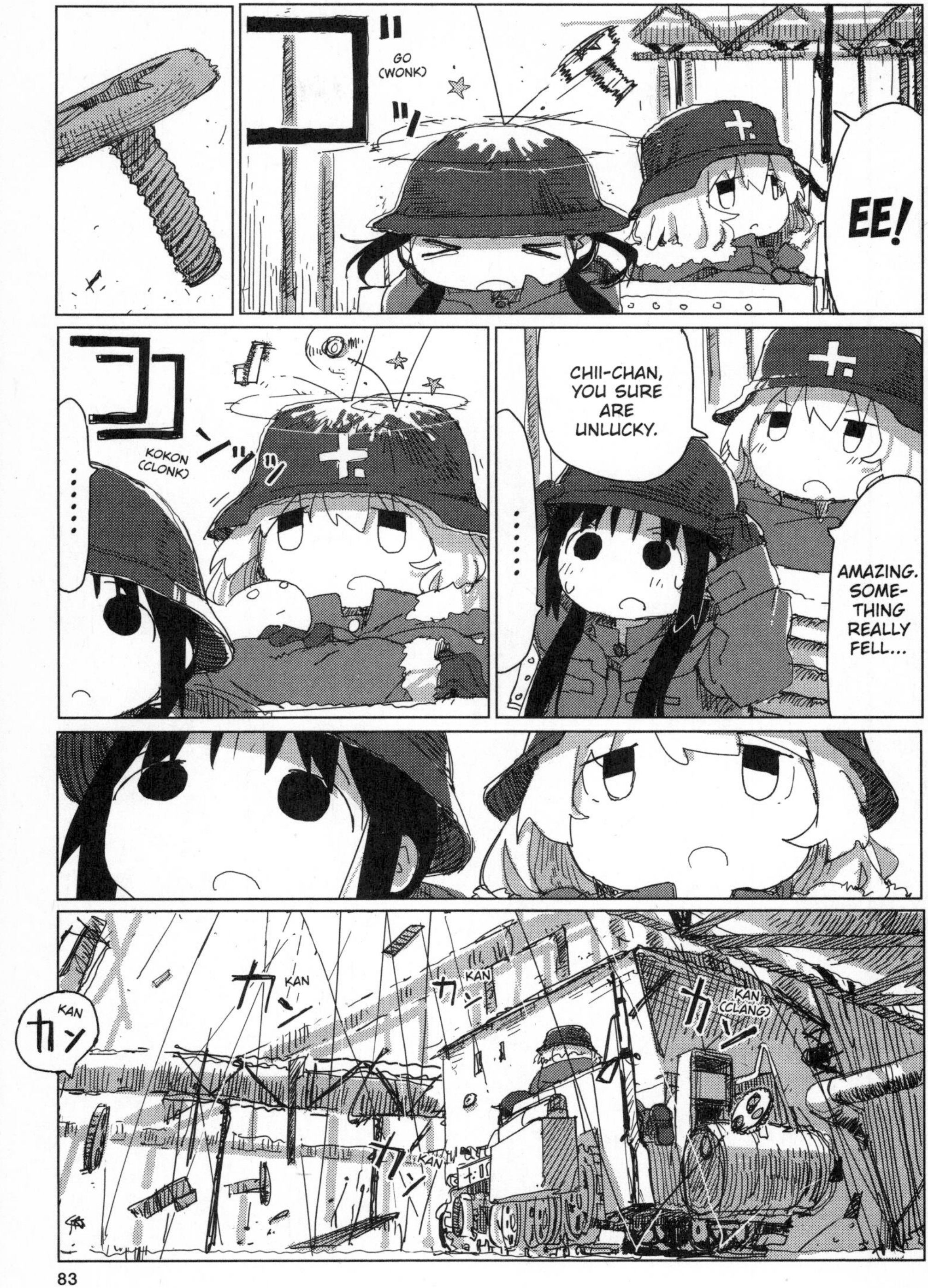

GO (WONK)
EE!
CHII-CHAN, YOU SURE ARE UNLUCKY.
......
AMAZING. SOMETHING REALLY FELL...
KOKON (CLONK)
......
KAN
KAN (CLANG)
KAN
KAN
KAN
カン

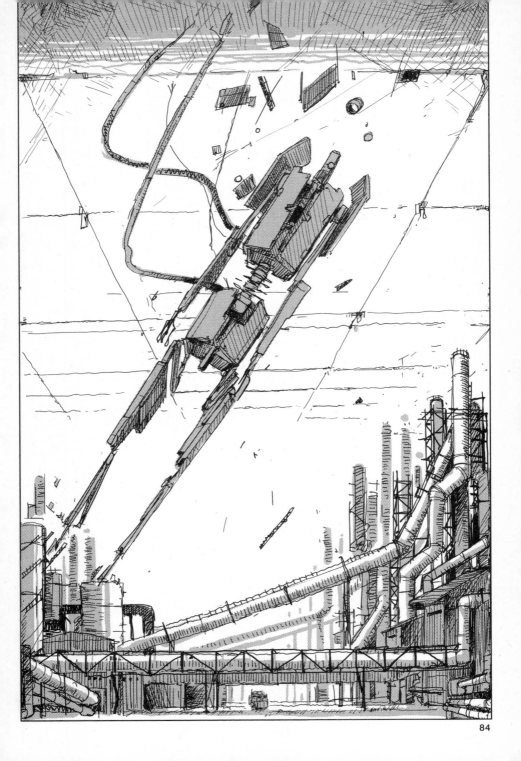

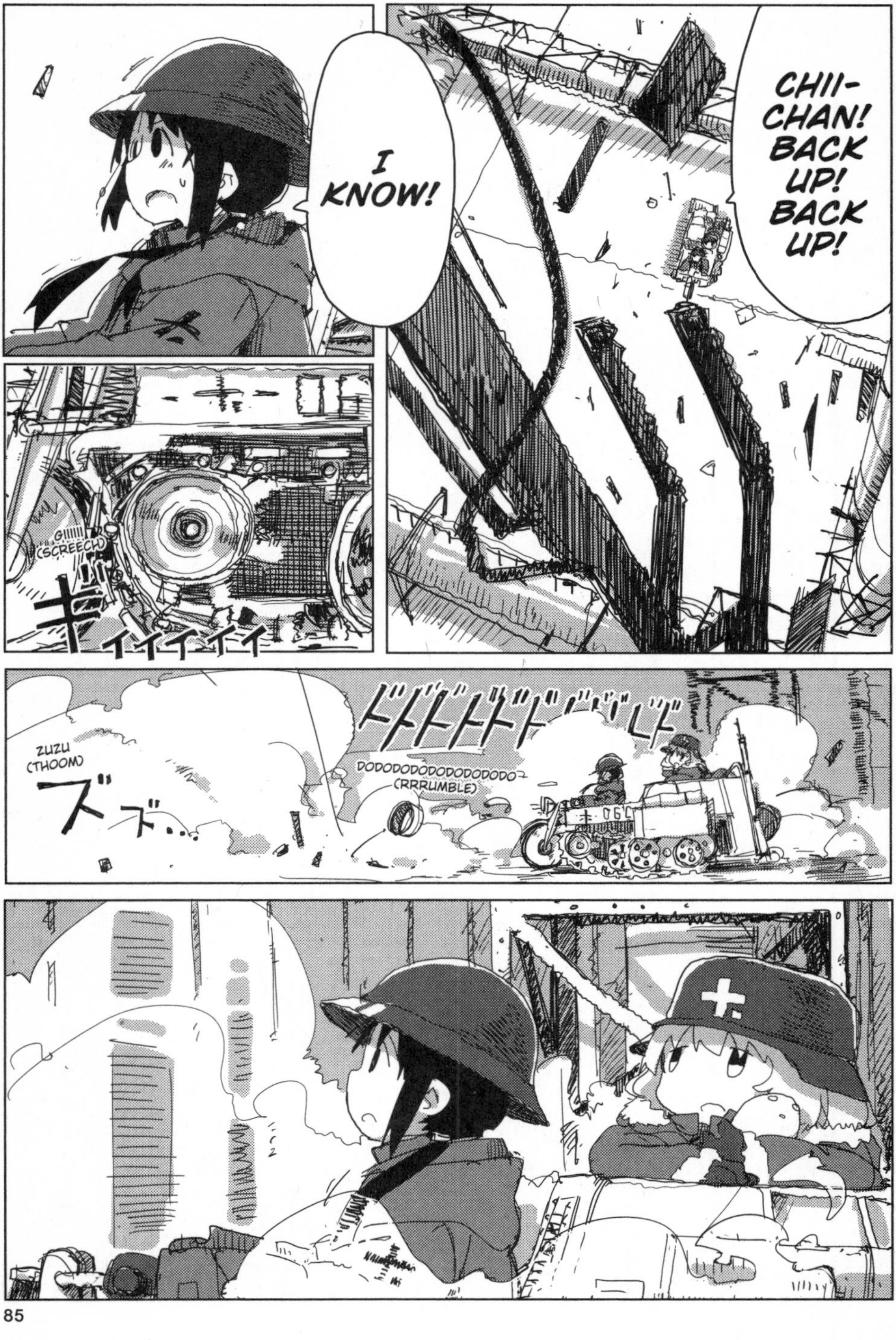
CHII-CHAN! BACK UP! BACK UP!
I KNOW!
GIIIIII
(SCREECH)
ギイイイイイ
ドドドドドドドドド
DODODODODODODODODO
(RRRUMBLE)
ZUZU
(THOOM)
ズズ…

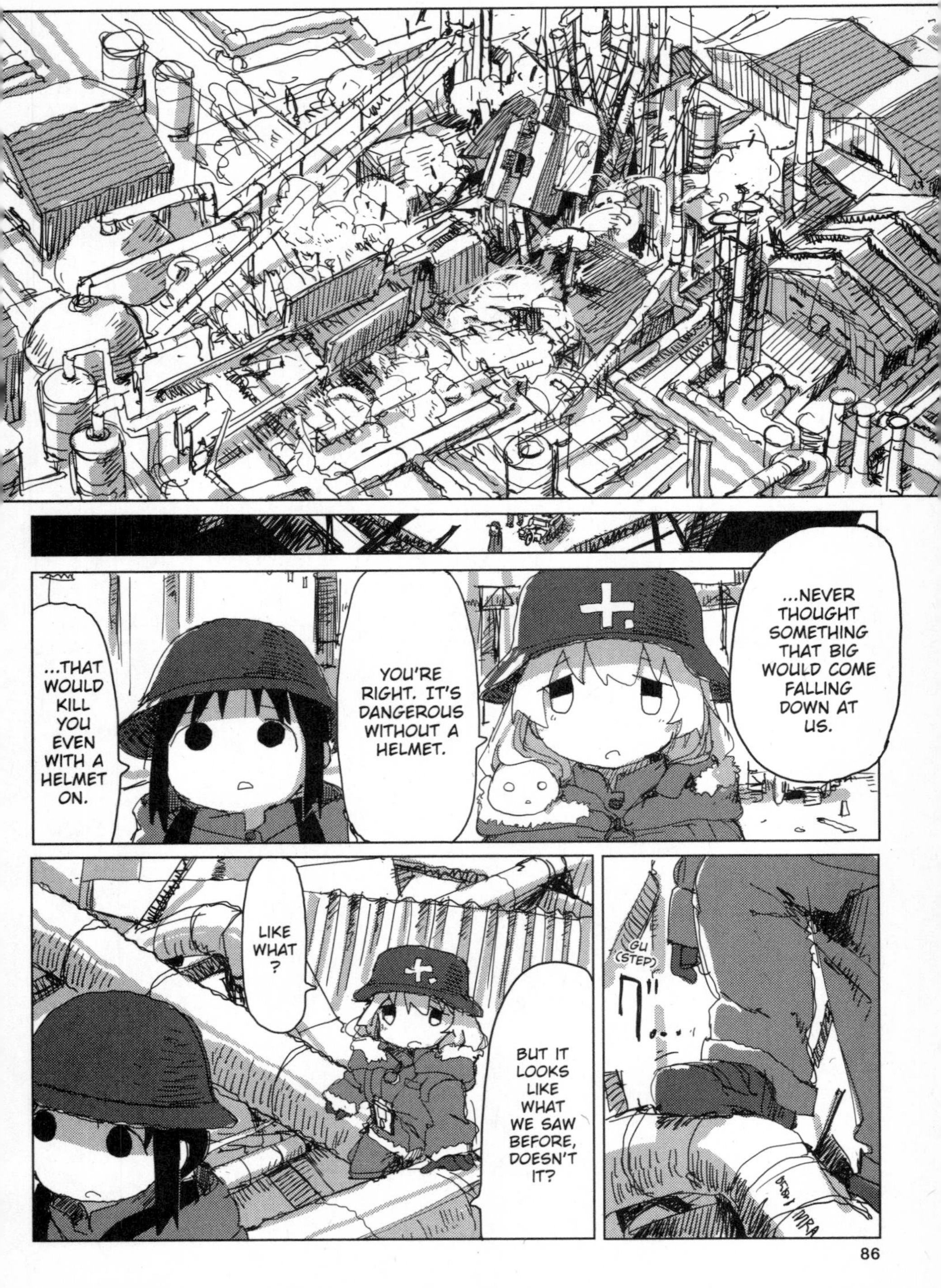

...NEVER THOUGHT SOMETHING THAT BIG WOULD COME FALLING DOWN AT US.
YOU'RE RIGHT. IT'S DANGEROUS WITHOUT A HELMET.
...THAT WOULD KILL YOU EVEN WITH A HELMET ON.
GU (STEP)
BUT IT LOOKS LIKE WHAT WE SAW BEFORE, DOESN'T IT?
LIKE WHAT?

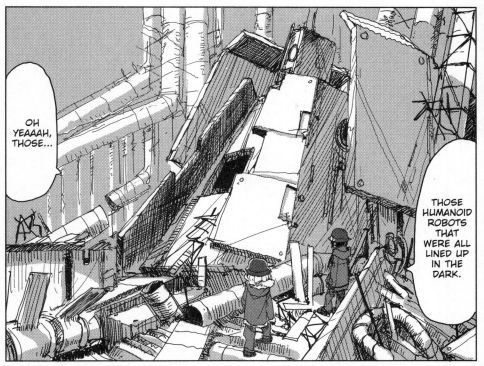

THOSE HUMANOID ROBOTS THAT WERE ALL LINED UP IN THE DARK.
OH YEAAAH, THOSE...
SURE IS HUGE.
YUU! OVER HERE!
CAN WE GET INSIDE?
MAY-BE.

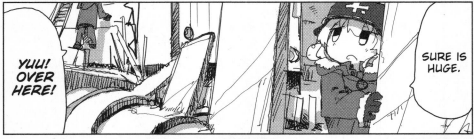

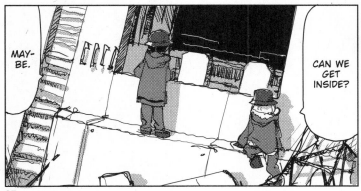

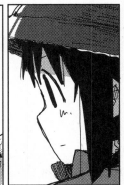

AH! KET...

...Nuii...

TOTE (STEP)

NYU (SLIP)

WANNA GO IN?

...YEAH.

TOTETE

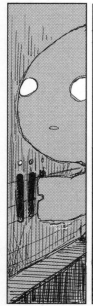

HUH? WHAT'S THIS?

IT'S DARK.

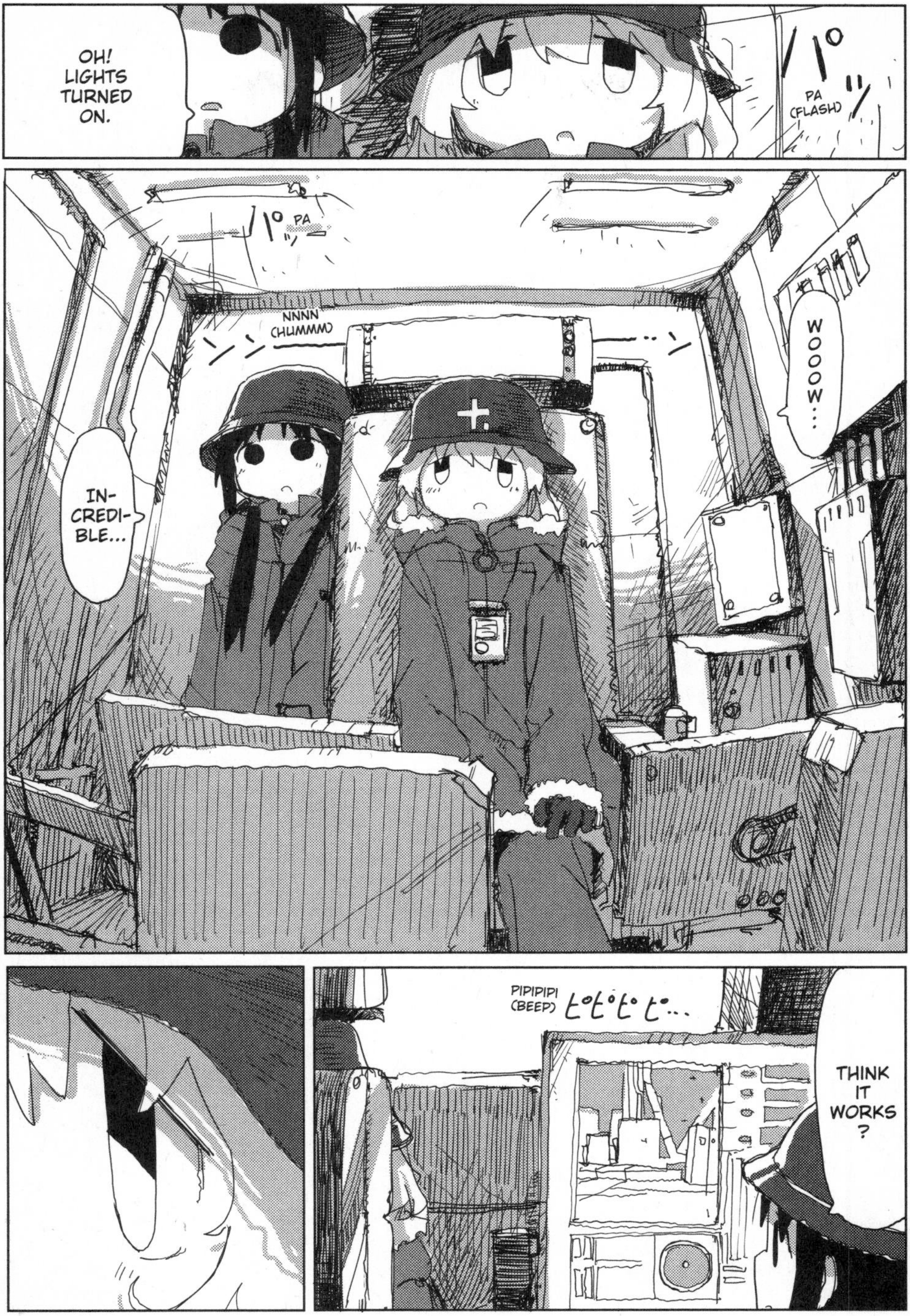

PA (FLASH)
OH! LIGHTS TURNED ON.
WOOOOW...
PA
NNNN (HUMMM)
IN-CREDI-BLE...
THINK IT WORKS?
PIPIPIPI (BEEP) ピピピピ...

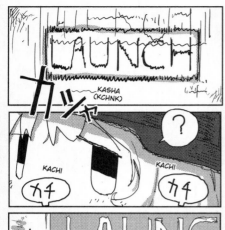

WHAT IS THIS...?
KACHI (CLICK)
カチ
LAUNCH
KASHA (KCHNK)
ガシャ
?
KACHI
カチ
KACHI
カチ
ピピッ
LAUNC
SFX: PI (BEEP) PI
PIPIPIPIPIPI
ピピピピピピ
...WHAT'S IT DOING?
BOSHU (BSHH)
ボシュ
WHO KNOWS ...?
SHU (FSHHT)
シュ
KASHA (KSHAK)
カシャ
BO (BOOF)
ボッ

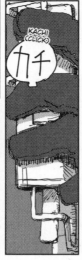

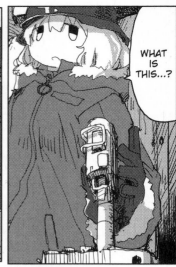

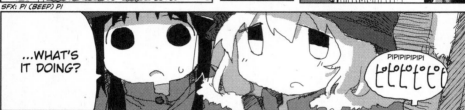

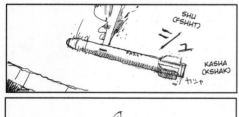

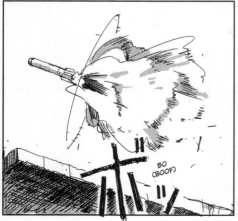

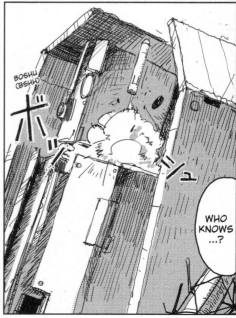

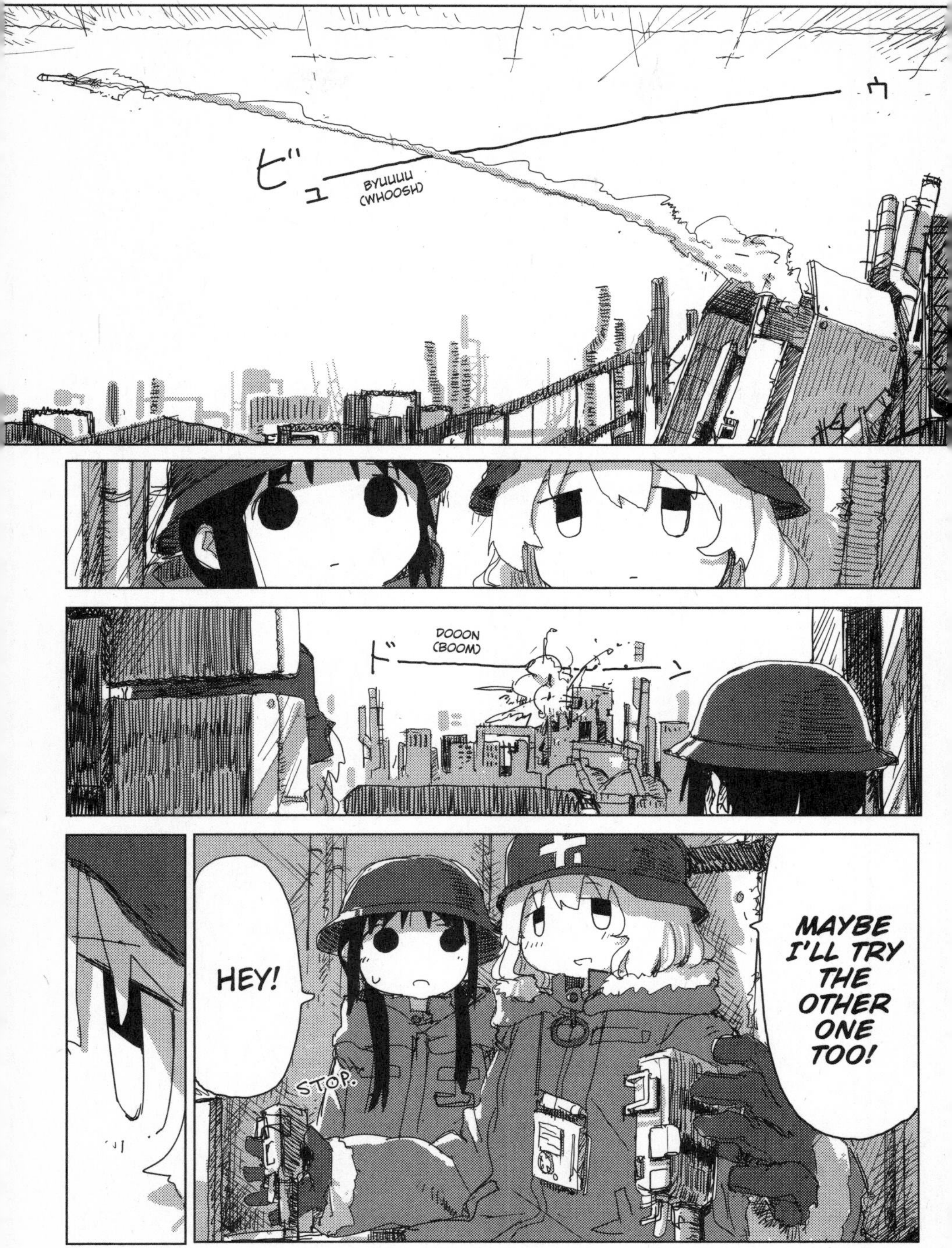
ビュ
ウ
BYUUUU (WHOOSH)
ド
ン
DOOON (BOOM)
MAYBE I'LL TRY THE OTHER ONE TOO!
HEY!
STOP.

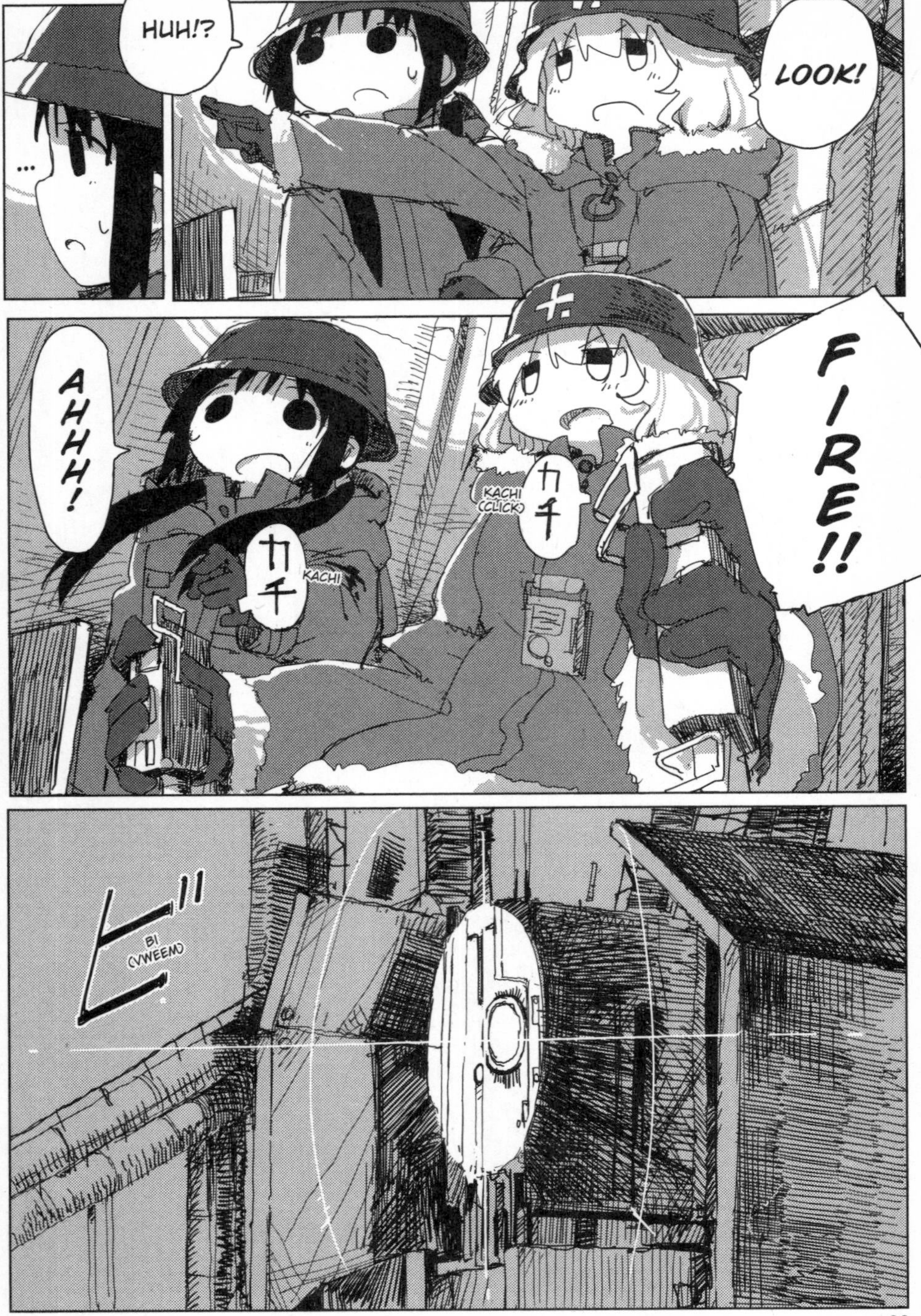
LOOK!
HUH!?
...
FIRE!!
カチ
KACHI (CLICK)
AHHHH!
カチ
KACHI
ビ
BI (VWEEM)

ビー
BIIIII
ドー
DO
(BOOM)
OOF!
DO
(WHUMP)
OW, OW, OW...

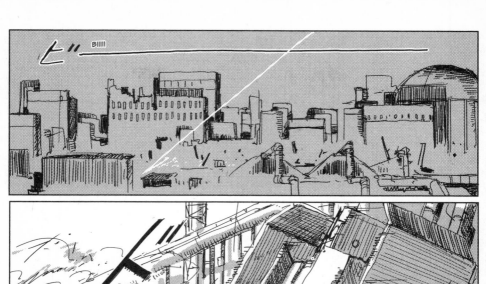

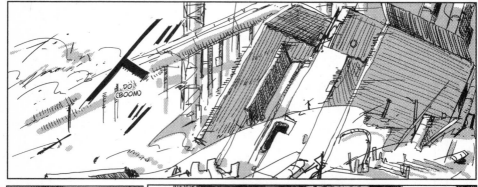

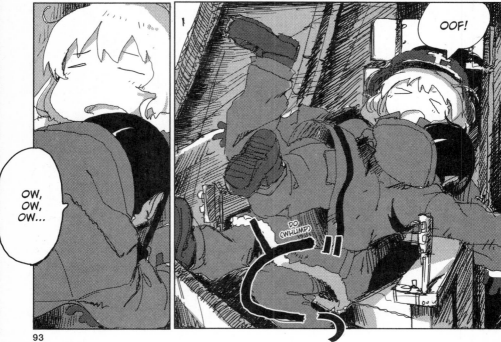

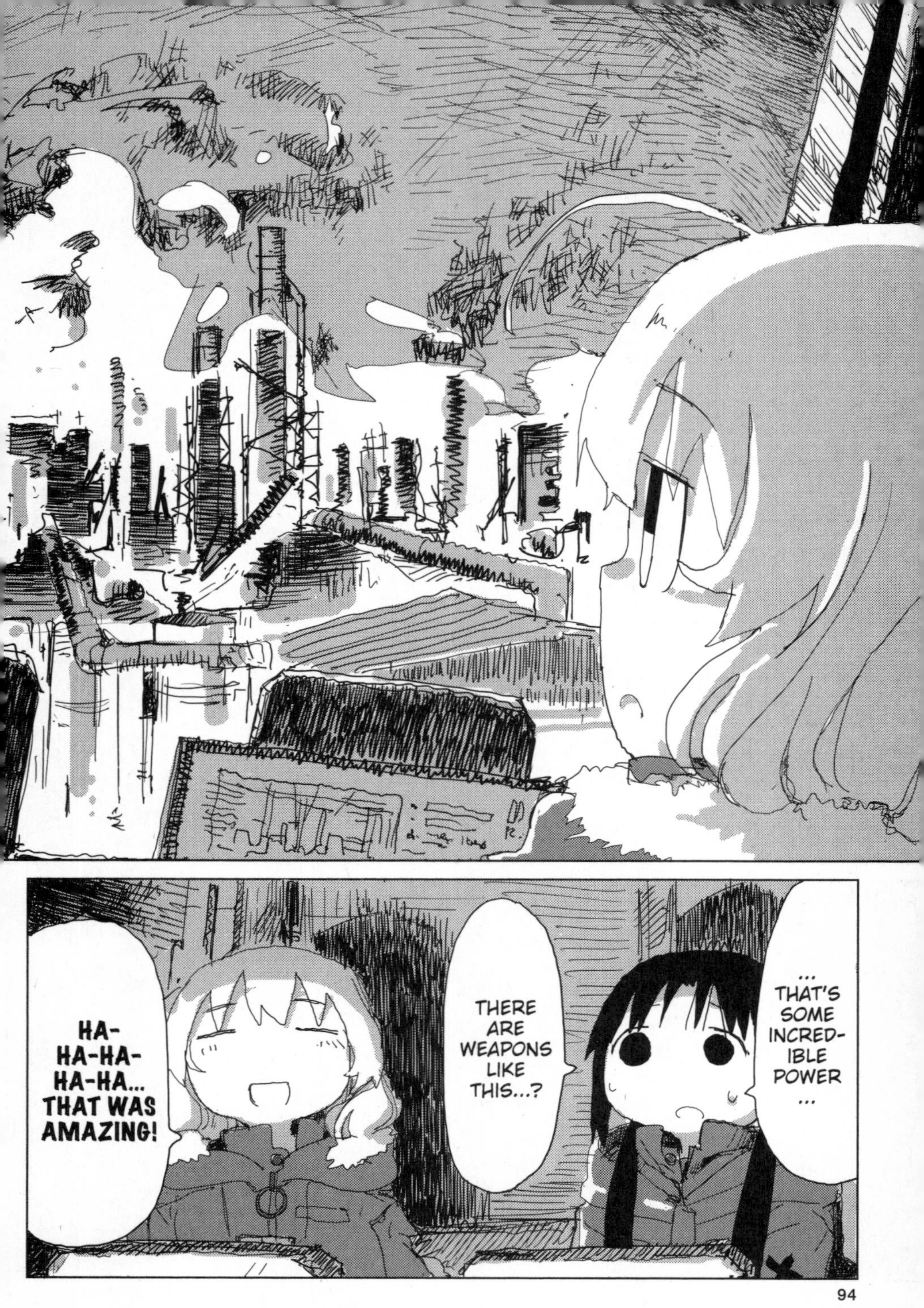
... THAT'S SOME INCREDIBLE POWER ...
THERE ARE WEAPONS LIKE THIS...?
HA-HA-HA-HA-HA... THAT WAS AMAZING!

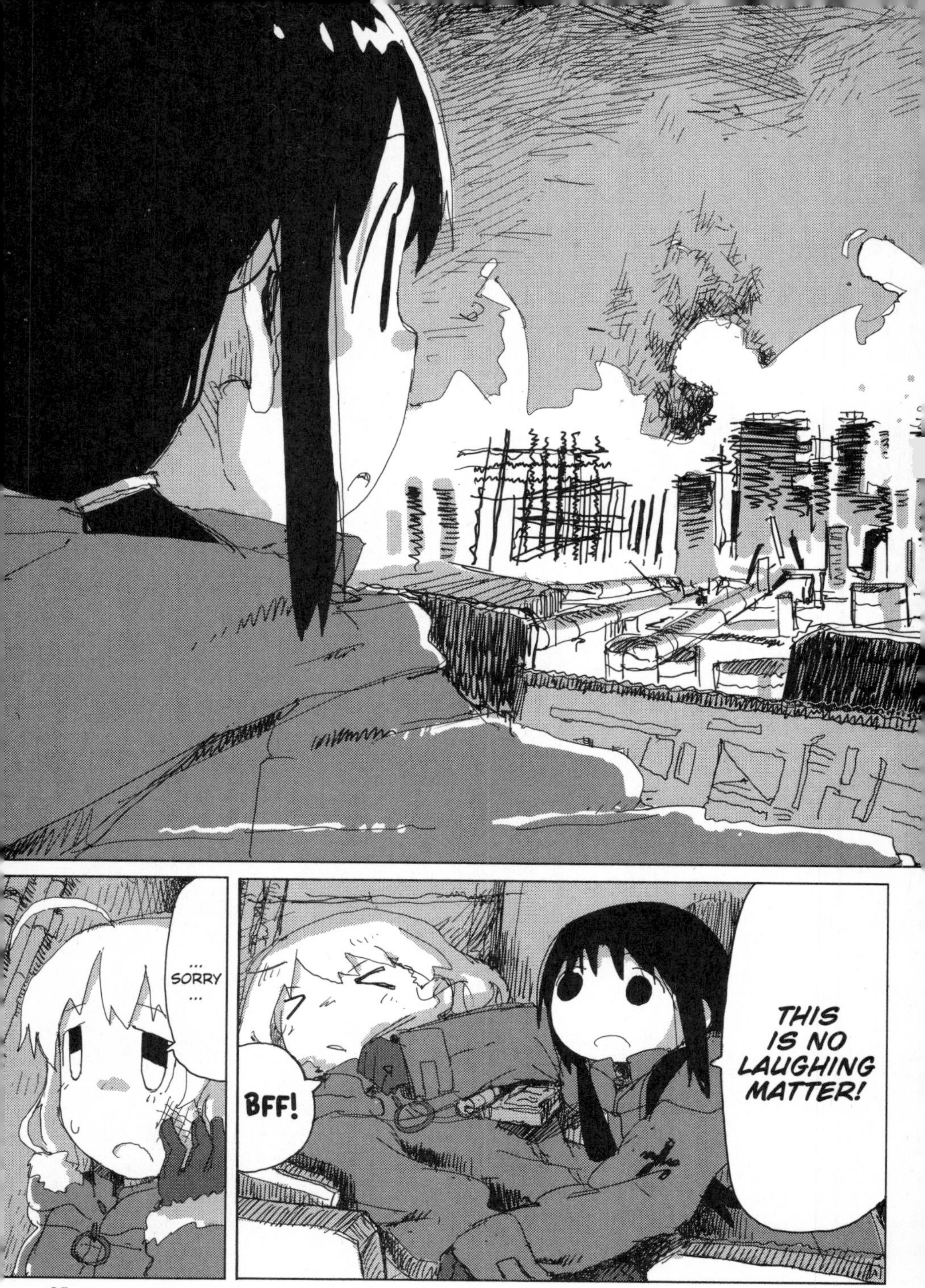
THIS IS NO LAUGHING MATTER!
BFF!
... SORRY ...

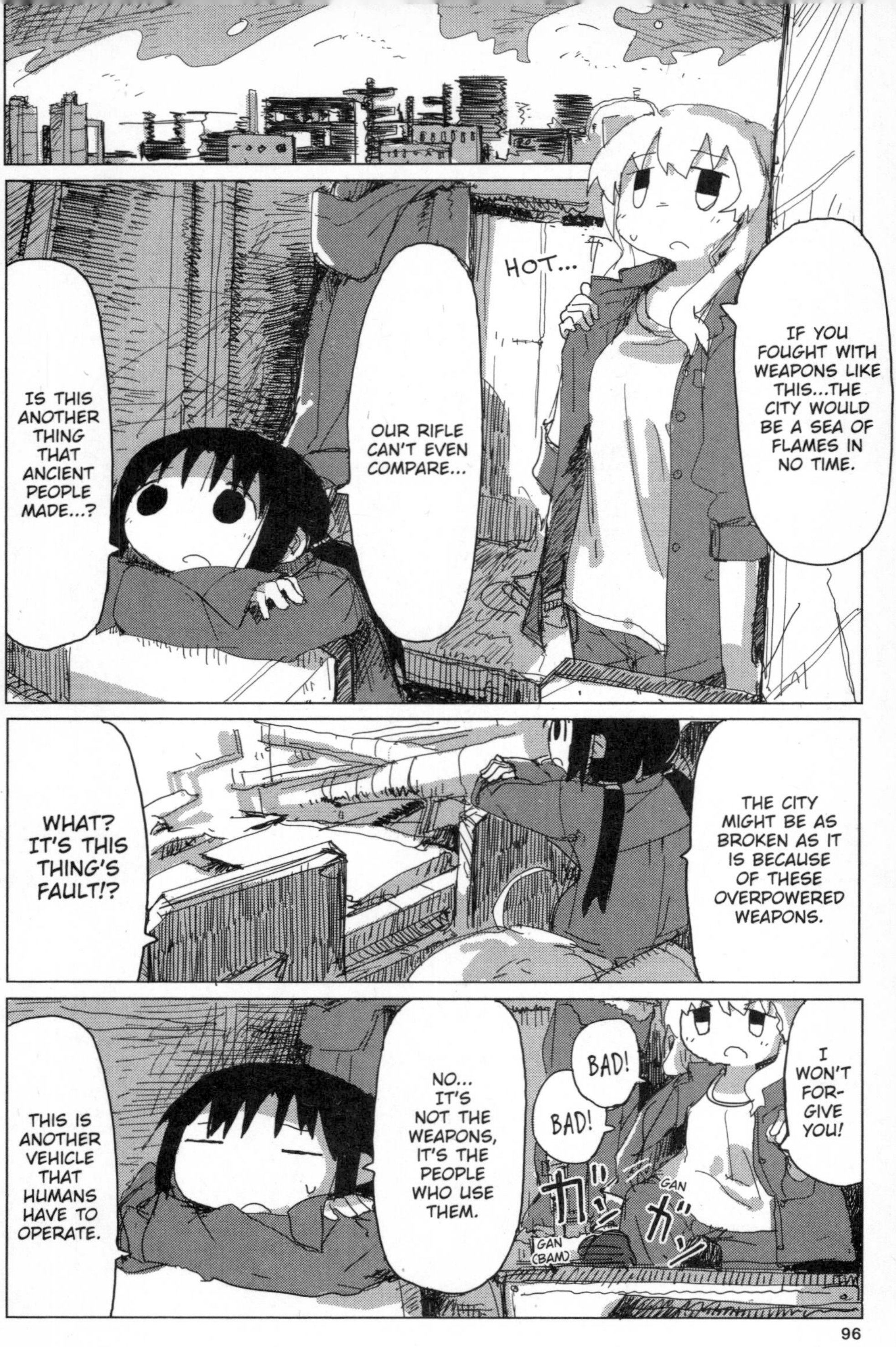
IF YOU FOUGHT WITH WEAPONS LIKE THIS...THE CITY WOULD BE A SEA OF FLAMES IN NO TIME.
HOT...
OUR RIFLE CAN'T EVEN COMPARE...
IS THIS ANOTHER THING THAT ANCIENT PEOPLE MADE...?
THE CITY MIGHT BE AS BROKEN AS IT IS BECAUSE OF THESE OVERPOWERED WEAPONS.
WHAT? IT'S THIS THING'S FAULT!?
I WON'T FOR-GIVE YOU!
BAD!
BAD!
ガン
GAN
ガン
GAN (BAM)
NO... IT'S NOT THE WEAPONS, IT'S THE PEOPLE WHO USE THEM.
THIS IS ANOTHER VEHICLE THAT HUMANS HAVE TO OPERATE.

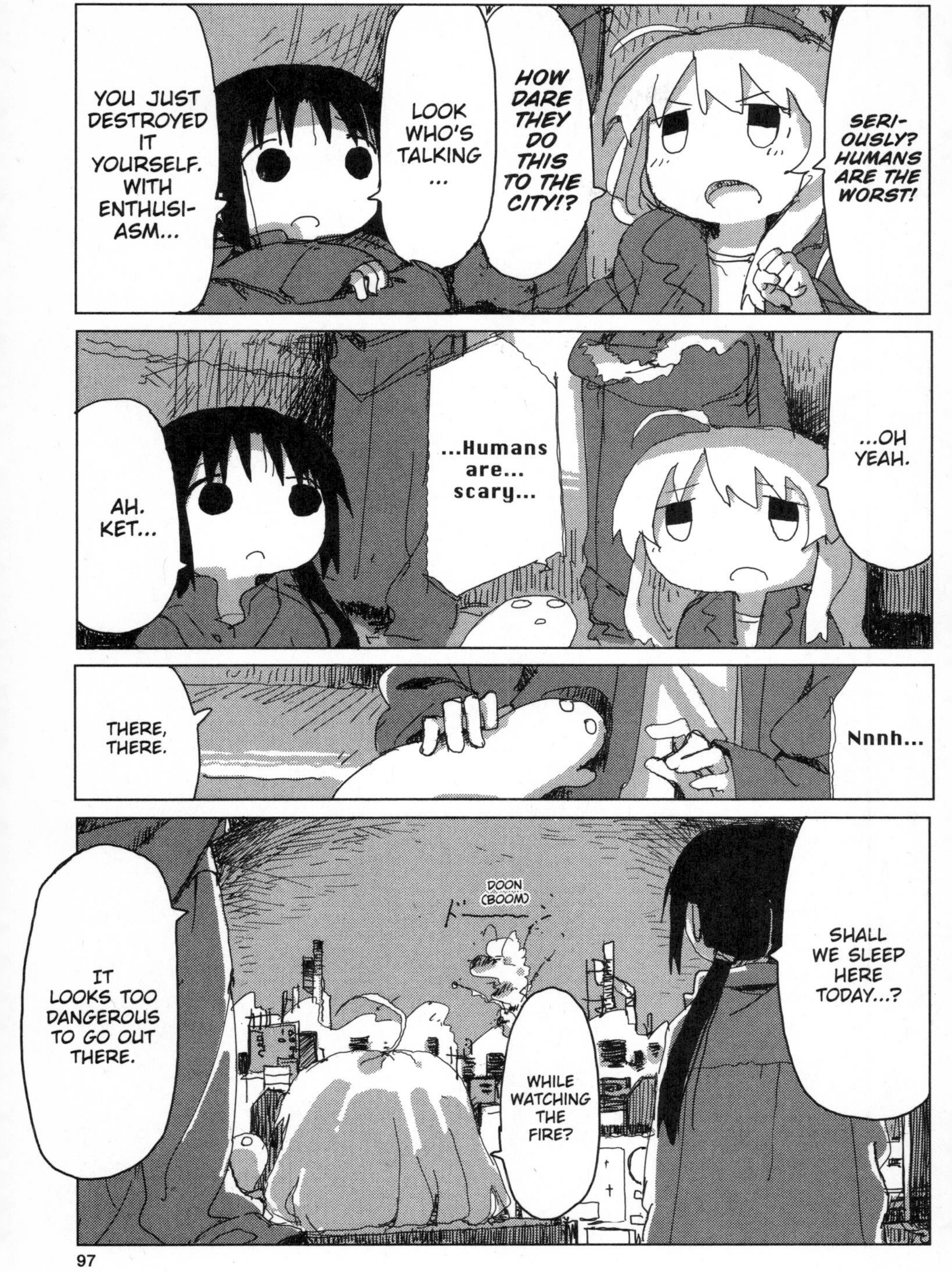
SERI-OUSLY? HUMANS ARE THE WORST!
HOW DARE THEY DO THIS TO THE CITY!?
LOOK WHO'S TALKING ...
YOU JUST DESTROYED IT YOURSELF. WITH ENTHUSI-ASM...
...OH YEAH.
...Humans are... scary...
AH. KET...
Nnnh...
THERE, THERE.
SHALL WE SLEEP HERE TODAY...?
WHILE WATCHING THE FIRE?
DOON (BOOM)
IT LOOKS TOO DANGEROUS TO GO OUT THERE.

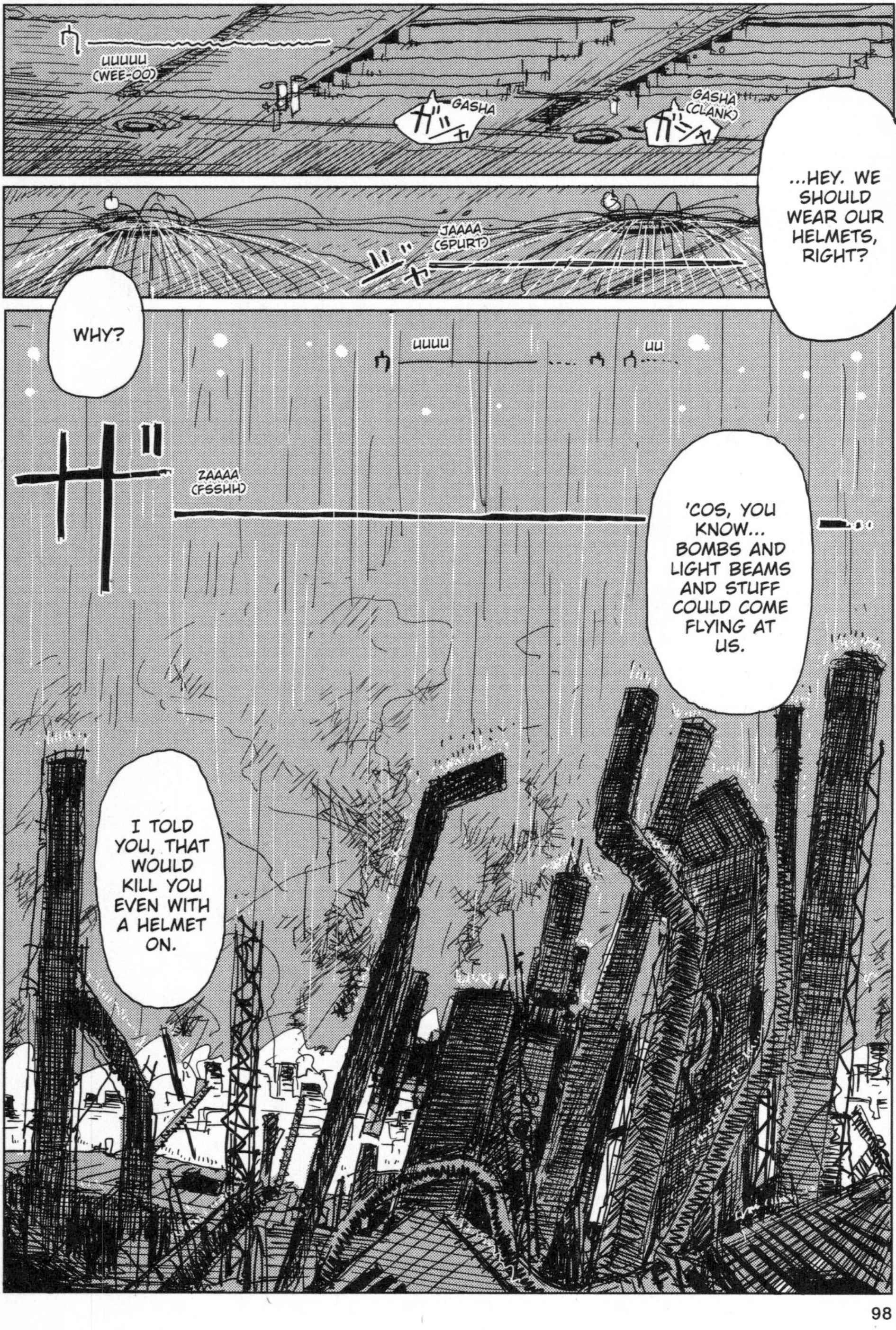
GASHA (CLANK)
GASHA
UUUUU (WEE-OO)
...HEY. WE SHOULD WEAR OUR HELMETS, RIGHT?
JAAAA (SPURT)
WHY?
UU
UUUU
ZAAAA (FSSHH)
'COS, YOU KNOW... BOMBS AND LIGHT BEAMS AND STUFF COULD COME FLYING AT US.
I TOLD YOU, THAT WOULD KILL YOU EVEN WITH A HELMET ON.

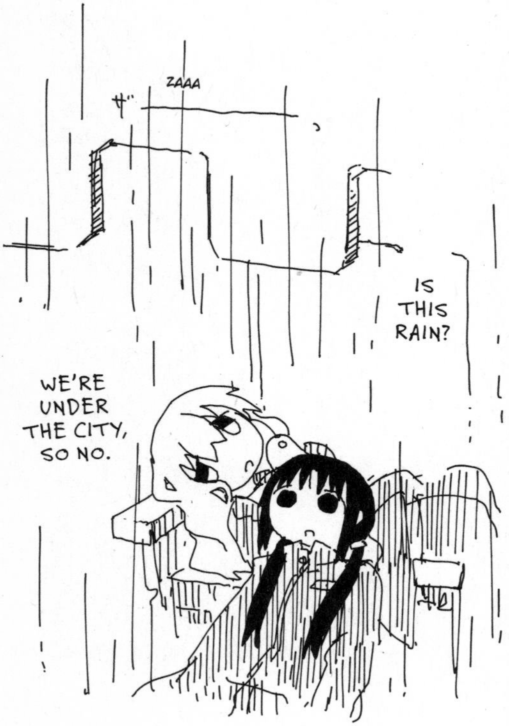
ZAAA
IS THIS RAIN?
WE'RE UNDER THE CITY, SO NO.

GIRLS' LAST TOUR

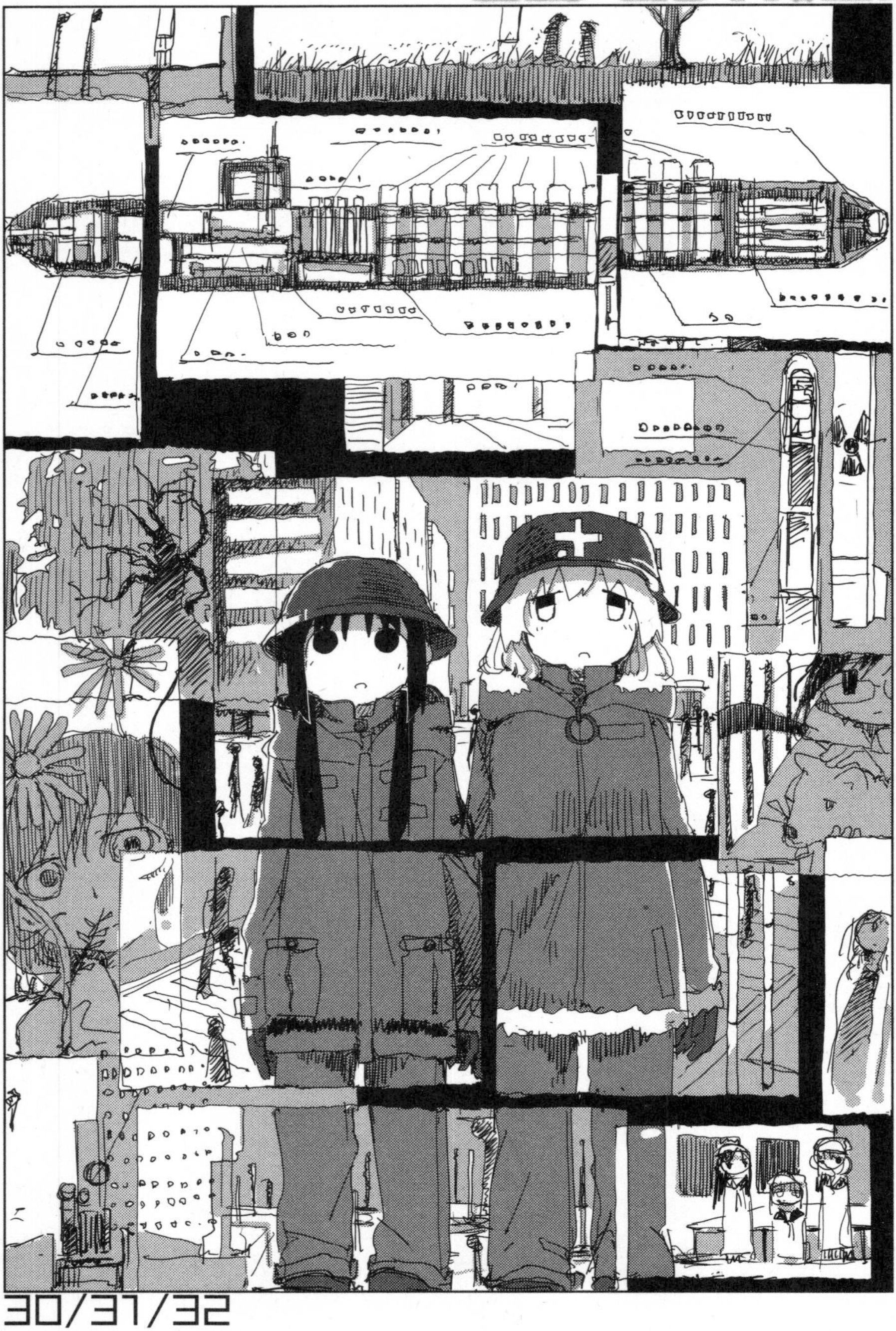

30/31/32

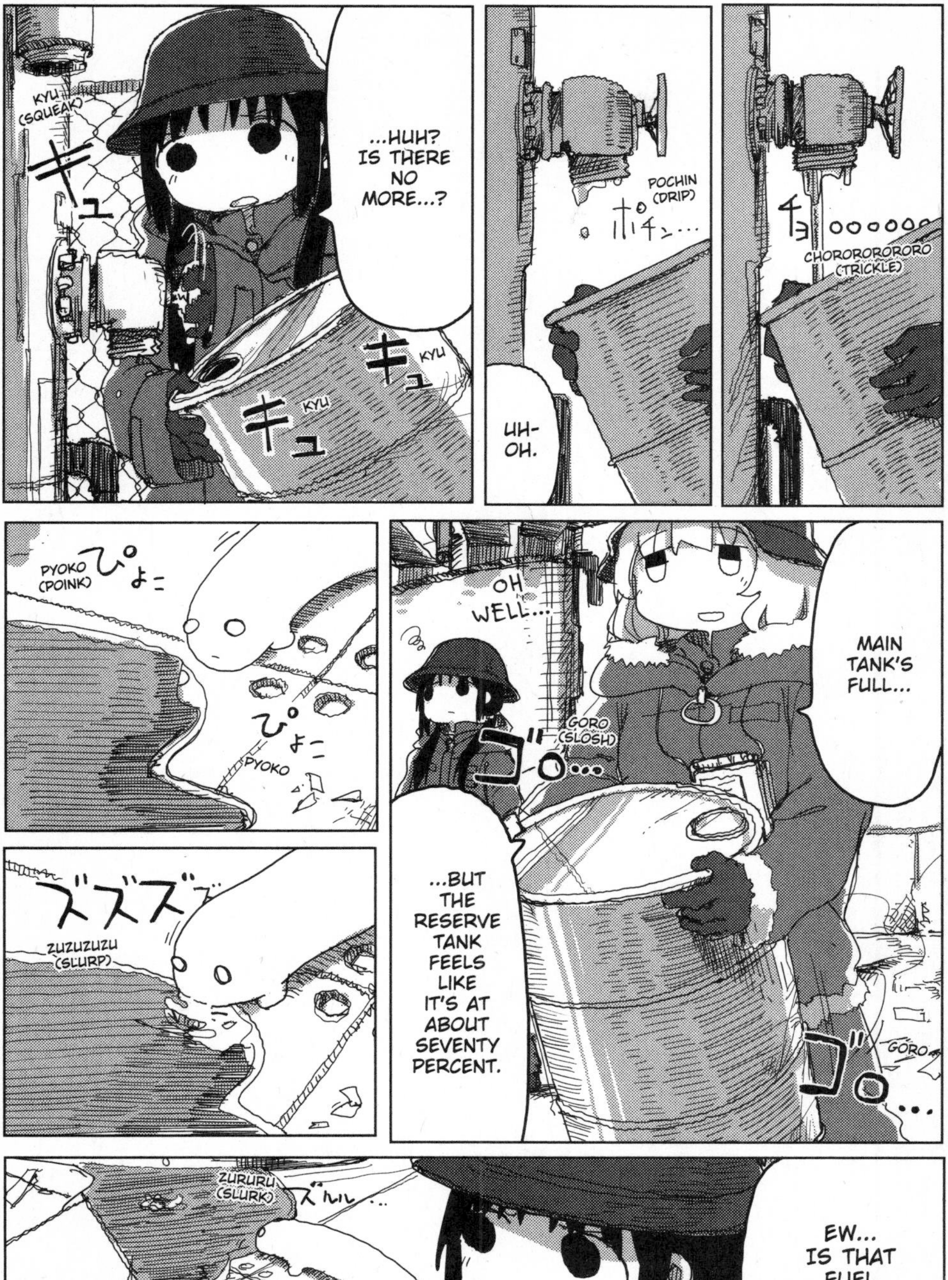
CHORORORORORO (TRICKLE)
POCHIN (DRIP)
UH-OH.
...HUH? IS THERE NO MORE...?
KYU (SQUEAK)
KYU
KYU
MAIN TANK'S FULL...
OH WELL...
...BUT THE RESERVE TANK FEELS LIKE IT'S AT ABOUT SEVENTY PERCENT.
GORO (SLOSH)
GORO
PYOKO (POINK)
PYOKO
ZUZUZUZU (SLURP)
EW... IS THAT FUEL TASTY?
ZURURU (SLURK)
...Tasty.

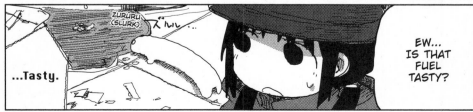

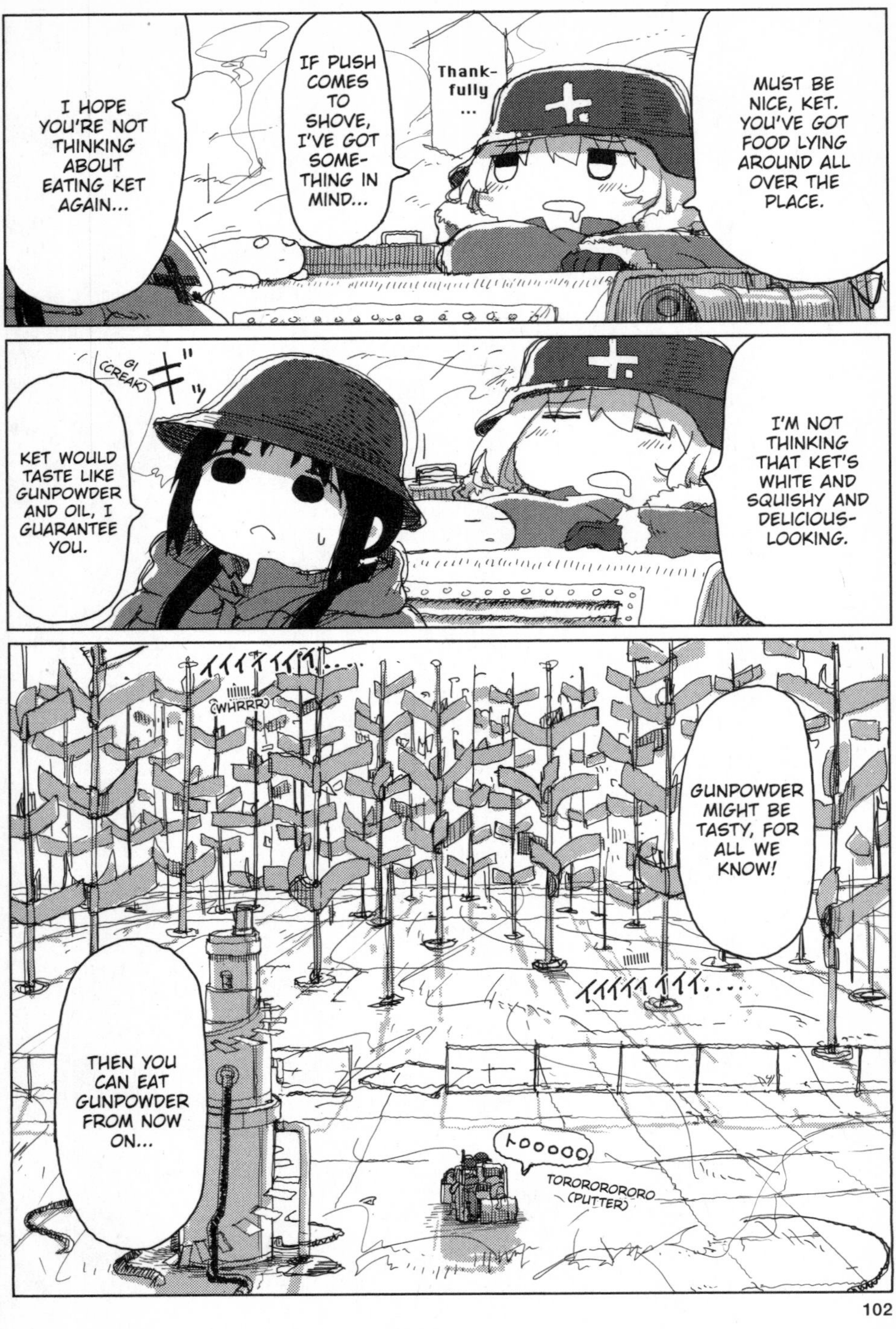
MUST BE NICE, KET. YOU'VE GOT FOOD LYING AROUND ALL OVER THE PLACE.
Thank-fully...
IF PUSH COMES TO SHOVE, I'VE GOT SOME-THING IN MIND...
I HOPE YOU'RE NOT THINKING ABOUT EATING KET AGAIN...
I'M NOT THINKING THAT KET'S WHITE AND SQUISHY AND DELICIOUS-LOOKING.
ギッ
GI (CREAK)
KET WOULD TASTE LIKE GUNPOWDER AND OIL, I GUARANTEE YOU.
GUNPOWDER MIGHT BE TASTY, FOR ALL WE KNOW!
イイイイイイイ…
(WHRRR)
イイイイイイイ…
THEN YOU CAN EAT GUNPOWDER FROM NOW ON...
トロロロロ
TORORORORORO (PUTTER)

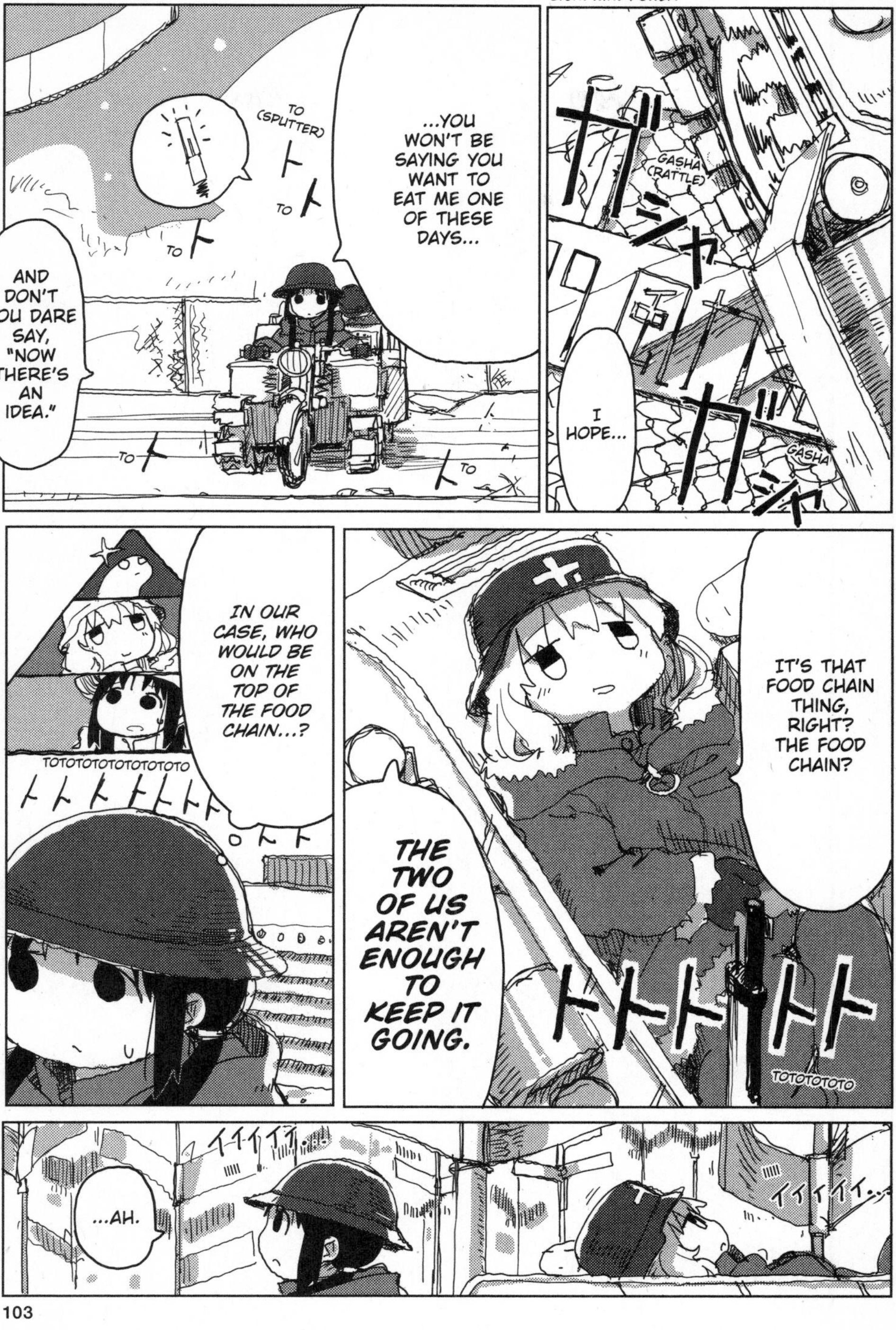
SIGN: WIND POWER
GASHA (RATTLE)
I HOPE...
GASHA
TO (SPUTTER)
...YOU WON'T BE SAYING YOU WANT TO EAT ME ONE OF THESE DAYS...
TO
TO
AND DON'T YOU DARE SAY, "NOW THERE'S AN IDEA."
TO
TO
IT'S THAT FOOD CHAIN THING, RIGHT? THE FOOD CHAIN?
THE TWO OF US AREN'T ENOUGH TO KEEP IT GOING.
TOTOTOTOTO
IN OUR CASE, WHO WOULD BE ON THE TOP OF THE FOOD CHAIN...?
TOTOTOTOTOTOTOTOTO
...AH.

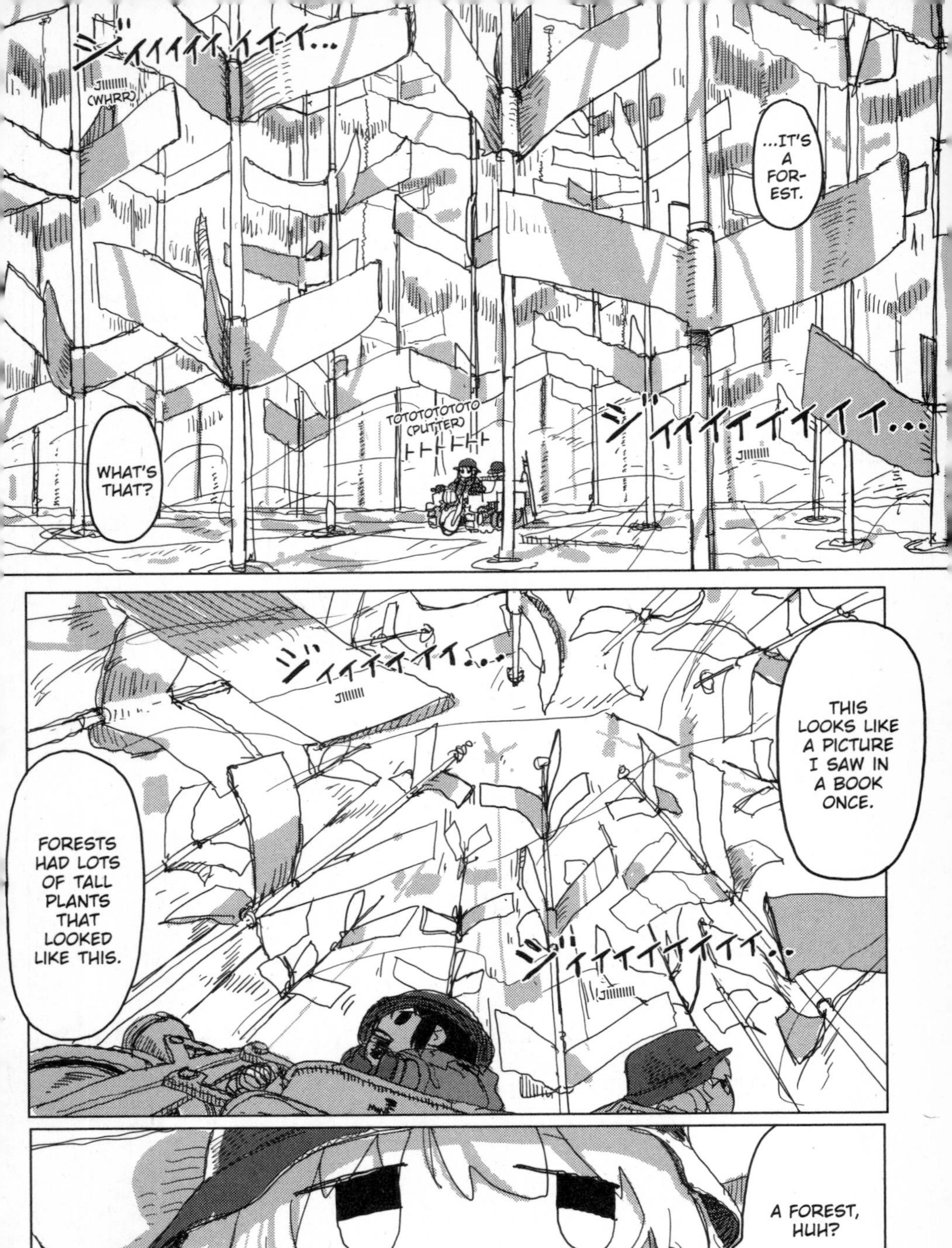
...IT'S A FOREST.
ジイイイイイイイ...
JIIIIIII (WHRR)
ジイイイイイイイイ...
JIIIIIII
TOTOTOTOTOTO (PUTTER)
トトトトトト
WHAT'S THAT?
THIS LOOKS LIKE A PICTURE I SAW IN A BOOK ONCE.
ジイイイイイ...
JIIIIII
FORESTS HAD LOTS OF TALL PLANTS THAT LOOKED LIKE THIS.
ジイイイイイイイ...
JIIIIIIII
A FOREST, HUH?

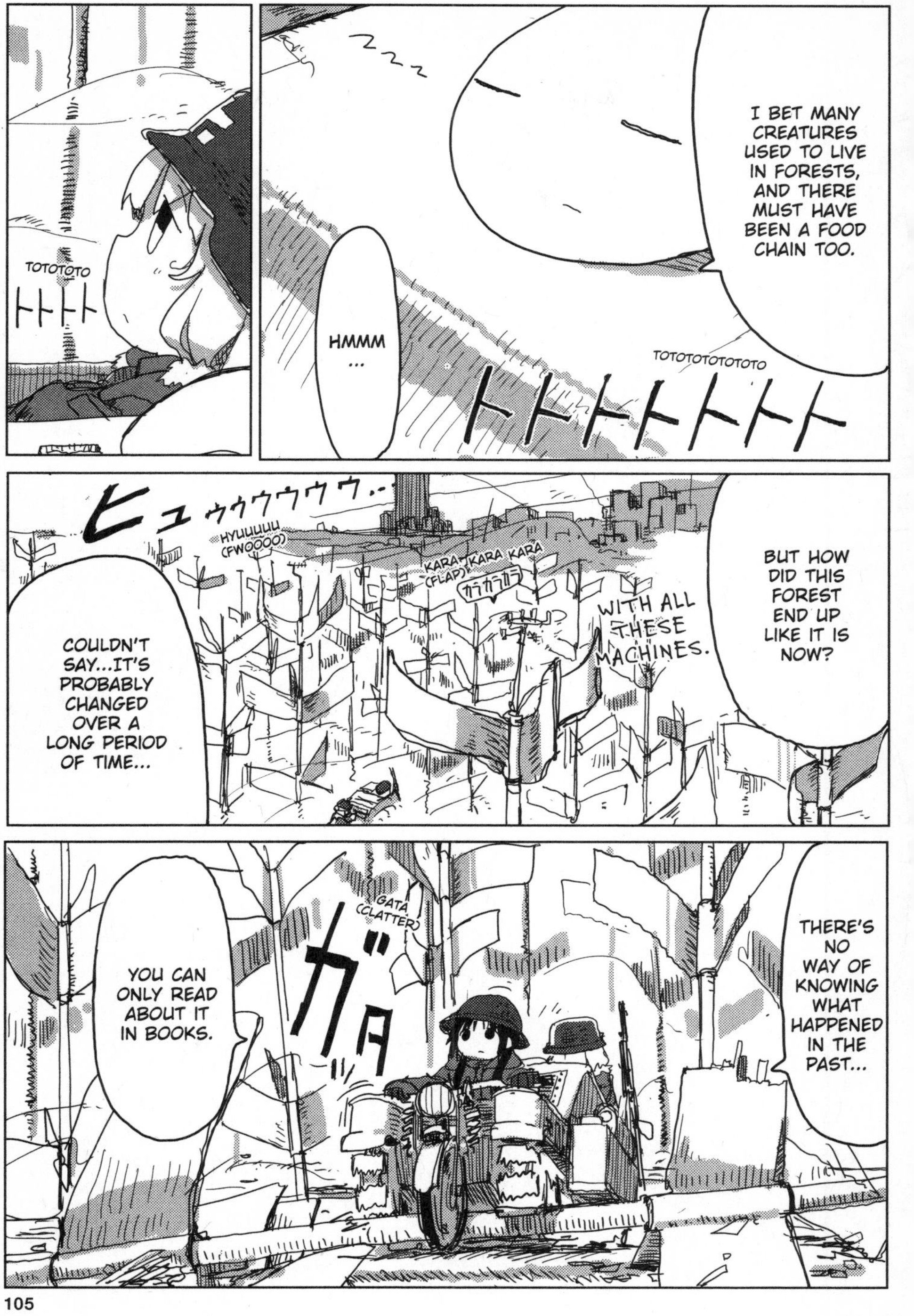
I BET MANY CREATURES USED TO LIVE IN FORESTS, AND THERE MUST HAVE BEEN A FOOD CHAIN TOO.
HMMM...
TOTOTOTOTOTOTO
トトトトトトトト
TOTOTOTO
トトトト
BUT HOW DID THIS FOREST END UP LIKE IT IS NOW?
WITH ALL THESE MACHINES.
KARA KARA KARA (FLAP)
カラカラカラ
HYUUUUUU (FWOOOO)
ヒュウウウウウウ…
COULDN'T SAY...IT'S PROBABLY CHANGED OVER A LONG PERIOD OF TIME...
THERE'S NO WAY OF KNOWING WHAT HAPPENED IN THE PAST...
GATA (CLATTER)
ガタ
YOU CAN ONLY READ ABOUT IT IN BOOKS.

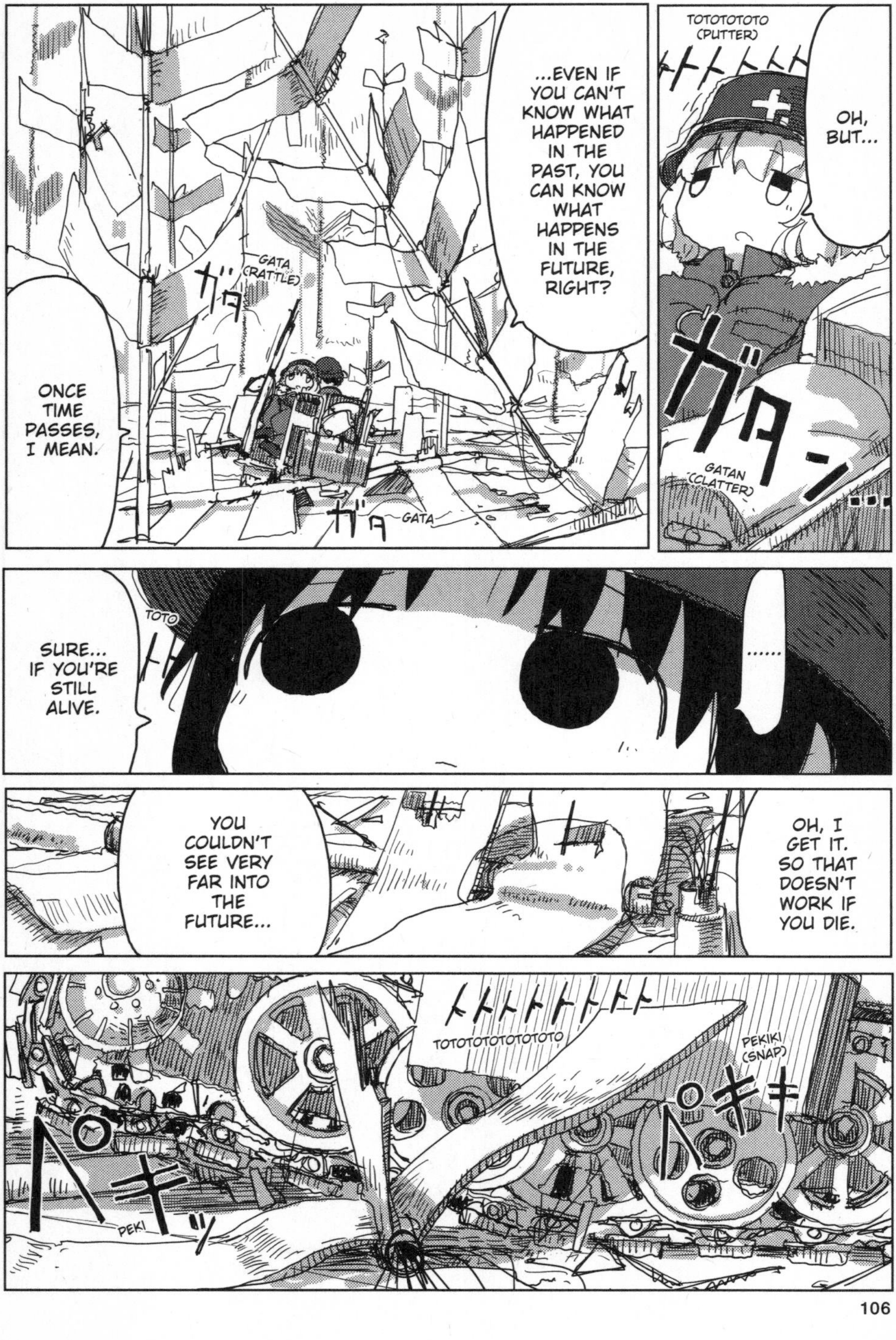
TOTOTOTOTO (PUTTER)
OH, BUT...
GATAN (CLATTER)
...EVEN IF YOU CAN'T KNOW WHAT HAPPENED IN THE PAST, YOU CAN KNOW WHAT HAPPENS IN THE FUTURE, RIGHT?
GATA (RATTLE)
ONCE TIME PASSES, I MEAN.
GATA
......
TOTO
SURE... IF YOU'RE STILL ALIVE.
OH, I GET IT. SO THAT DOESN'T WORK IF YOU DIE.
YOU COULDN'T SEE VERY FAR INTO THE FUTURE...
PEKIKI (SNAP)
TOTOTOTOTOTOTOTO
PEKI

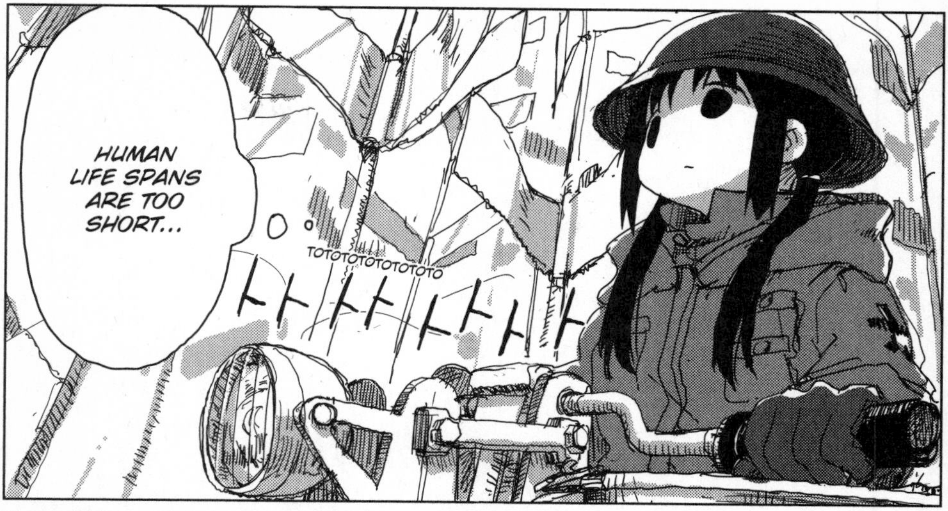
HUMAN LIFE SPANS ARE TOO SHORT...
トトトトトトトトト
TOTOTOTOTOTOTOTO

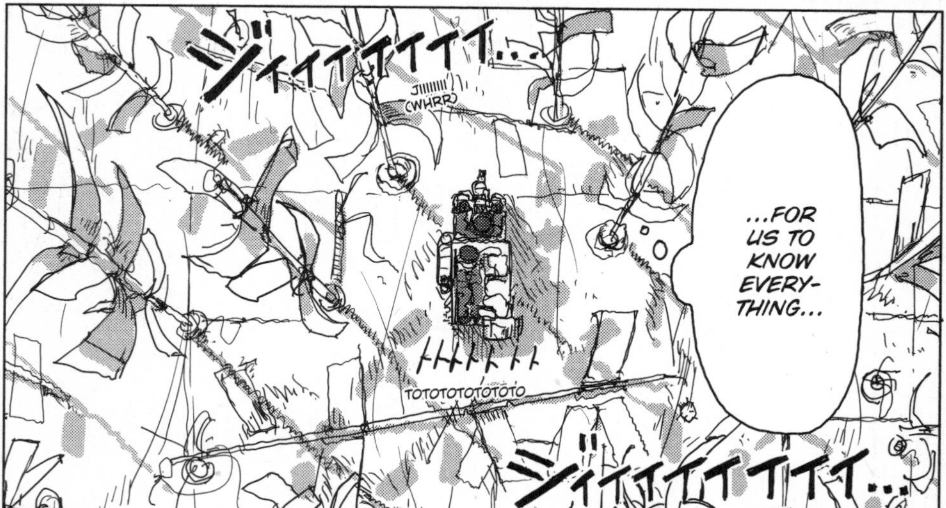
ジィイイイイイイ...
(WHRR)
...FOR US TO KNOW EVERY-THING...
トトトトトトト
TOTOTOTOTOTOTO
ジィイイイイイイイイ...

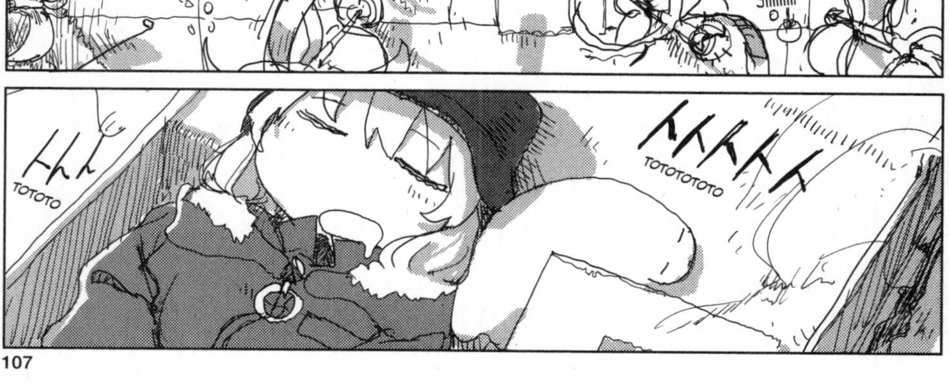
トトトトトト
TOTOTOTOTO
トトト
TOTOTO

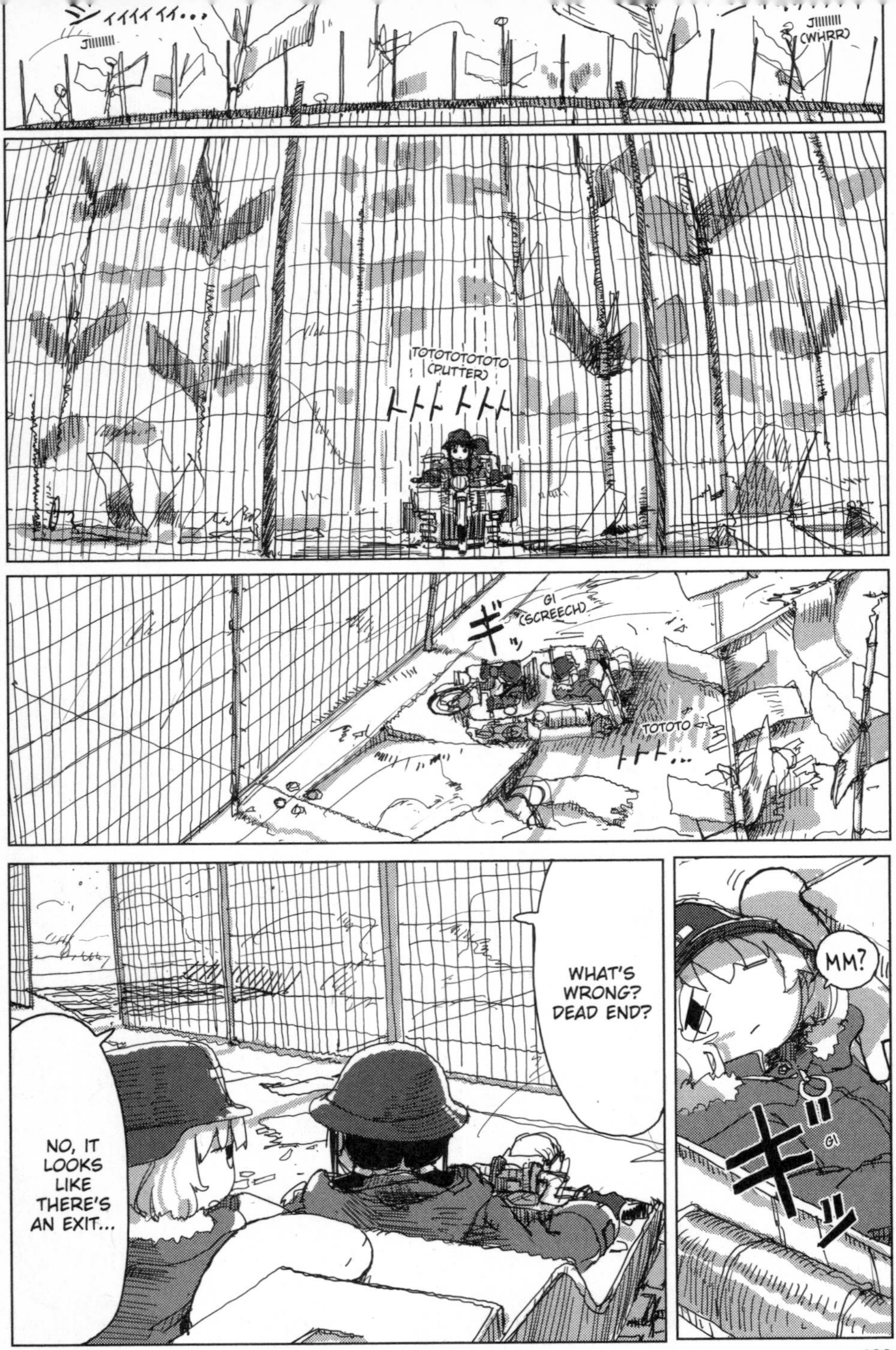
JIIIIIIII
(WHRR)
シィィィィィィ・・・
JIIIIIIII
TOTOTOTOTOTO
(PUTTER)
トトトトトト
GI
(SCREECH)
ギッ
TOTOTO
トトト…
MM?
GI
ギッ
WHAT'S WRONG? DEAD END?
NO, IT LOOKS LIKE THERE'S AN EXIT...

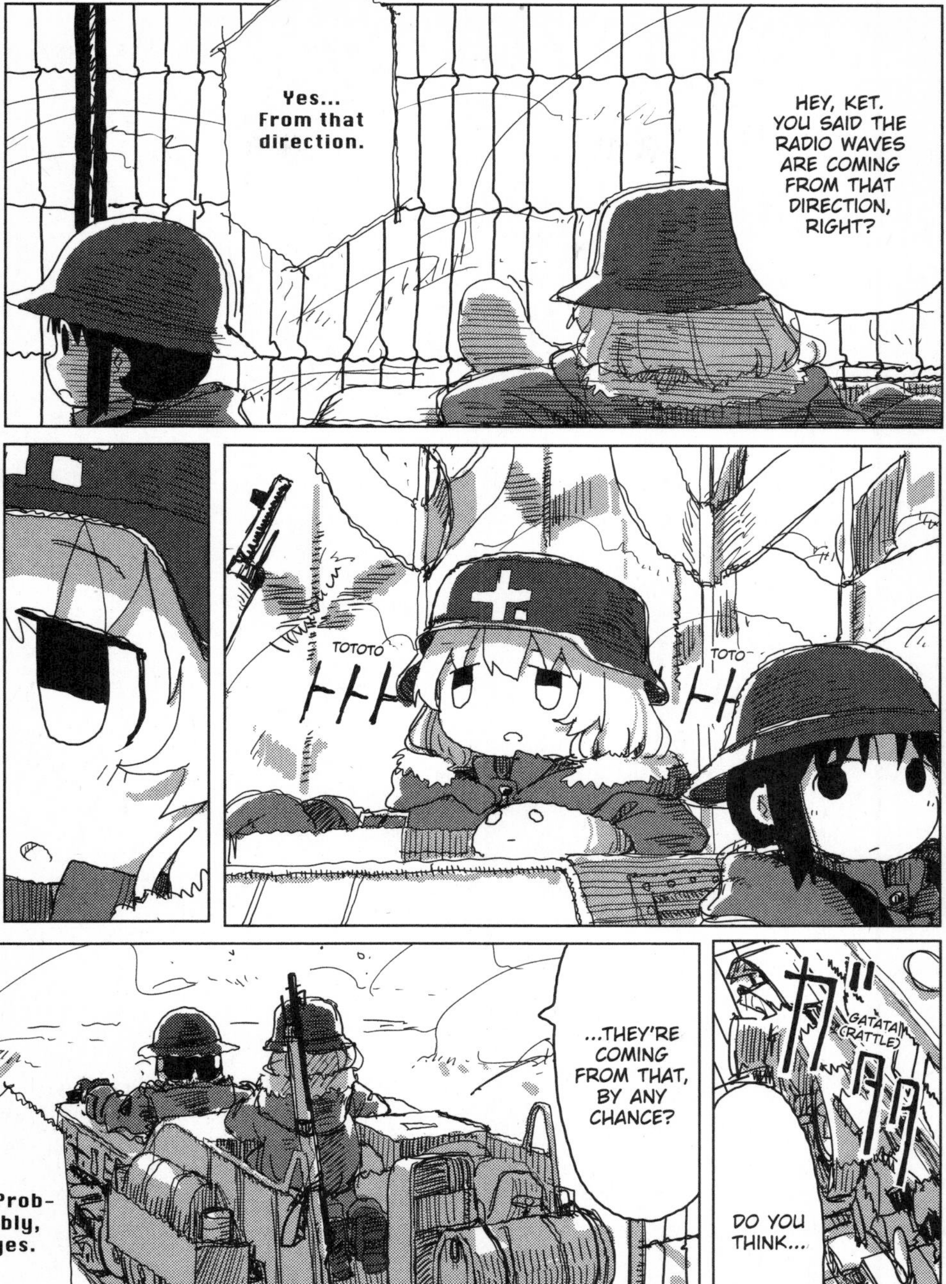
HEY, KET. YOU SAID THE RADIO WAVES ARE COMING FROM THAT DIRECTION, RIGHT?
Yes... From that direction.
TOTO
トト
TOTOTO
トトト
ガタタ
GATATA (RATTLE)
DO YOU THINK...
...THEY'RE COMING FROM THAT, BY ANY CHANCE?
...Prob-ably, yes.

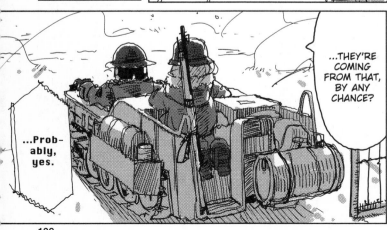

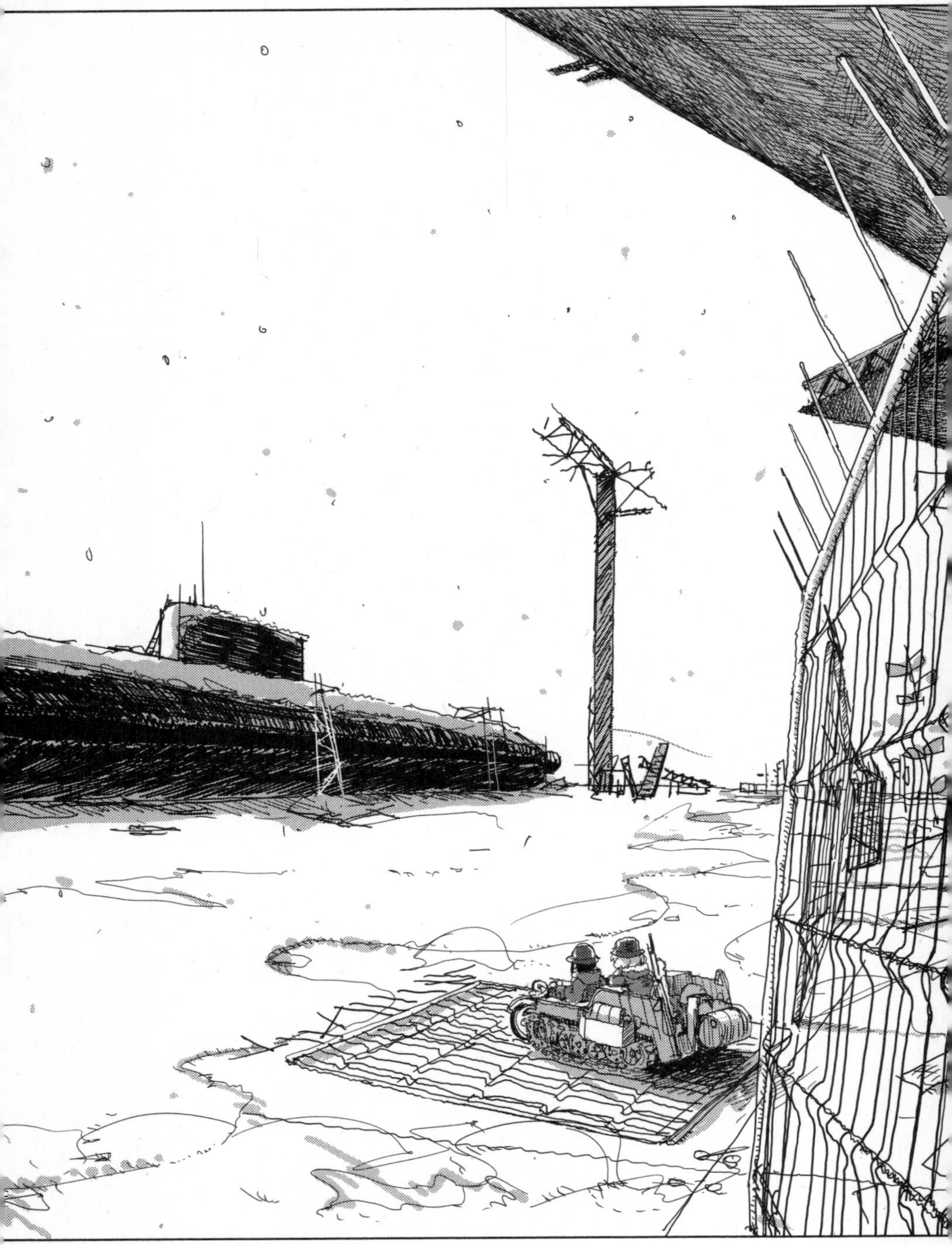

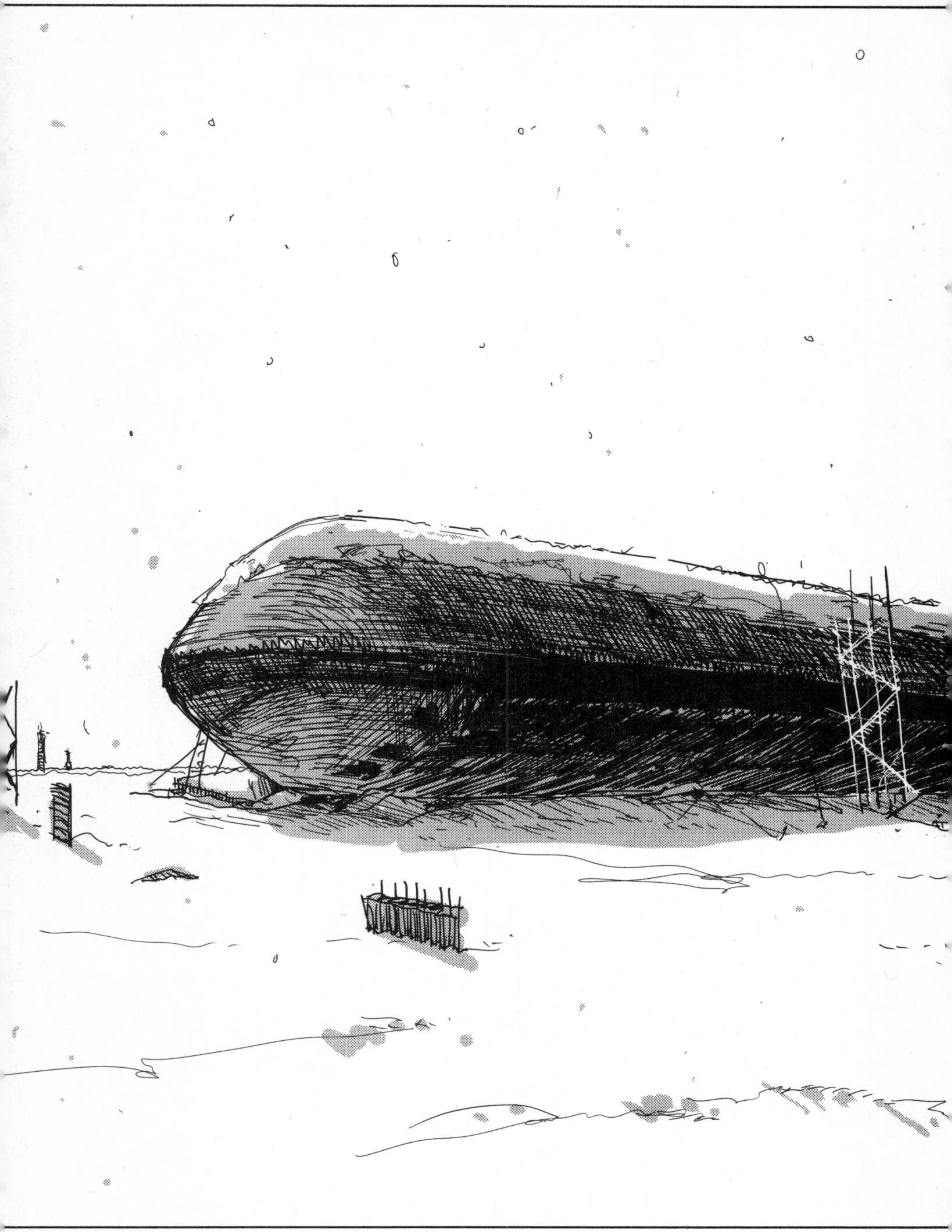

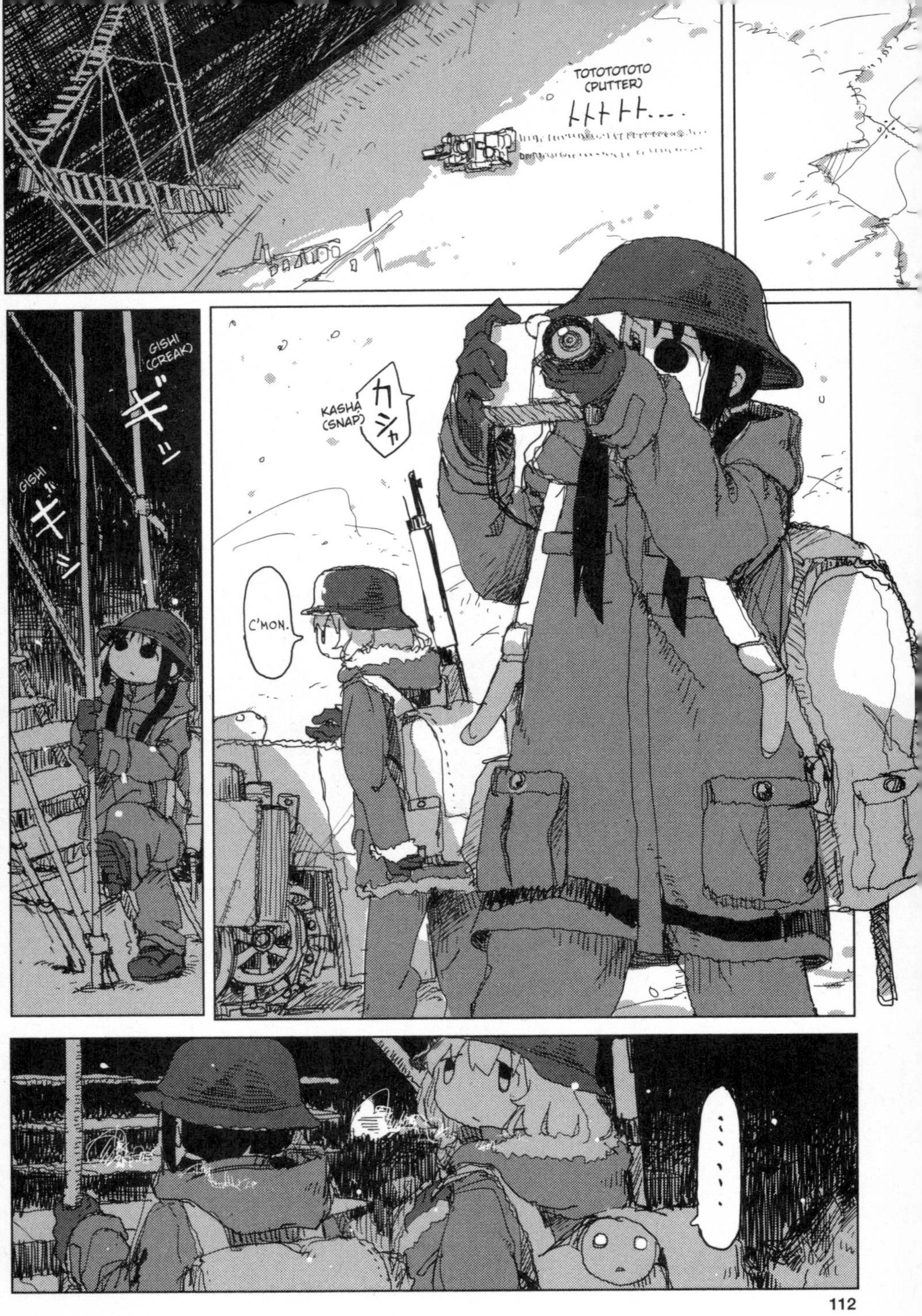
TOTOTOTOTO (PUTTER)
トトトトト….
カシャ
KASHA (SNAP)
C'MON.
GISHI (CREAK)
ギッ
GISHI
ギシ
……

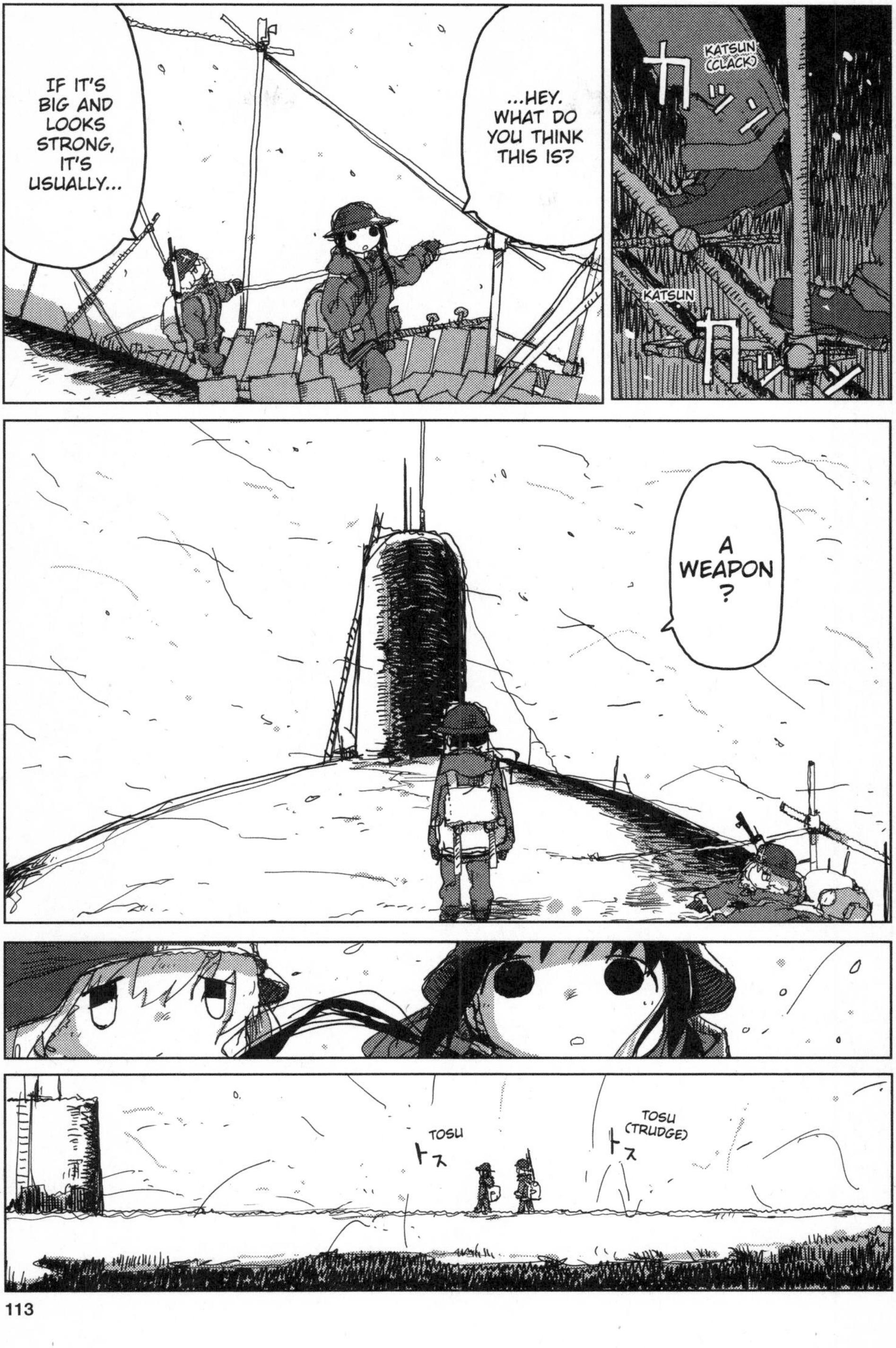

カツン
KATSUN (CLACK)
カツン
KATSUN
...HEY. WHAT DO YOU THINK THIS IS?
IF IT'S BIG AND LOOKS STRONG, IT'S USUALLY...
A WEAPON?
トス
TOSU (TRUDGE)
トス
TOSU

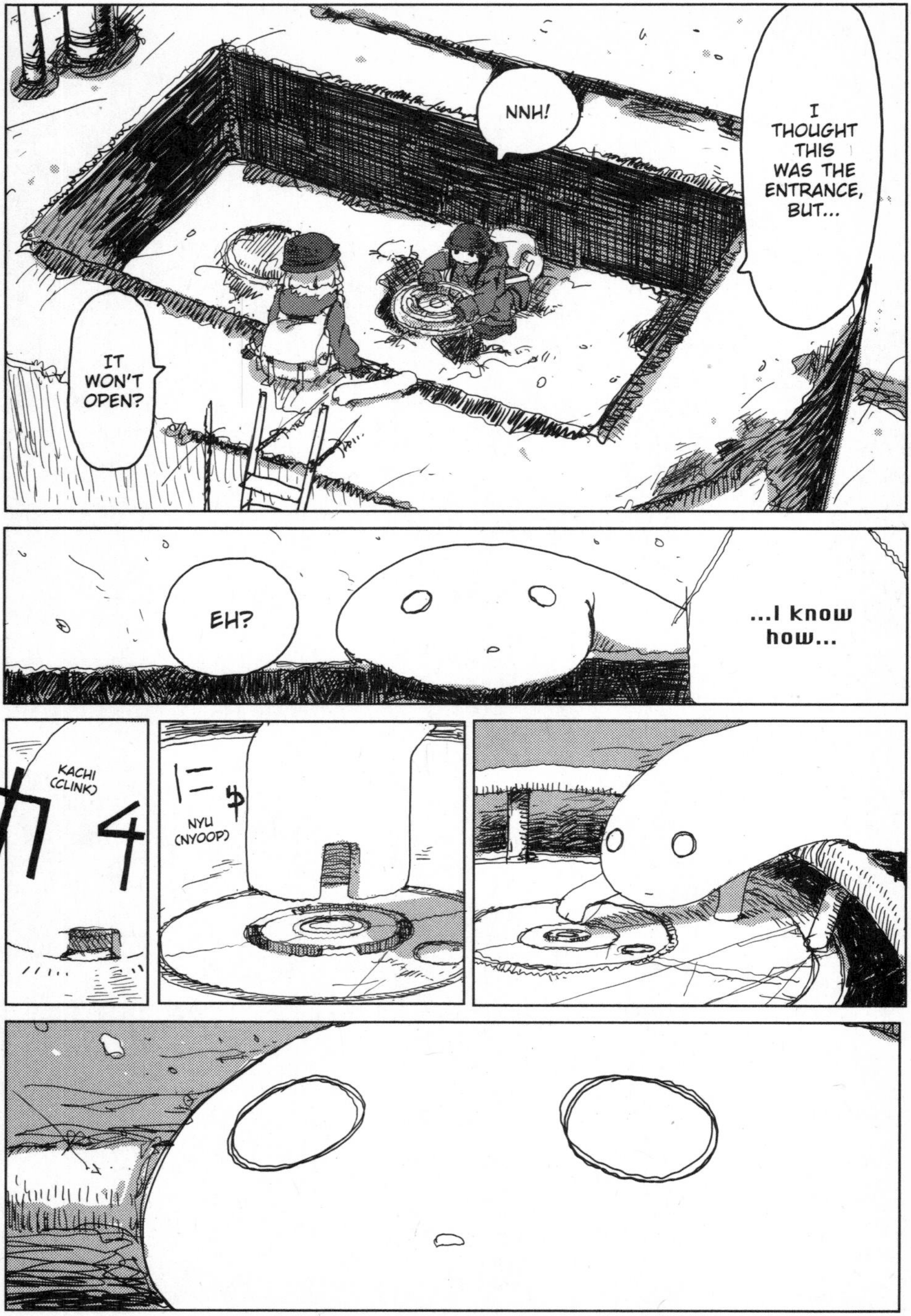
I THOUGHT THIS WAS THE ENTRANCE, BUT...
NNH!
IT WON'T OPEN?
...I know how...
EH?
にゅ
NYU (NYOOP)
カチ
KACHI (CLINK)

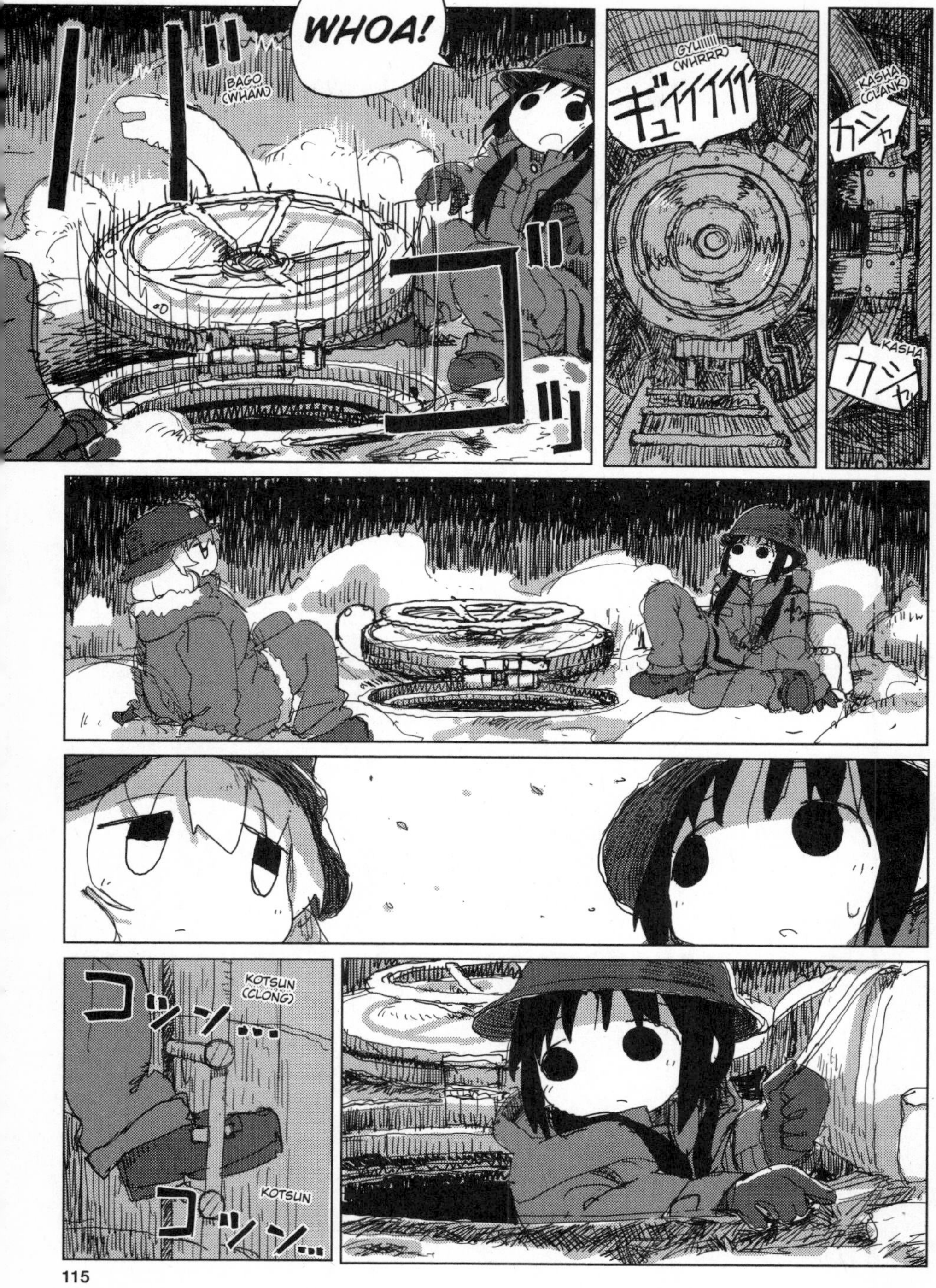
KASHA (CLANK)
カシャ
KASHA
カシャ
GYUIIIII (WHRRR)
ギュイイイイイ
WHOA!
BAGO (WHAM)
KOTSUN (CLONG)
コツン…
KOTSUN
コツン…

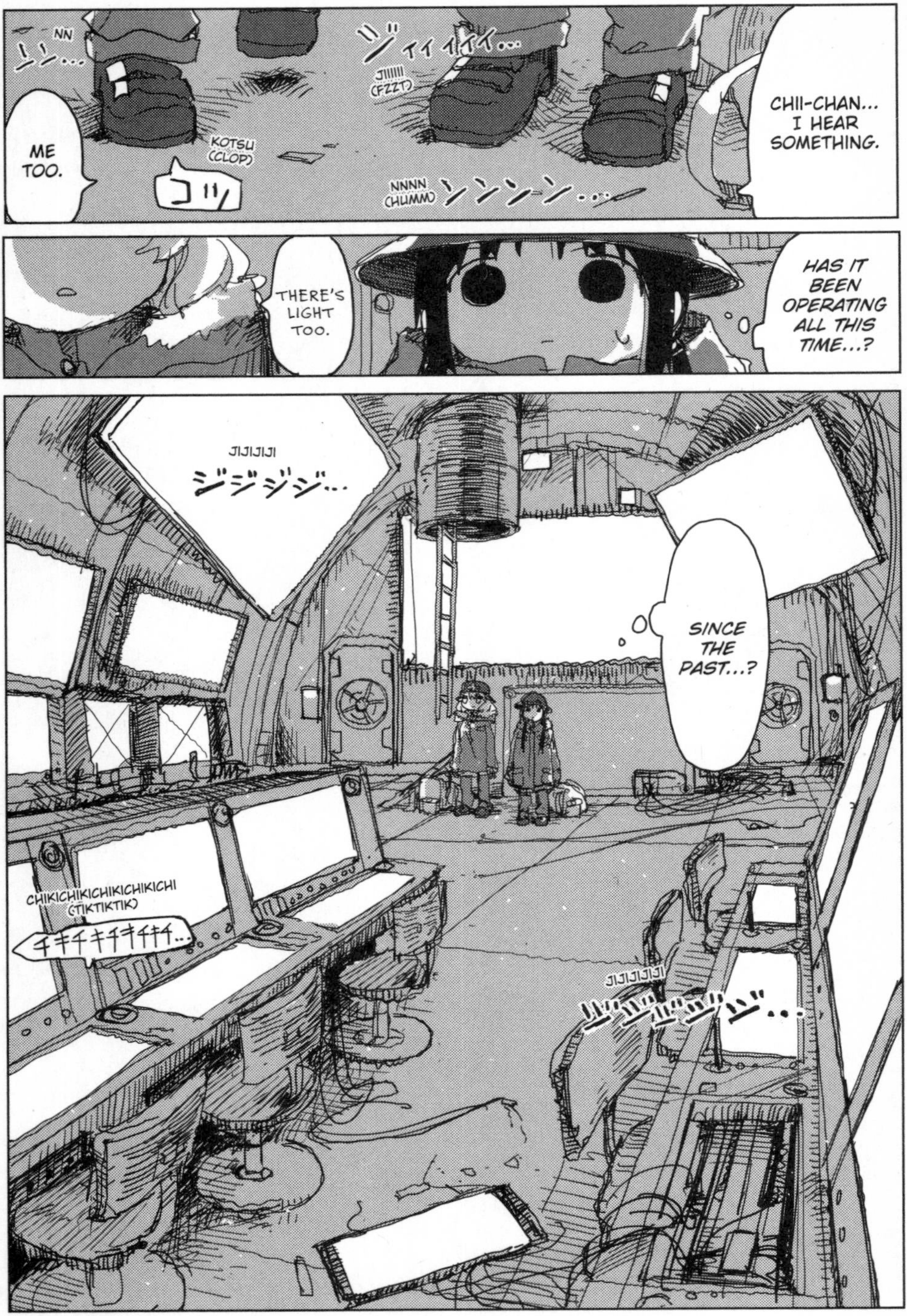
CHII-CHAN... I HEAR SOMETHING.
NNNN (HUMM) ンンンン...
KOTSU (CLOP) コッ
JIIIIII (FZZT) ジィイイイ...
NN ンン...
ME TOO.
HAS IT BEEN OPERATING ALL THIS TIME...?
THERE'S LIGHT TOO.
SINCE THE PAST...?
JIJIJIJI ジジジジ...
JIJIJIJIJI
CHIKICHIKICHIKICHIKICHI (TIKTIKTIK) チキチキチキチキ...

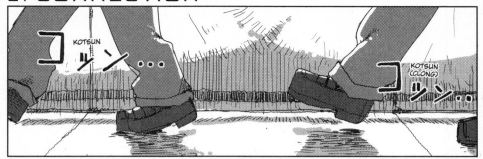

31 CONNECTION

コッン…
KOTSUN (CLONG)
コッン…
KOTSUN
コッン…
KOTSUN
コッン…
KOTSUN
静粛
SIGN: SILENCE
コッン…
KOTSU
ルルルル……
RURURURU (LOOLOOLOO)
ルルルルル……
RURURURURU

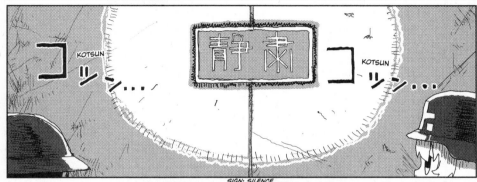

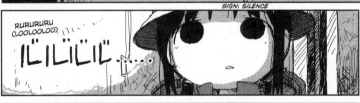

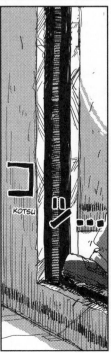

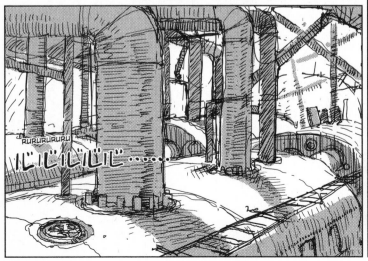

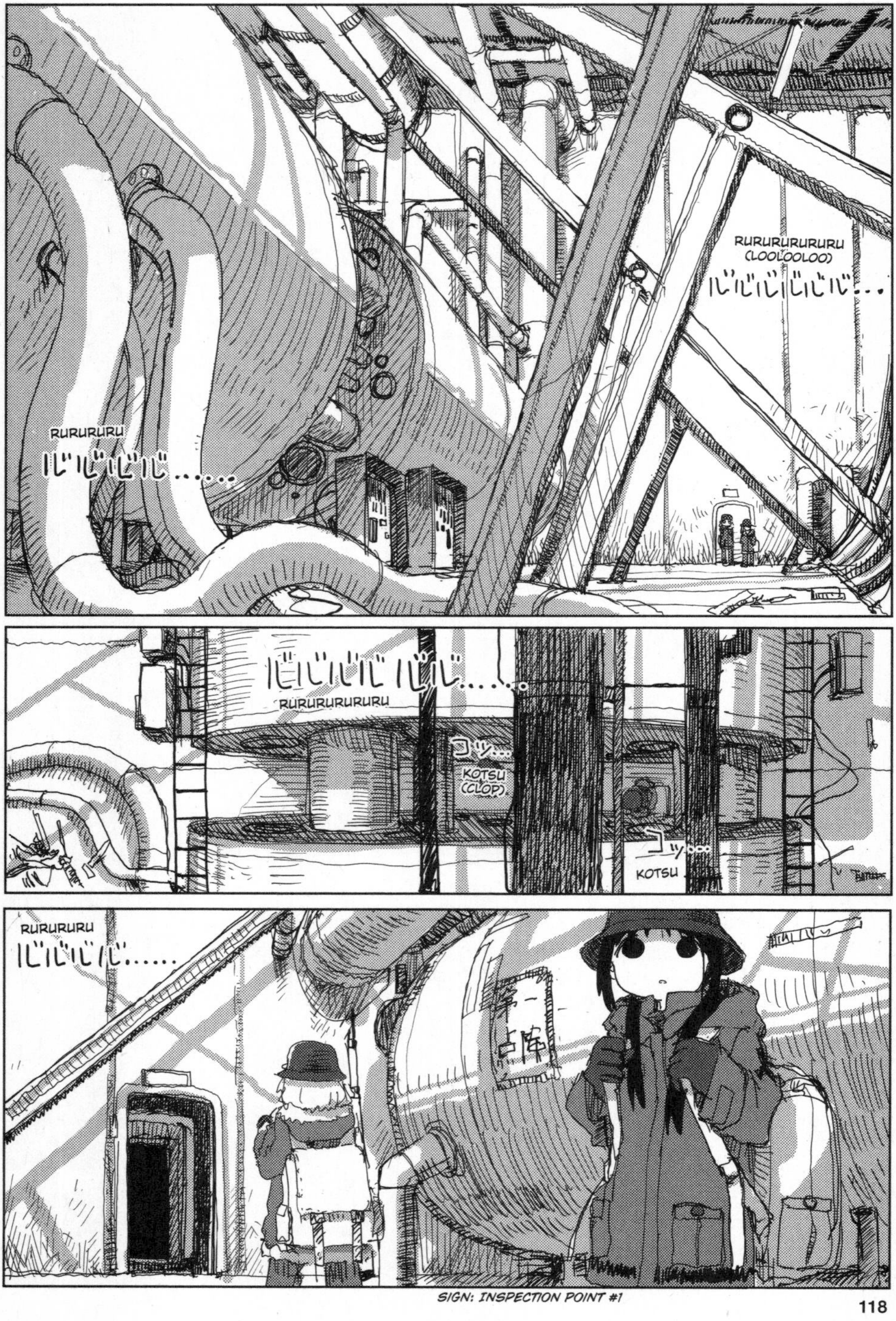
RURURURURURU
(LOOLOOLOO)
ルルルルルル...
RURURURU
ルルルル......
ルルルルルル......
RURURURURURU
コツ...
KOTSU
(CLOP)
コツ...
KOTSU
RURURURU
ルルルル......

SIGN: INSPECTION POINT #1

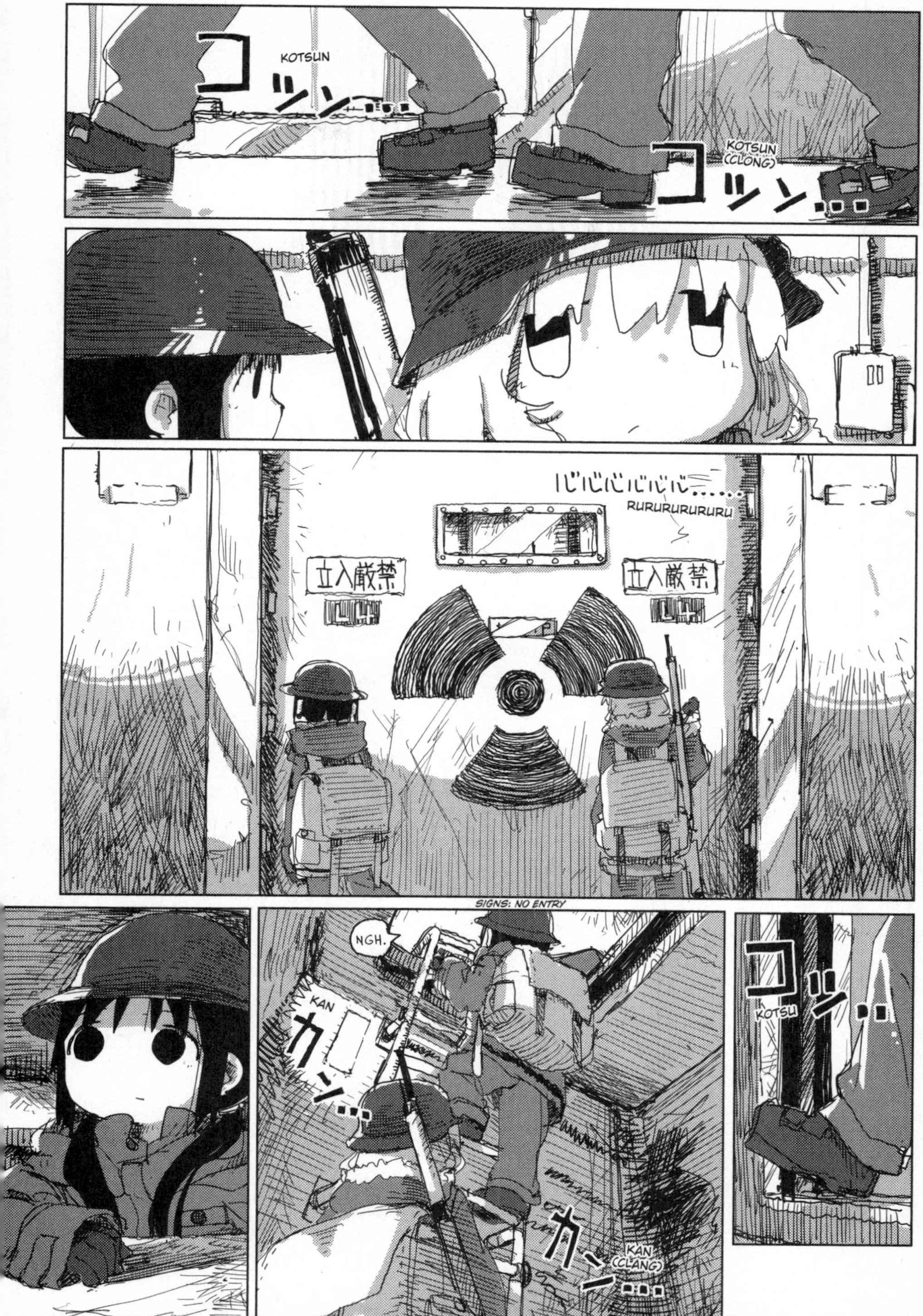

コツン…
KOTSUN
コツン…
KOTSUN (CLONG)
ルルルルルル……
RURURURURURU
立入厳禁
立入厳禁
SIGNS: NO ENTRY
コツ…
KOTSU
NGH.
カン…
KAN
カーン…
KAN (CLANG)

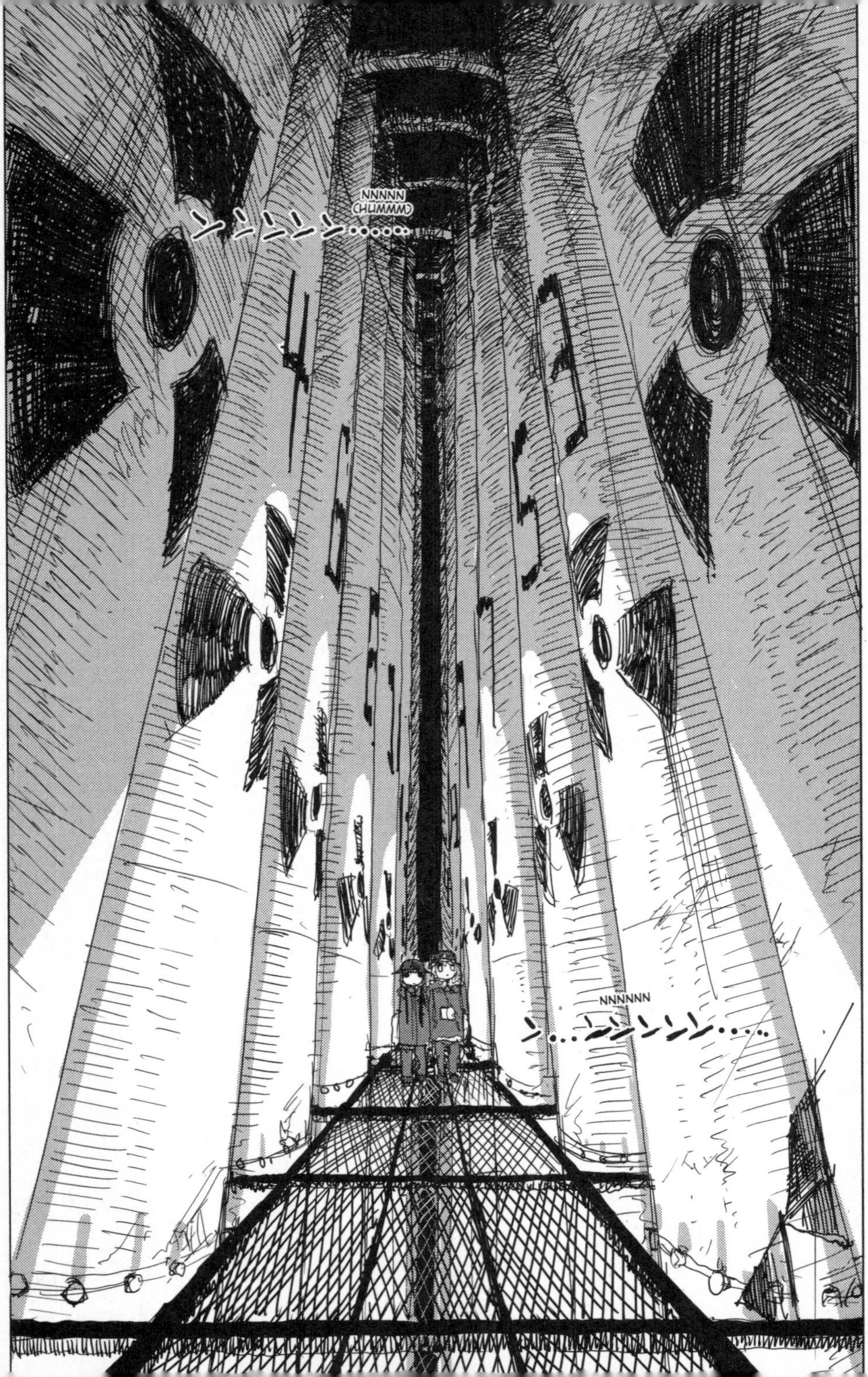
NNNNN (HUMMM)
NNNNNN

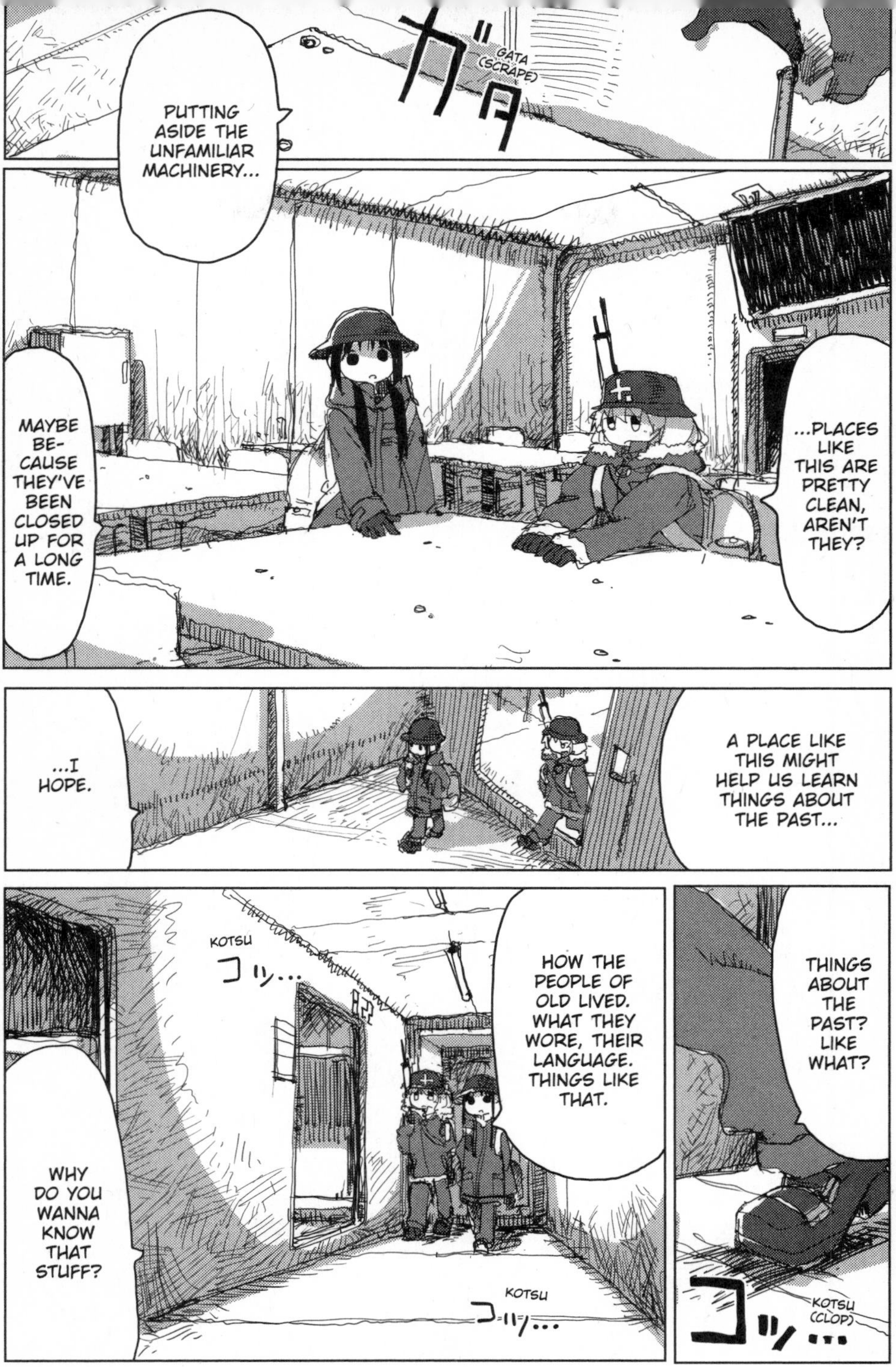
GATA (SCRAPE)
PUTTING ASIDE THE UNFAMILIAR MACHINERY...
...PLACES LIKE THIS ARE PRETTY CLEAN, AREN'T THEY?
MAYBE BE-CAUSE THEY'VE BEEN CLOSED UP FOR A LONG TIME.
A PLACE LIKE THIS MIGHT HELP US LEARN THINGS ABOUT THE PAST...
...I HOPE.
THINGS ABOUT THE PAST? LIKE WHAT?
KOTSU (CLOP)
HOW THE PEOPLE OF OLD LIVED. WHAT THEY WORE, THEIR LANGUAGE. THINGS LIKE THAT.
KOTSU
WHY DO YOU WANNA KNOW THAT STUFF?
KOTSU

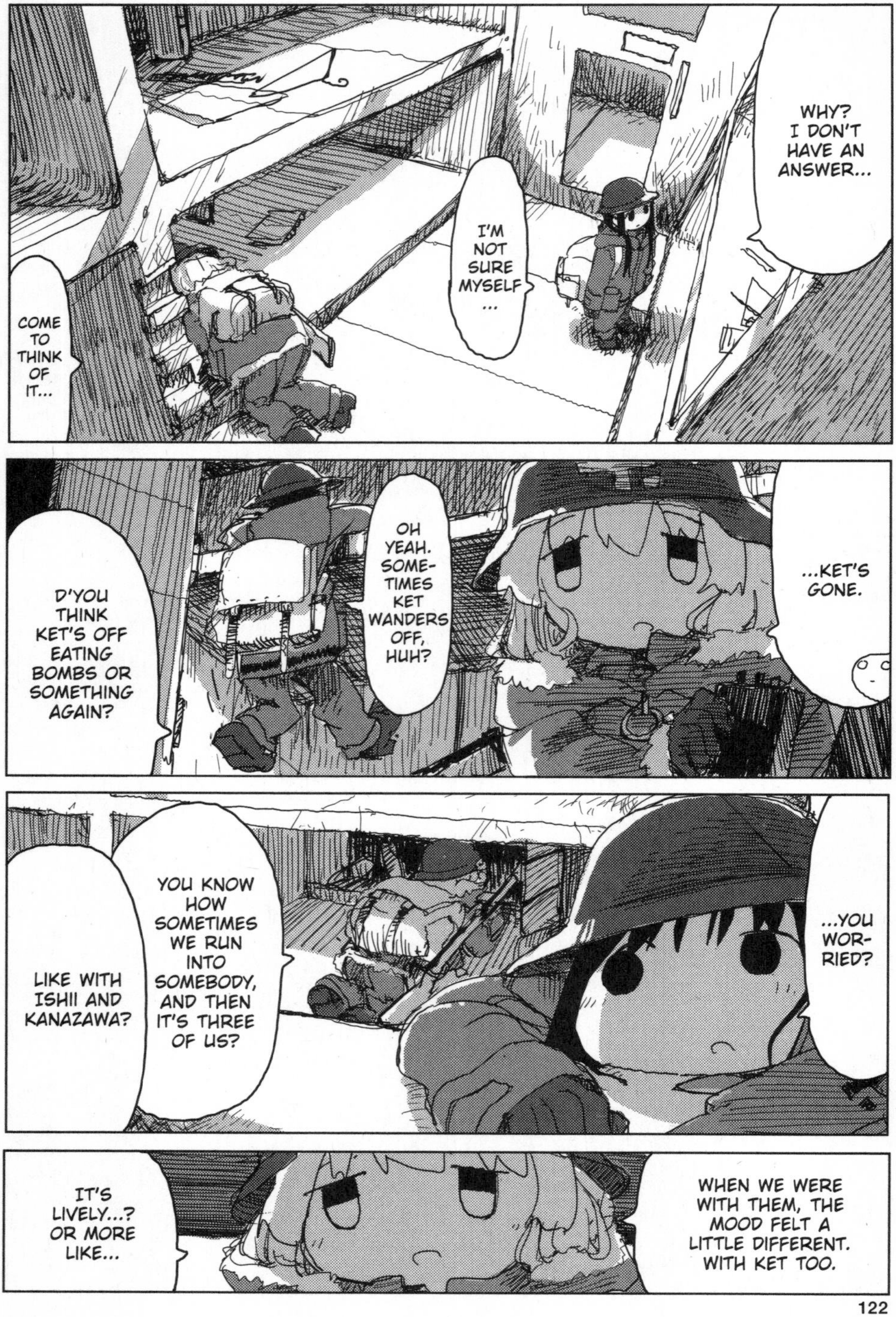
WHY? I DON'T HAVE AN ANSWER...
I'M NOT SURE MYSELF ...
COME TO THINK OF IT...
...KET'S GONE.
OH YEAH. SOMETIMES KET WANDERS OFF, HUH?
D'YOU THINK KET'S OFF EATING BOMBS OR SOMETHING AGAIN?
...YOU WORRIED?
YOU KNOW HOW SOMETIMES WE RUN INTO SOMEBODY, AND THEN IT'S THREE OF US?
LIKE WITH ISHII AND KANAZAWA?
WHEN WE WERE WITH THEM, THE MOOD FELT A LITTLE DIFFERENT. WITH KET TOO.
IT'S LIVELY...? OR MORE LIKE...

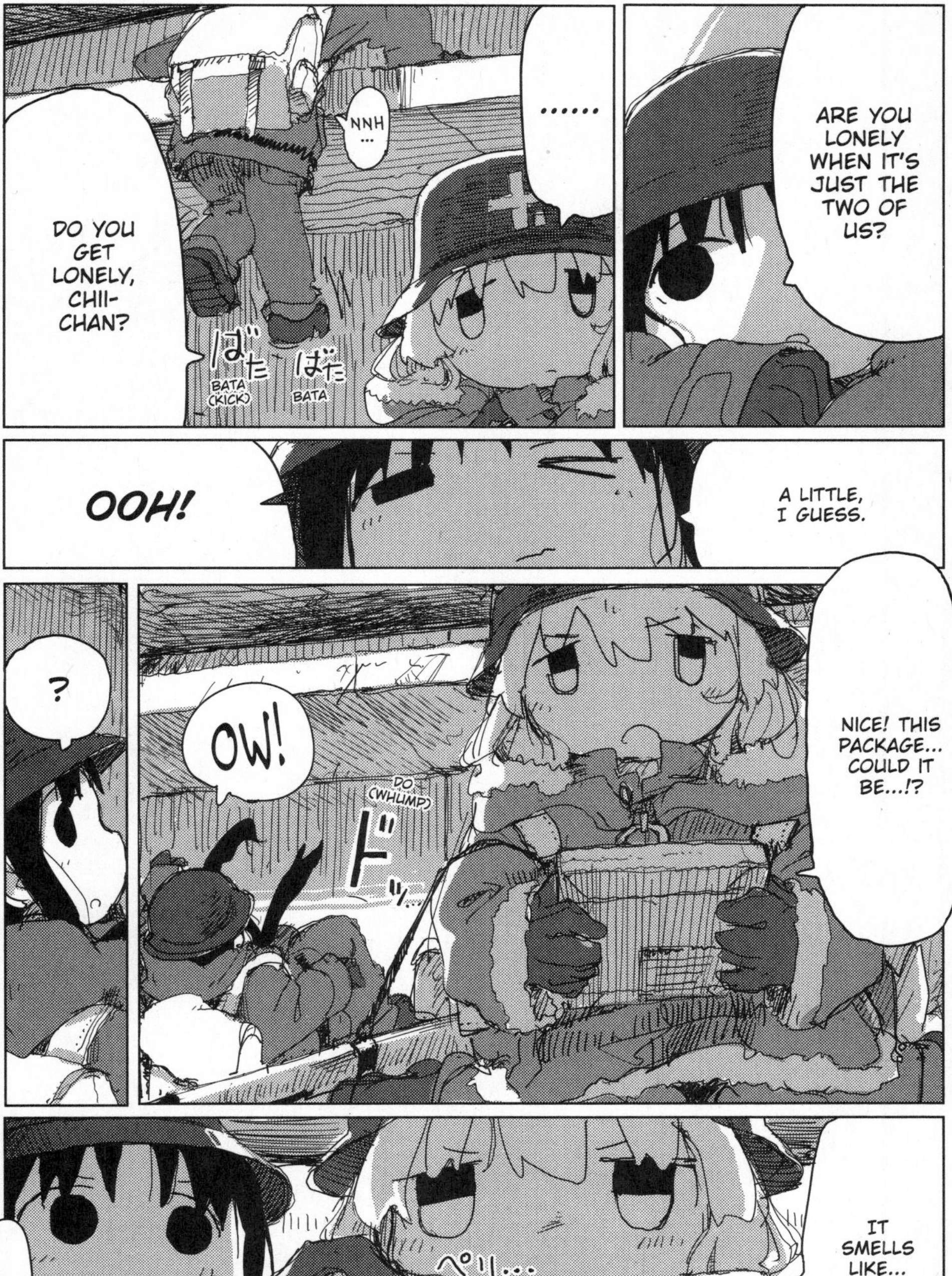

ARE YOU LONELY WHEN IT'S JUST THE TWO OF US?
......
NNH ...
DO YOU GET LONELY, CHII-CHAN?
ばた
BATA
ばた
BATA (KICK)
A LITTLE, I GUESS.
OOH!
NICE! THIS PACKAGE... COULD IT BE...!?
ドッ...
DO (WHUMP)
OW!
?
IT SMELLS LIKE...
ぺり...
PERI (RIP)
LIKE?

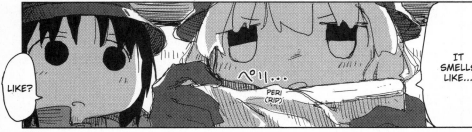

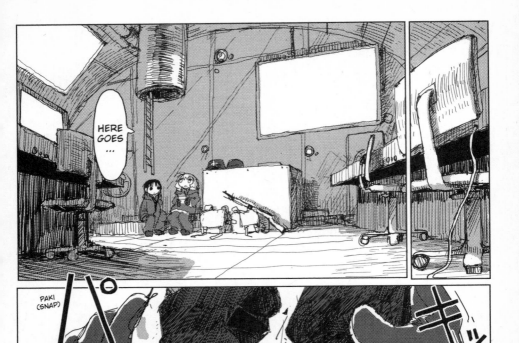

HERE GOES ...

PAKI (SNAP)

IT'S BLACK...

IS THIS SAFE...?

HERE.

PAKUN (CHOMP)

...YOU CAN EAT IT!

D...!

AHHH...

IF YOU CAN EAT IT...

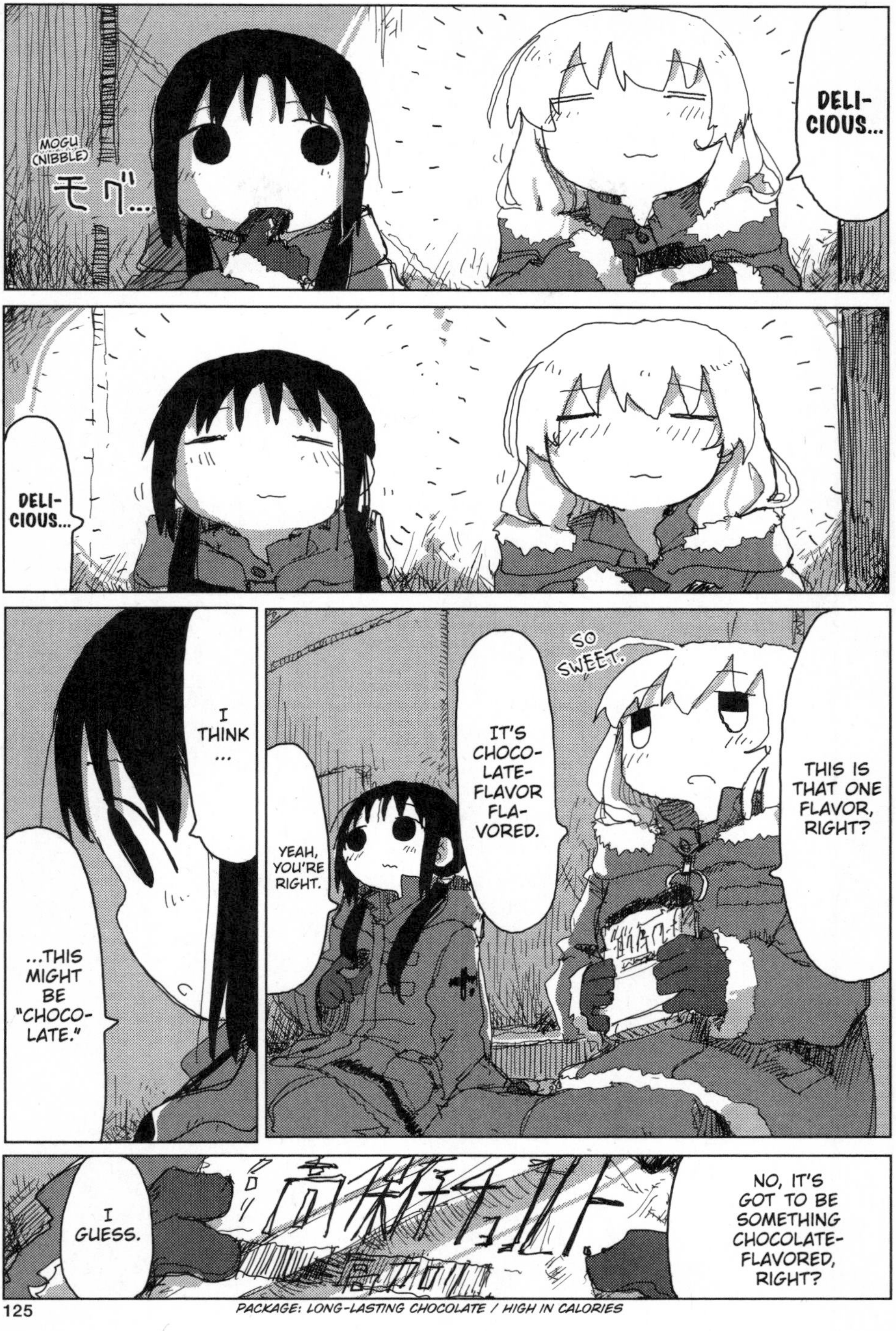
DELI-CIOUS...
MOGU (NIBBLE)
モグ…
DELI-CIOUS...
THIS IS THAT ONE FLAVOR, RIGHT?
SO SWEET.
IT'S CHOCO-LATE-FLAVOR FLA-VORED.
YEAH, YOU'RE RIGHT.
I THINK ...
...THIS MIGHT BE "CHOCO-LATE."
NO, IT'S GOT TO BE SOMETHING CHOCOLATE-FLAVORED, RIGHT?
I GUESS.

PACKAGE: LONG-LASTING CHOCOLATE / HIGH IN CALORIES

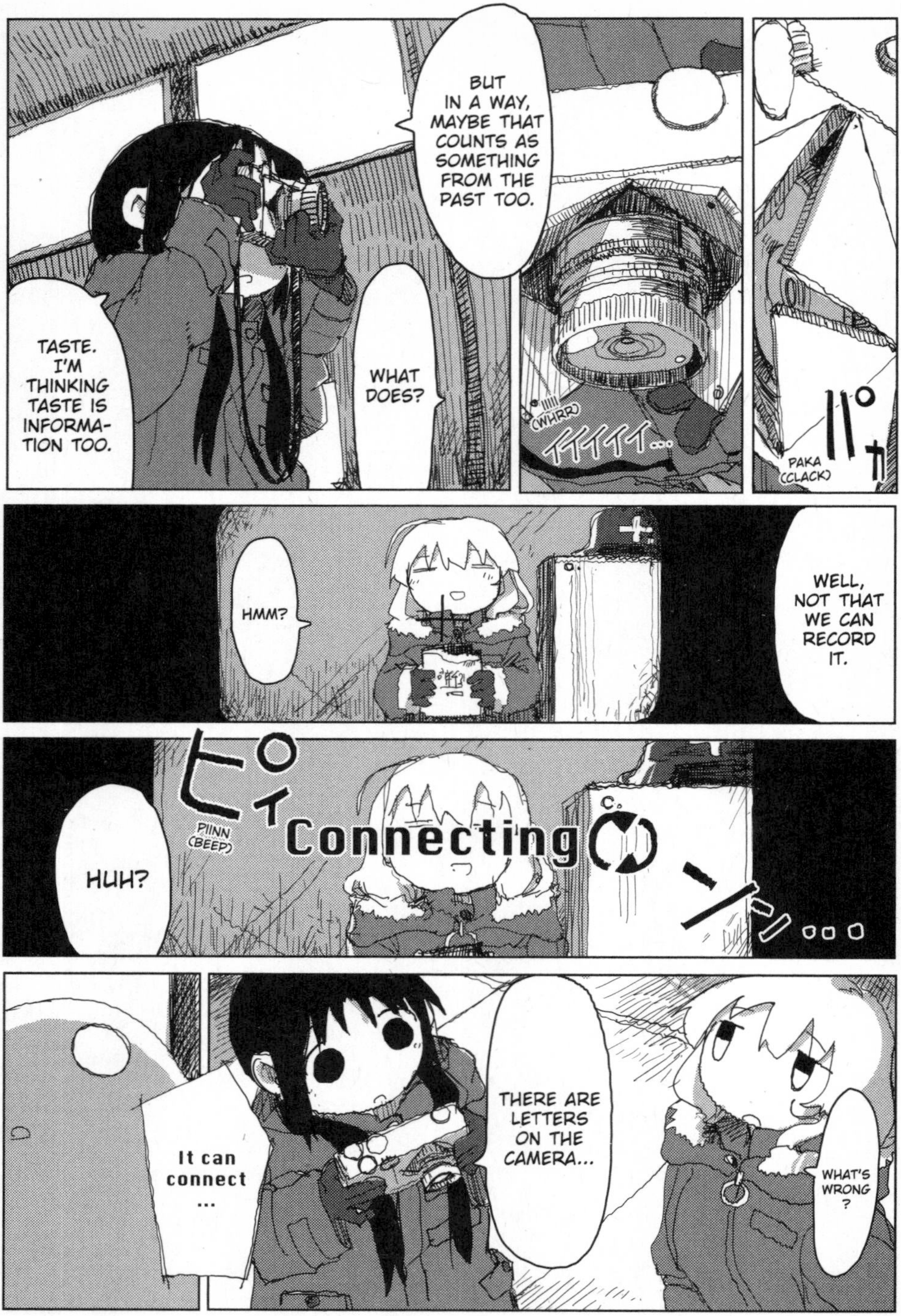
PAKA (CLACK)
(WHRR)
BUT IN A WAY, MAYBE THAT COUNTS AS SOMETHING FROM THE PAST TOO.
WHAT DOES?
TASTE. I'M THINKING TASTE IS INFORMATION TOO.
WELL, NOT THAT WE CAN RECORD IT.
HMM?
Connecting
PIINN (BEEP)
HUH?
WHAT'S WRONG?
THERE ARE LETTERS ON THE CAMERA...
It can connect ...

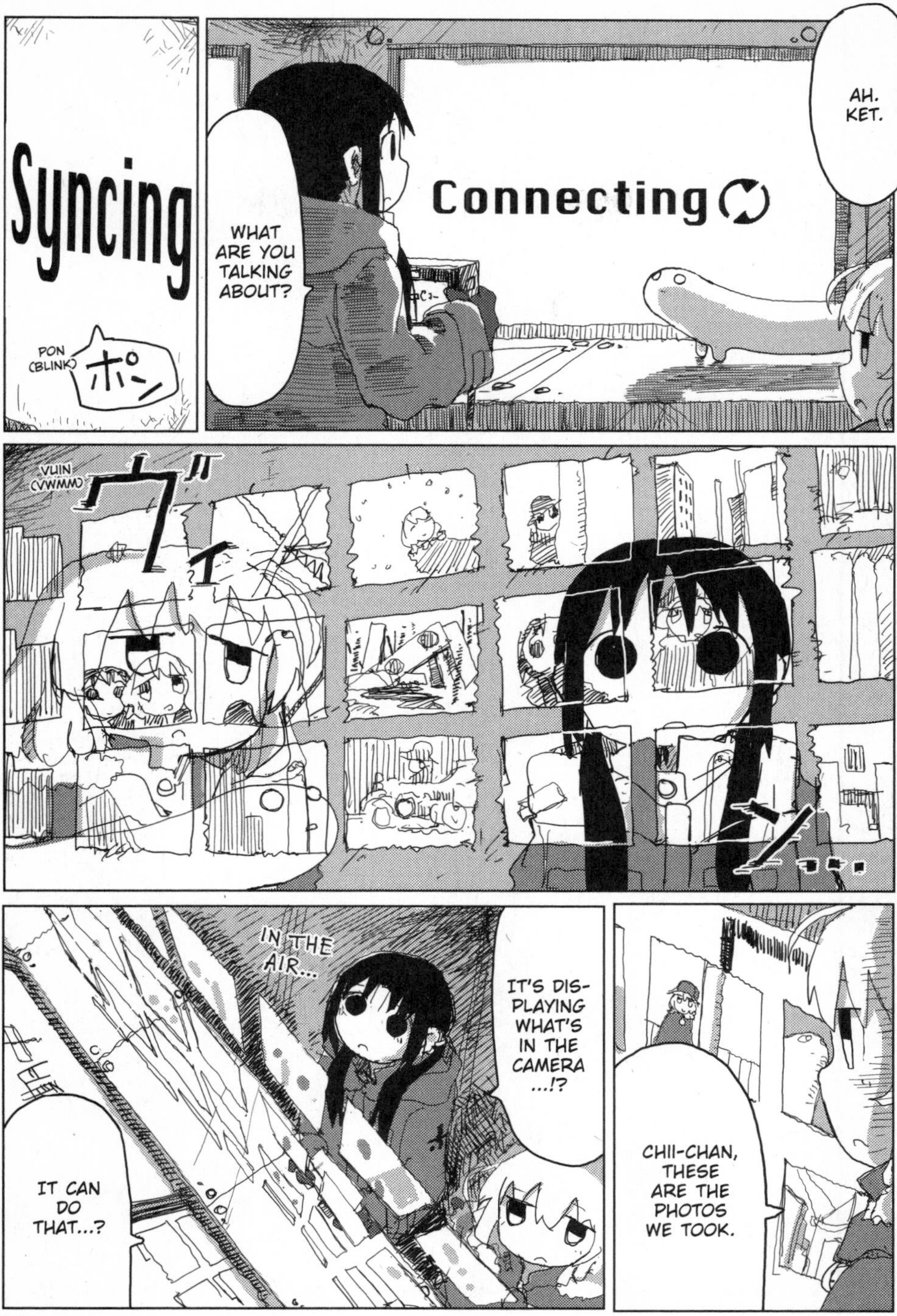
AH. KET.
Connecting
WHAT ARE YOU TALKING ABOUT?
Syncing
PON (BLINK)
ポン
VUIN (VWMM)
ヴィ
CHII-CHAN, THESE ARE THE PHOTOS WE TOOK.
IT'S DIS-PLAYING WHAT'S IN THE CAMERA ...!?
IN THE AIR...
IT CAN DO THAT...?

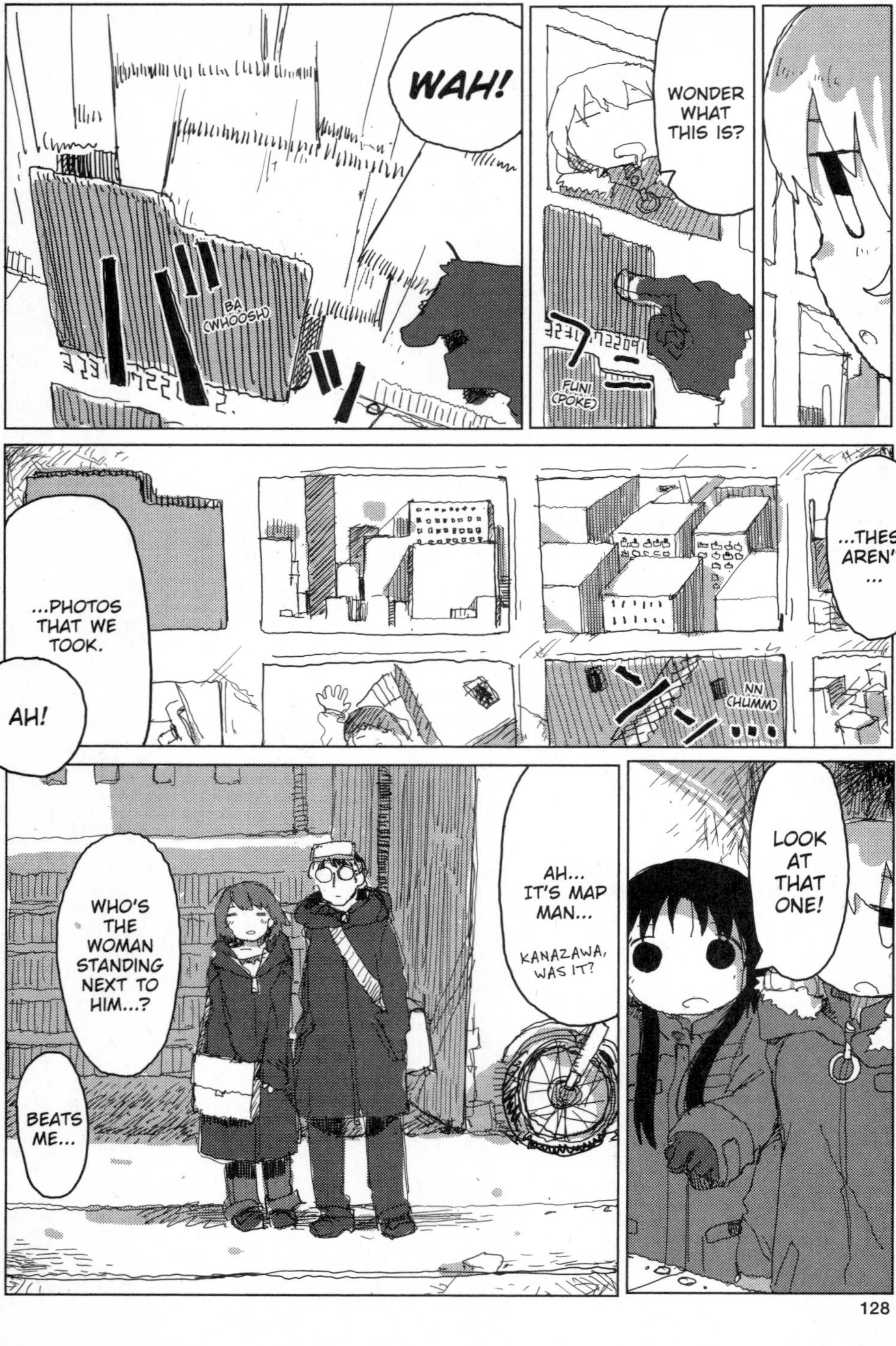
WONDER WHAT THIS IS?
FUNI (POKE)
WAH!
BA (WHOOSH)
...THESE AREN'T ...
NN (HUMM)
...PHOTOS THAT WE TOOK.
AH!
LOOK AT THAT ONE!
AH... IT'S MAP MAN...
KANAZAWA, WAS IT?
WHO'S THE WOMAN STANDING NEXT TO HIM...?
BEATS ME...

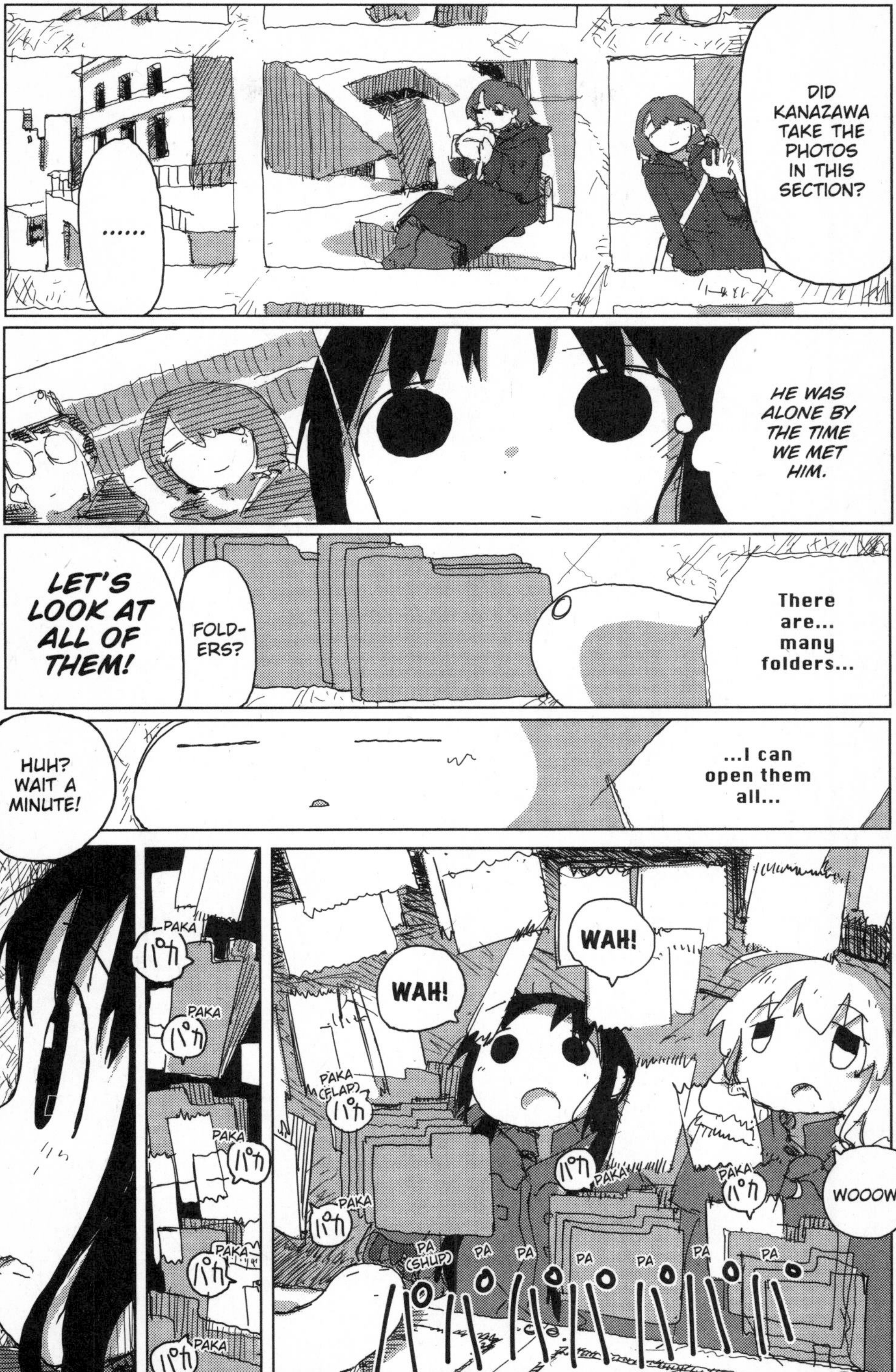
DID KANAZAWA TAKE THE PHOTOS IN THIS SECTION?
......
HE WAS ALONE BY THE TIME WE MET HIM.
There are... many folders...
FOLDERS?
LET'S LOOK AT ALL OF THEM!
...I can open them all...
HUH? WAIT A MINUTE!
WOOOW.
PAKA パカ
WAH!
WAH!
PAKA パカ
PAKA (FLAP) パカ
PAKA パカ
PA (SHUP) PA PA PA PA PA PA
PAKA パカ
PAKA パカ
PAKA パカ
PAKA パカ
PAKA パカ

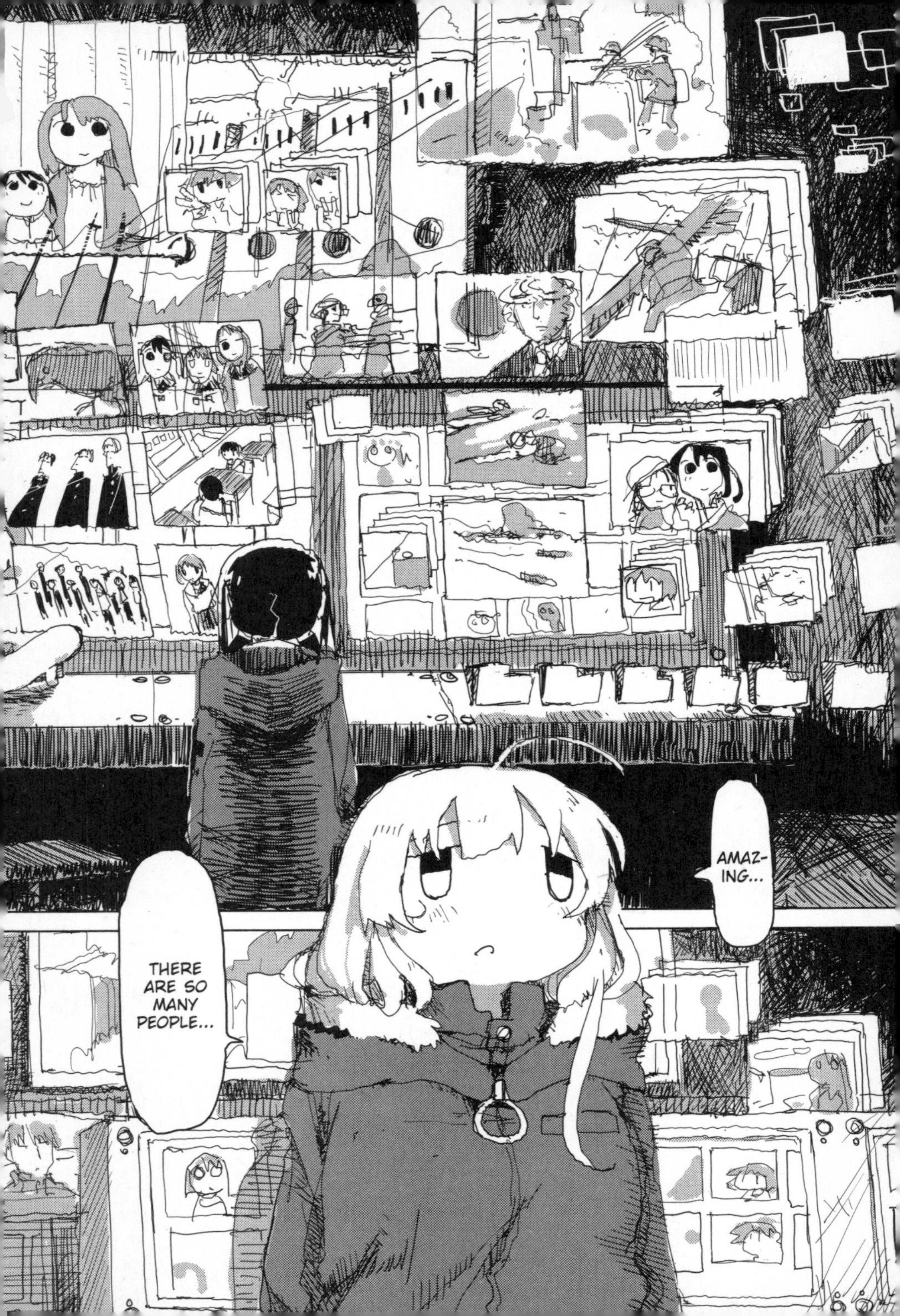
AMAZ-
ING...
THERE ARE SO MANY PEOPLE...

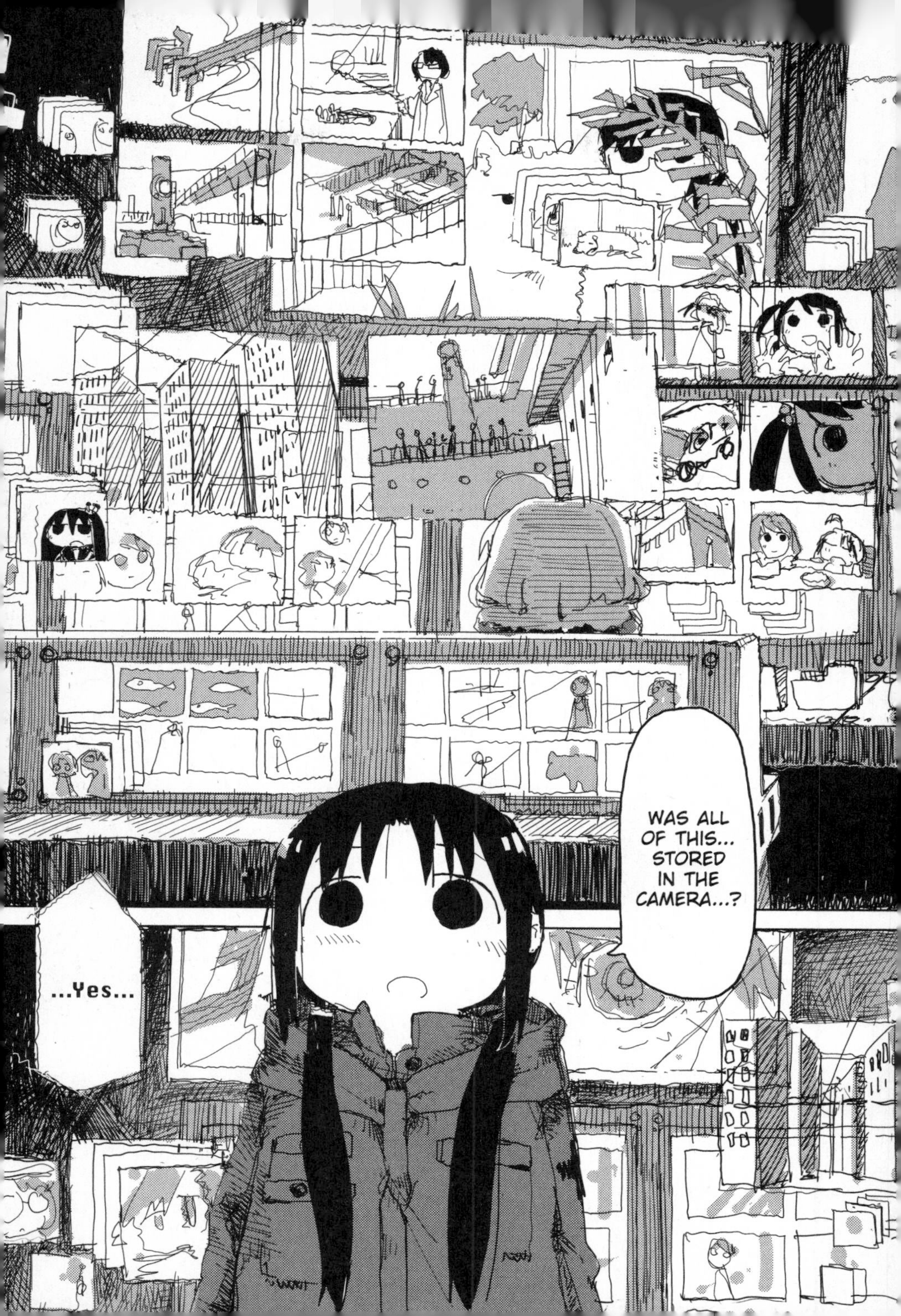
WAS ALL OF THIS... STORED IN THE CAMERA...?
...Yes...

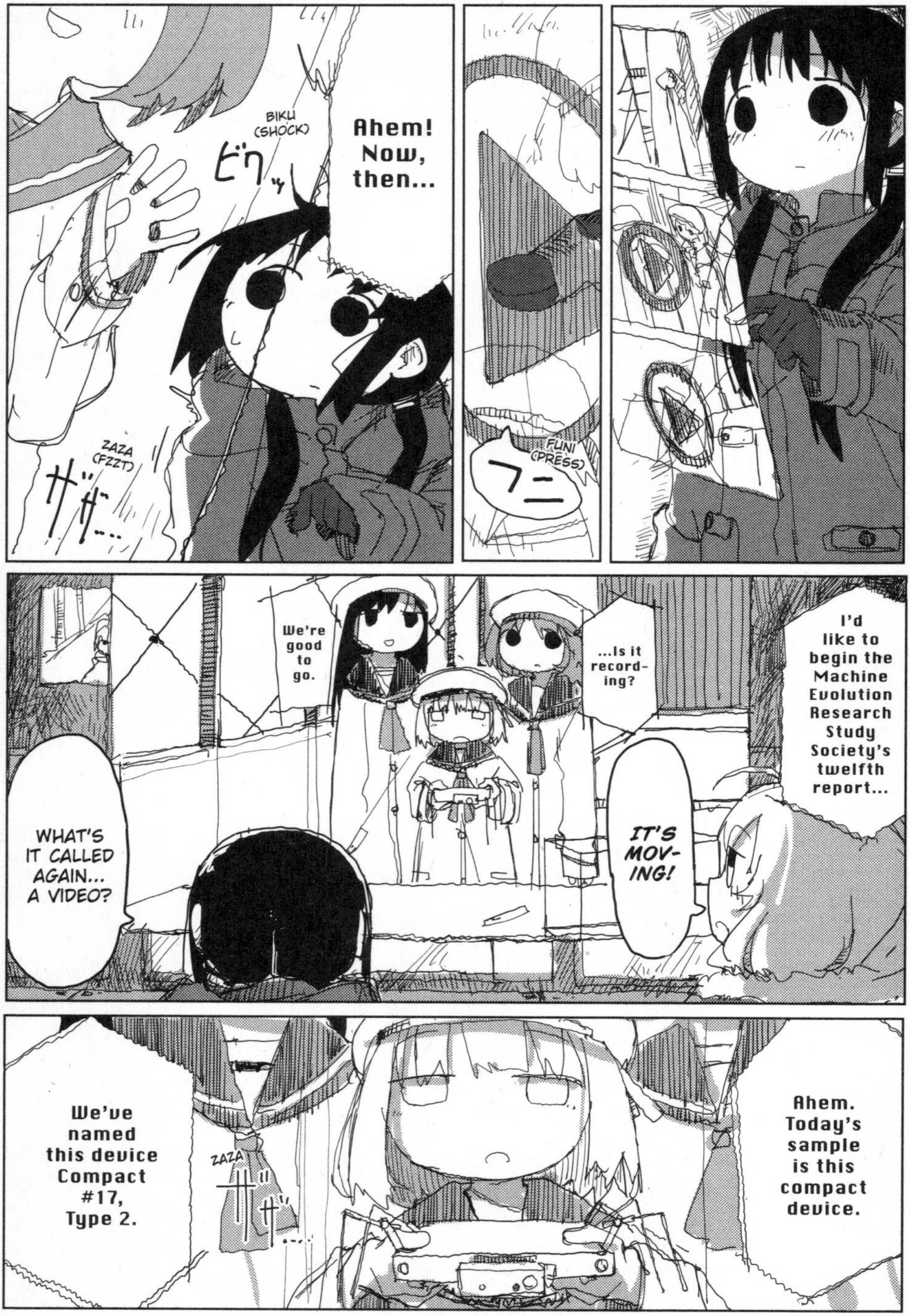
FUNI (PRESS)
フニ
Ahem! Now, then...
BIKU (SHOCK)
ビクッ
ZAZA (FZZT)
ザザ...
I'd like to begin the Machine Evolution Research Study Society's twelfth report...
...Is it recording?
We're good to go.
IT'S MOVING!
WHAT'S IT CALLED AGAIN... A VIDEO?
Ahem. Today's sample is this compact device.
ZAZA
ザザ...
We've named this device Compact #17, Type 2.

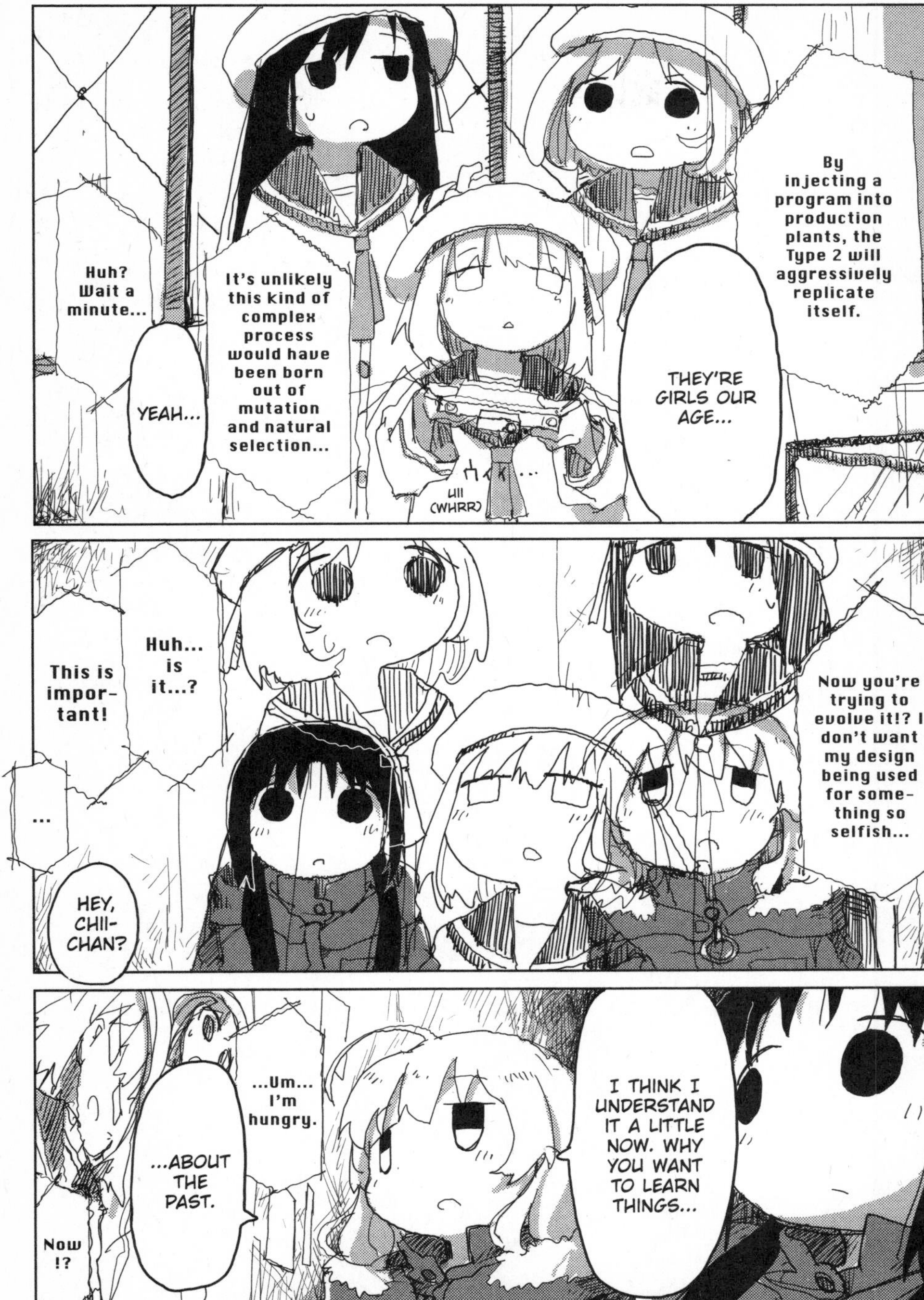
By injecting a program into production plants, the Type 2 will aggressively replicate itself.
THEY'RE GIRLS OUR AGE...
It's unlikely this kind of complex process would have been born out of mutation and natural selection...
UII (WHRR)
Huh? Wait a minute...
YEAH...
Now you're trying to evolve it!? I don't want my design being used for some-thing so selfish...
Huh... is it...?
This is impor-tant!
...
HEY, CHII-CHAN?
I THINK I UNDERSTAND IT A LITTLE NOW. WHY YOU WANT TO LEARN THINGS...
...Um... I'm hungry.
...ABOUT THE PAST.
Now !?

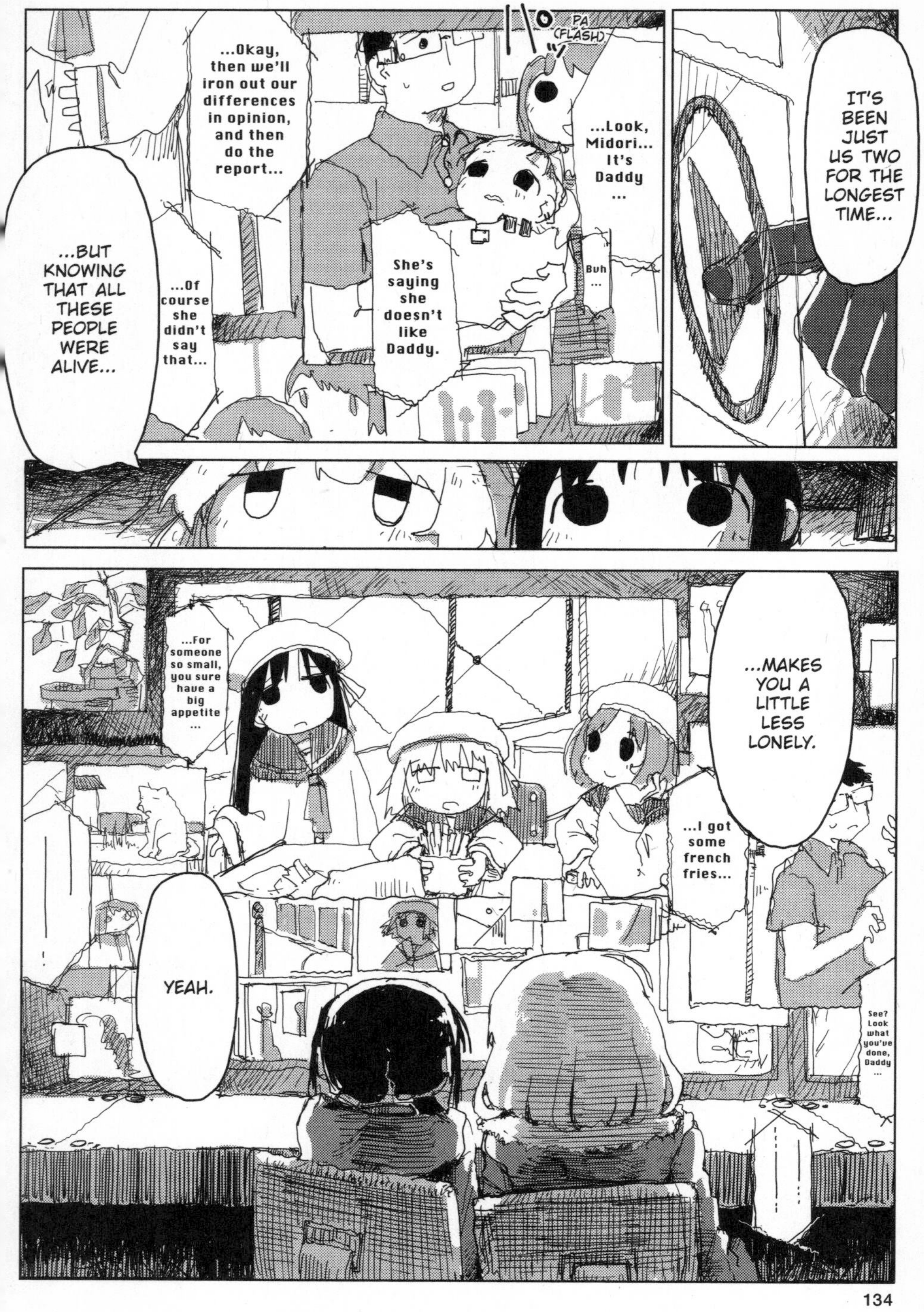
IT'S BEEN JUST US TWO FOR THE LONGEST TIME...
PA (FLASH)
...Look, Midori... It's Daddy ...
...Okay, then we'll iron out our differences in opinion, and then do the report...
Buh ...
She's saying she doesn't like Daddy.
...Of course she didn't say that...
...BUT KNOWING THAT ALL THESE PEOPLE WERE ALIVE...
...MAKES YOU A LITTLE LESS LONELY.
...For someone so small, you sure have a big appetite ...
...I got some french fries...
See? Look what you've done, Daddy ...
YEAH.

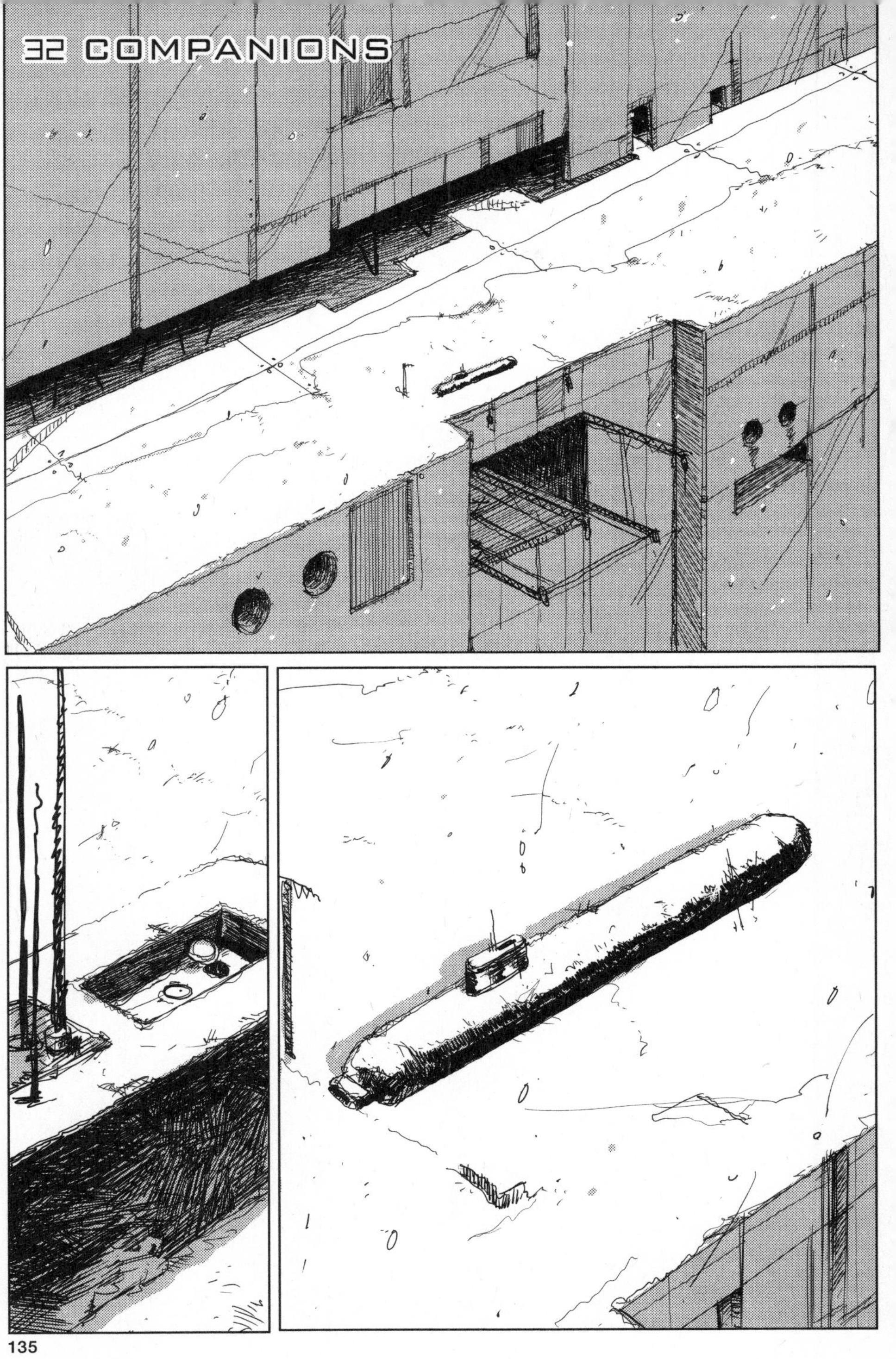
32 COMPANIONS

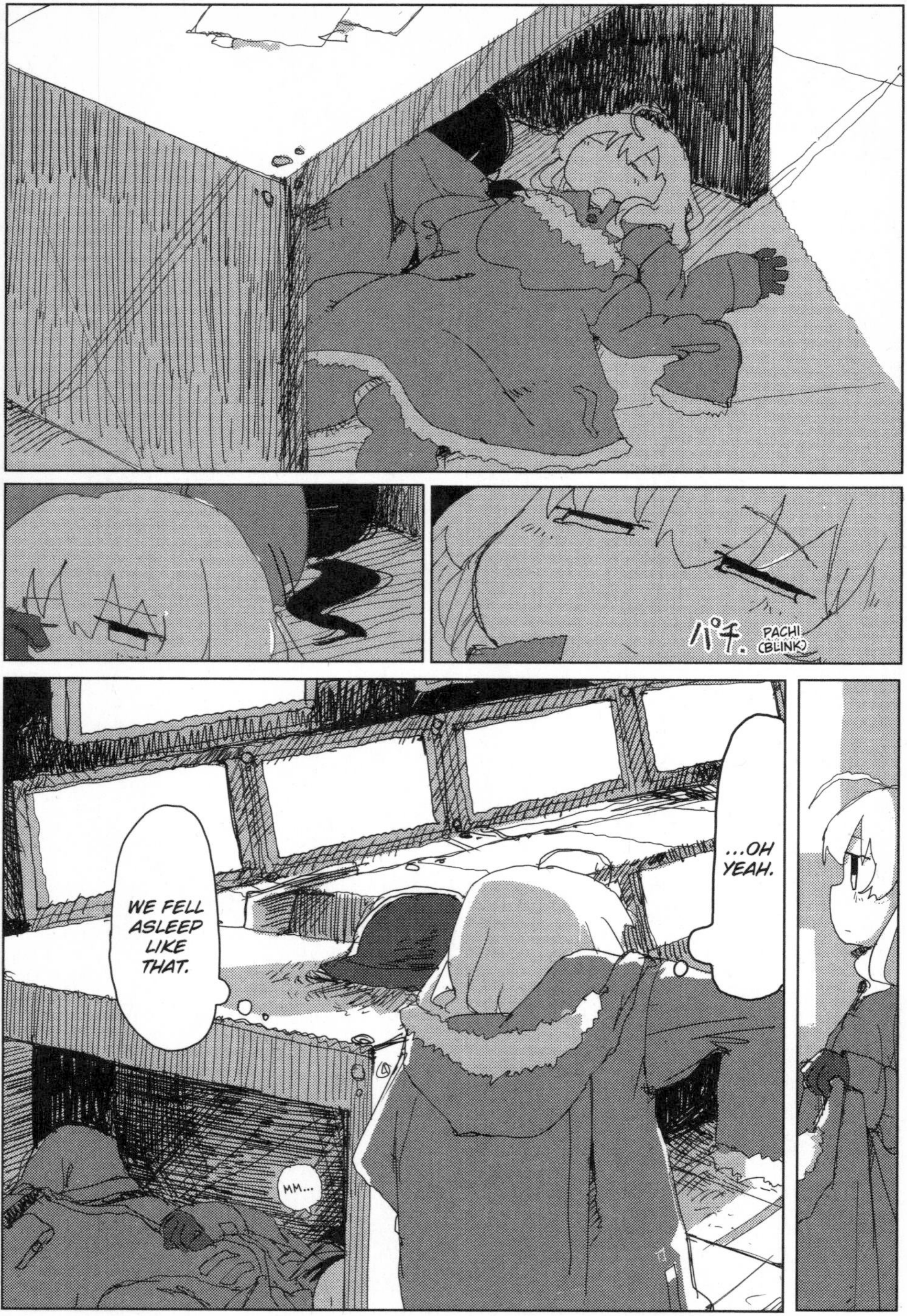
パチ。
PACHI (BLINK)
...OH YEAH.
WE FELL ASLEEP LIKE THAT.
MM...

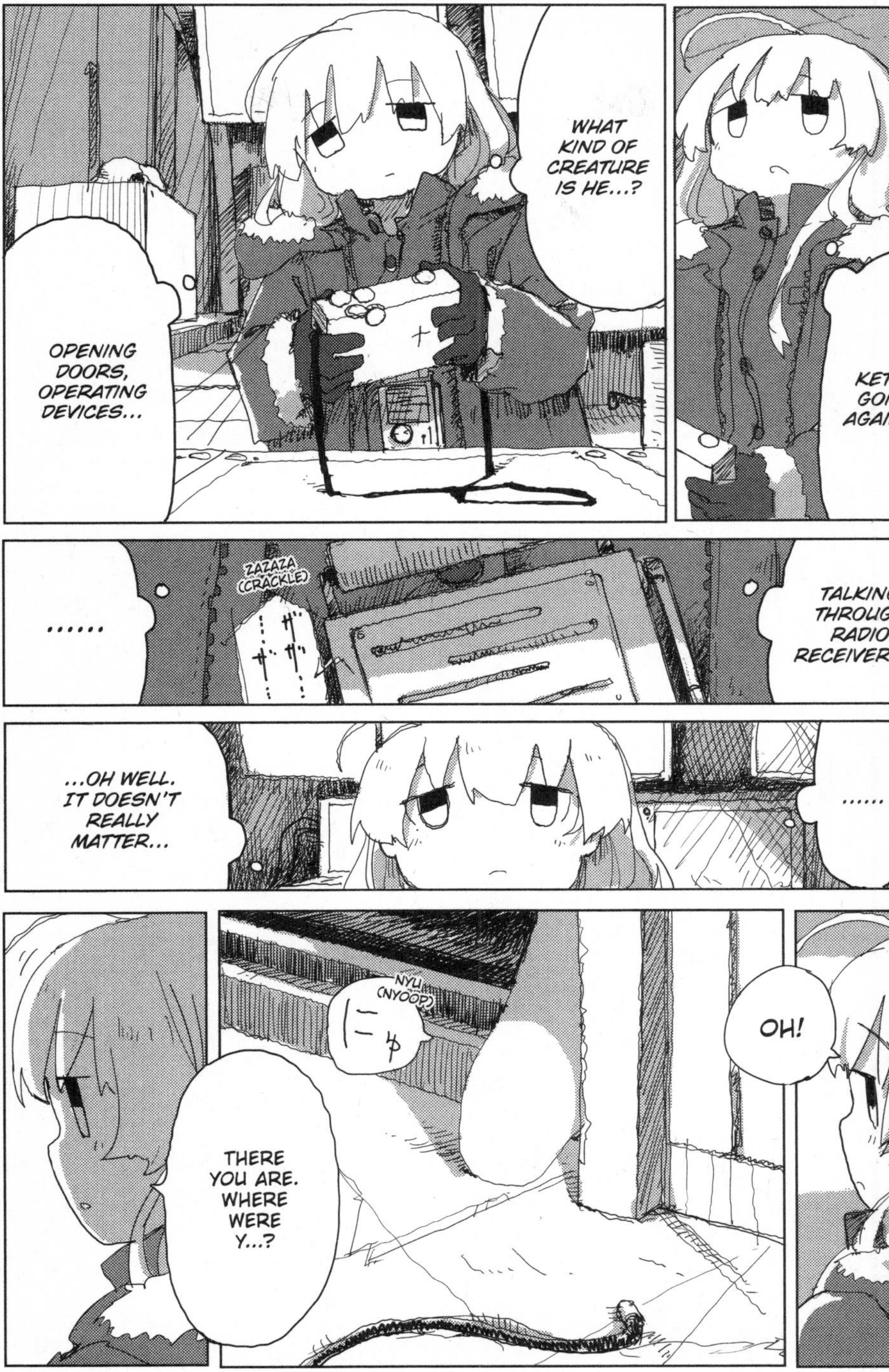
KET'S GONE AGAIN...
WHAT KIND OF CREATURE IS HE...?
OPENING DOORS, OPERATING DEVICES...
TALKING THROUGH RADIO RECEIVERS...
ZAZAZA (CRACKLE)
......
......
...OH WELL. IT DOESN'T REALLY MATTER...
OH!
NYU (NYOOP)
THERE YOU ARE. WHERE WERE Y...?

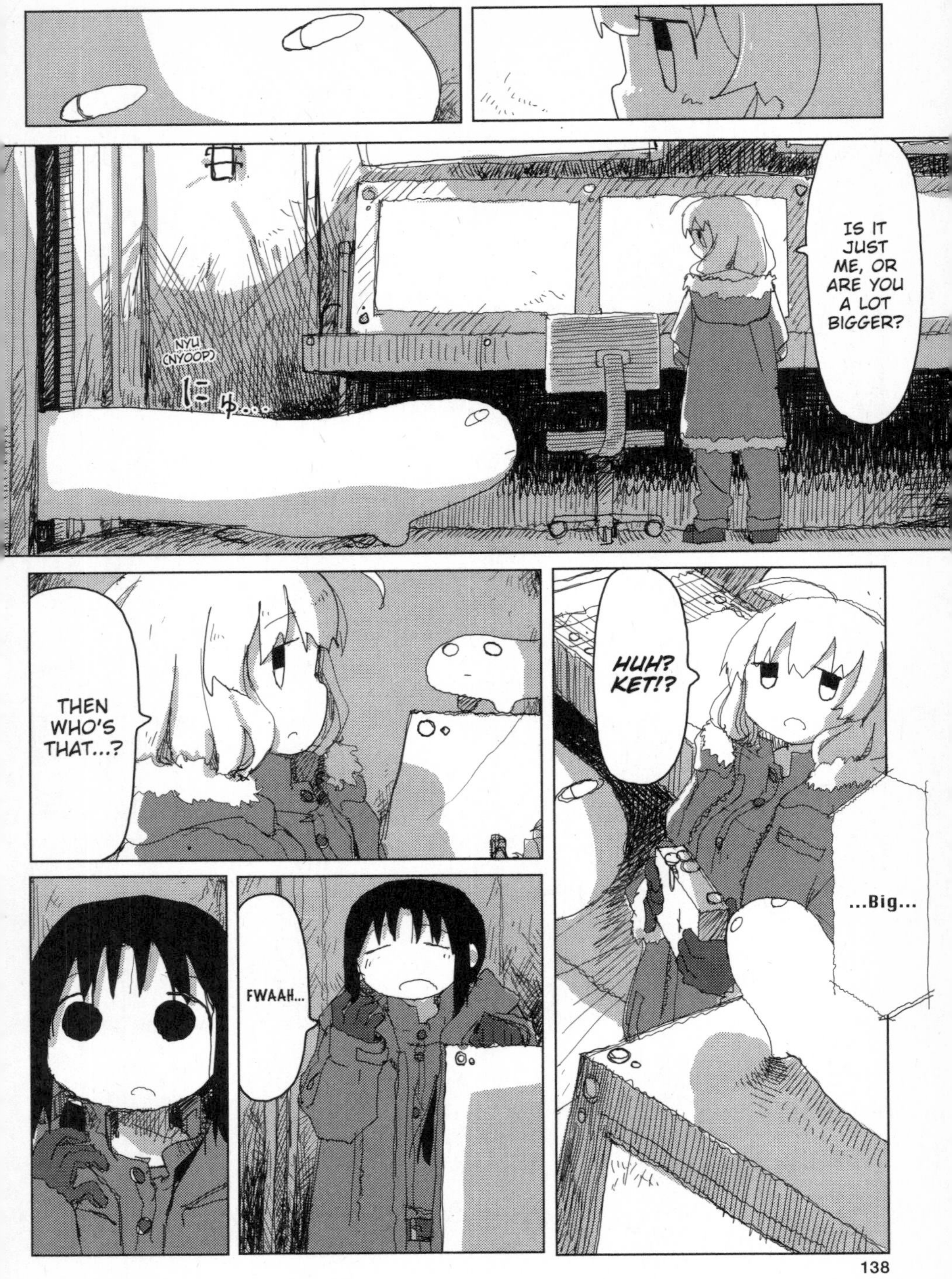
IS IT JUST ME, OR ARE YOU A LOT BIGGER?
NYU (NYOOP)
にゅ…
HUH? KET!?
...Big...
THEN WHO'S THAT...?
FWAAH...

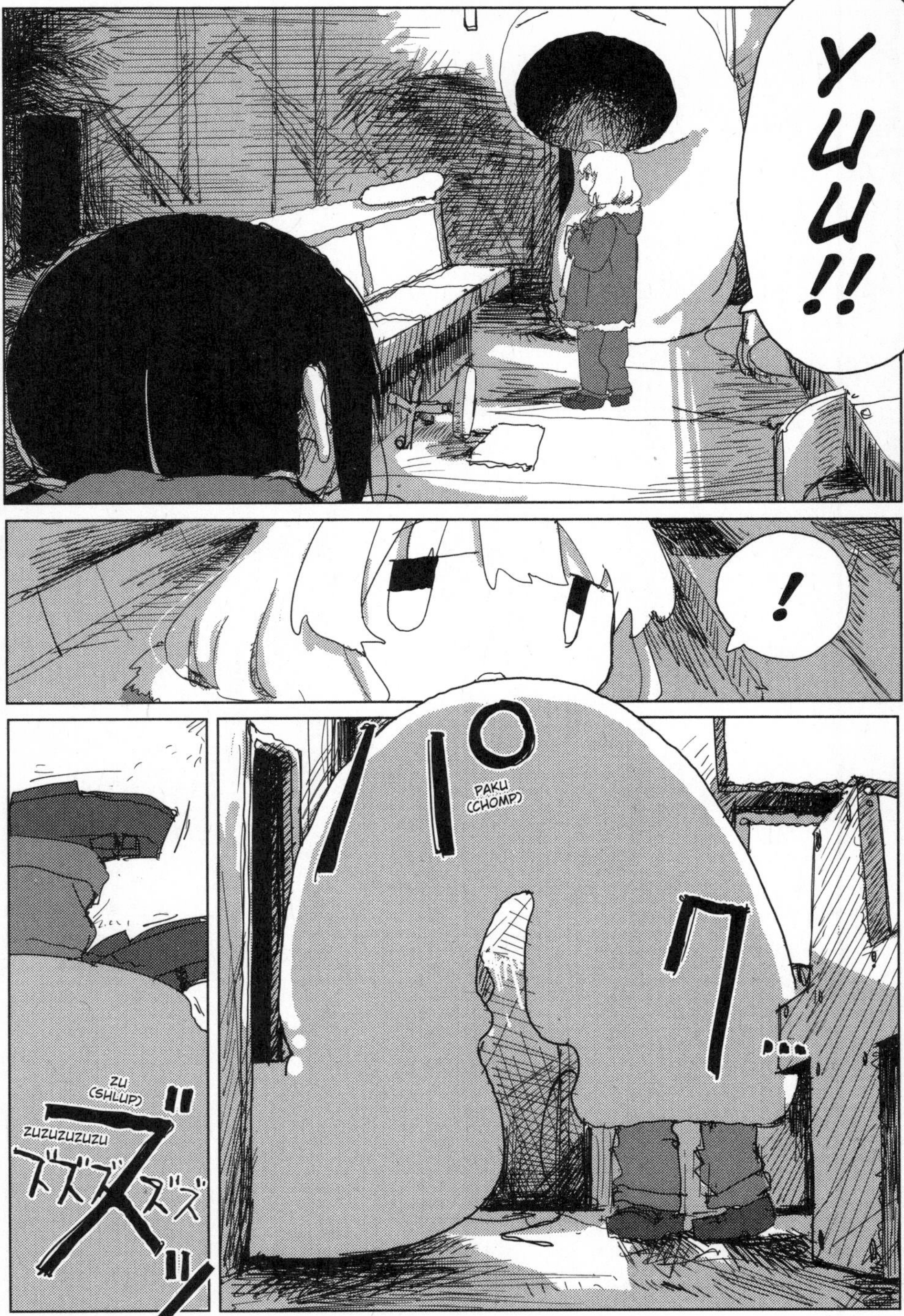
YUUU!!
!
パク…
PAKU (CHOMP)
ZU (SHLUP)
ZUZUZUZUZU
ズズズズズズ

ゴクン…
GOKUN (GULP)
ズズズ…
ZUZUZU (SLITHER)

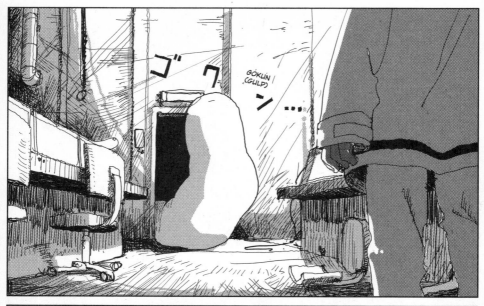

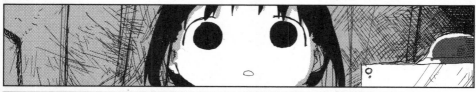

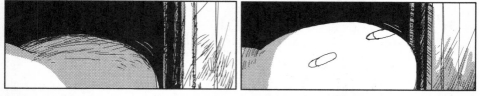

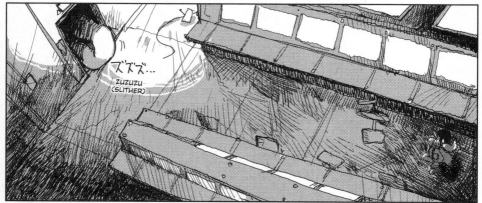

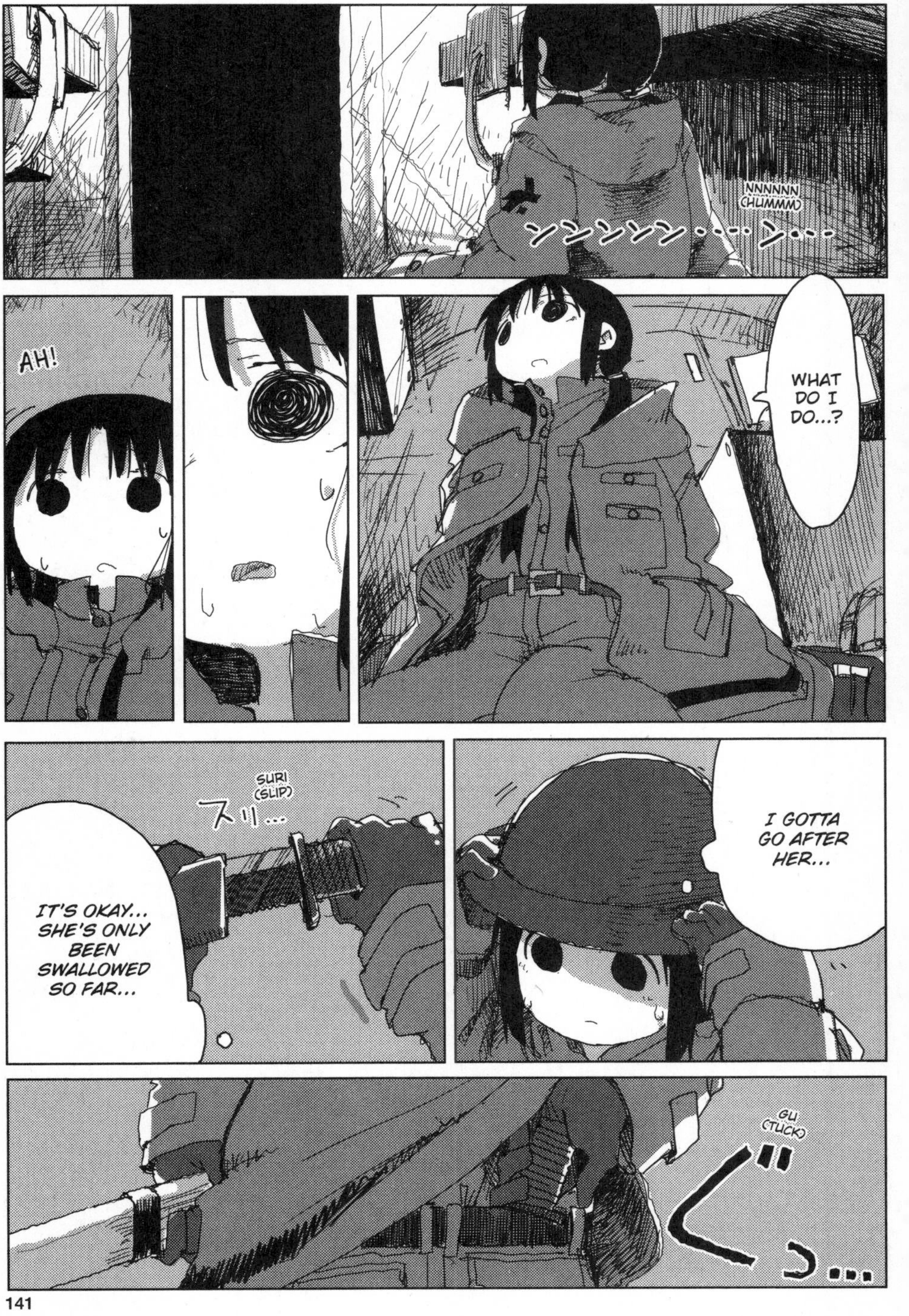
NNNNNN (HUMMM)
ンンンンンン・・・ン・・・
WHAT DO I DO...?
AH!
I GOTTA GO AFTER HER...
SURI (SLIP)
スリ…
IT'S OKAY... SHE'S ONLY BEEN SWALLOWED SO FAR...
GU (TUCK)
ぐっ...

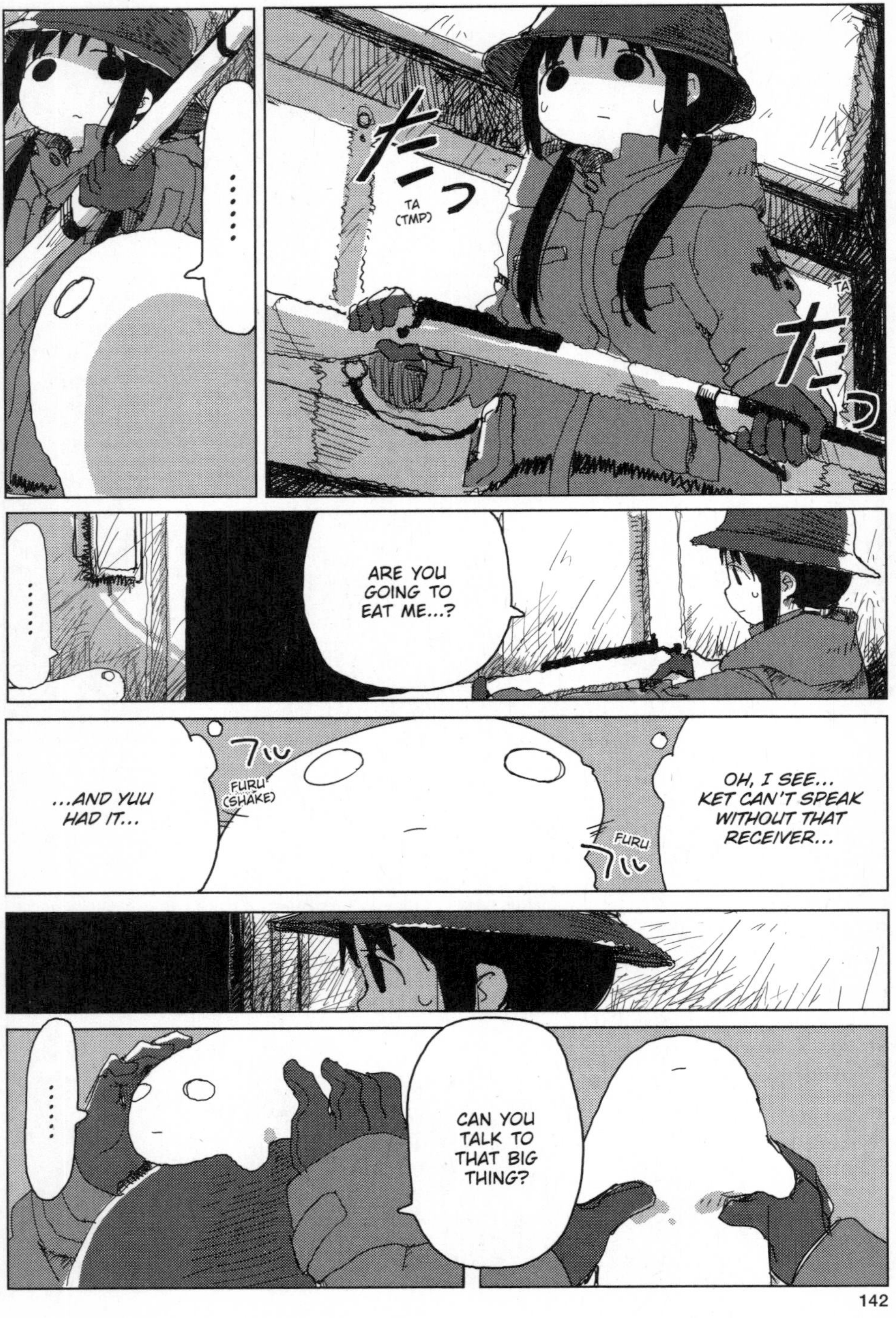
たーっ
TA (TMP)
たっ
TA
......
ARE YOU GOING TO EAT ME...?
......
OH, I SEE... KET CAN'T SPEAK WITHOUT THAT RECEIVER...
フル
FURU
フル
FURU (SHAKE)
...AND YUU HAD IT...
CAN YOU TALK TO THAT BIG THING?
......

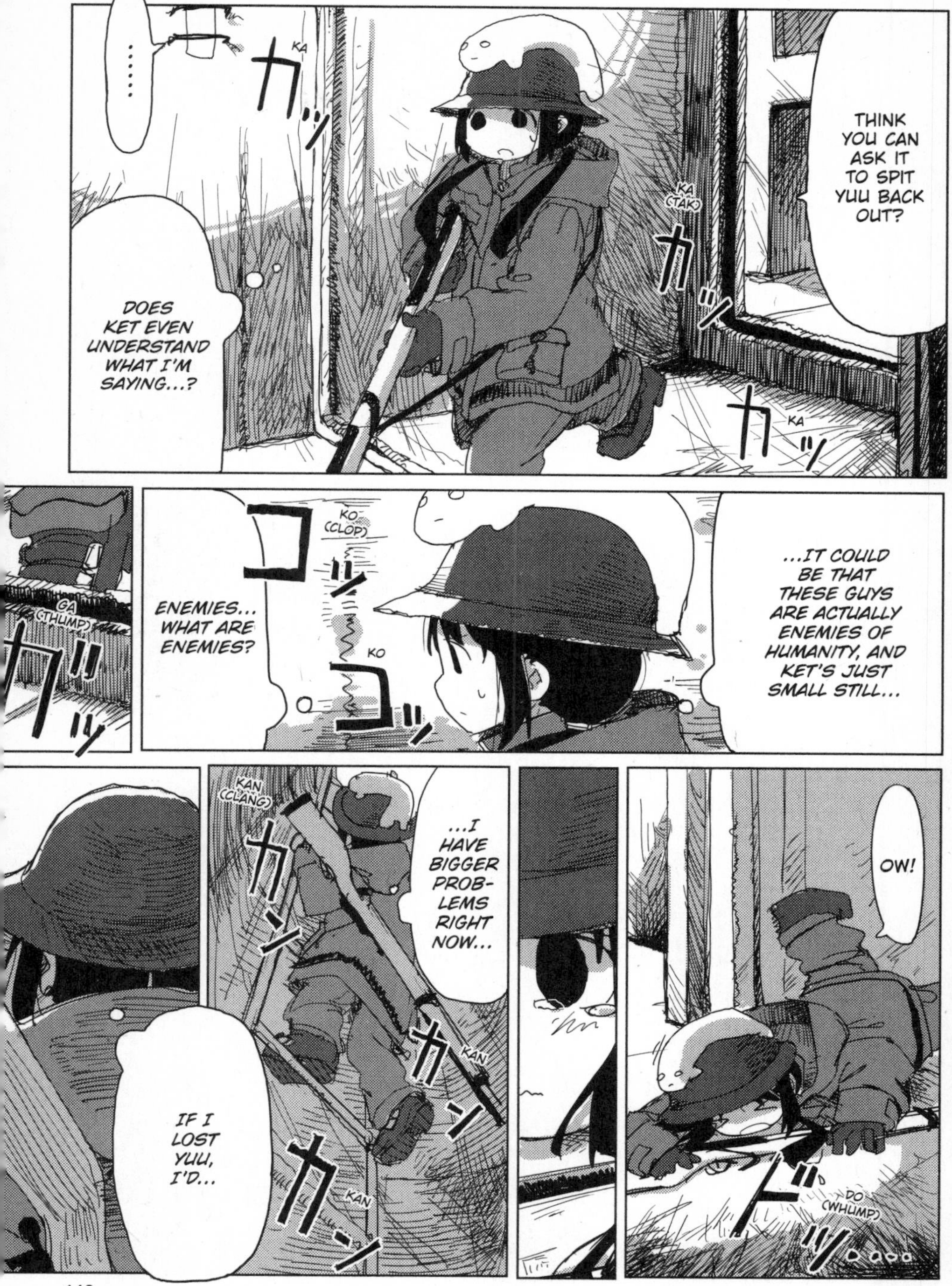
THINK YOU CAN ASK IT TO SPIT YUU BACK OUT?
KA
KA (TAK)
KA
......
DOES KET EVEN UNDERSTAND WHAT I'M SAYING...?
...IT COULD BE THAT THESE GUYS ARE ACTUALLY ENEMIES OF HUMANITY, AND KET'S JUST SMALL STILL...
KO (CLOP)
KO
ENEMIES... WHAT ARE ENEMIES?
GA (THUMP)
OW!
DO (WHUMP)
...I HAVE BIGGER PROB-LEMS RIGHT NOW...
KAN (CLANG)
KAN
KAN
IF I LOST YUU, I'D...

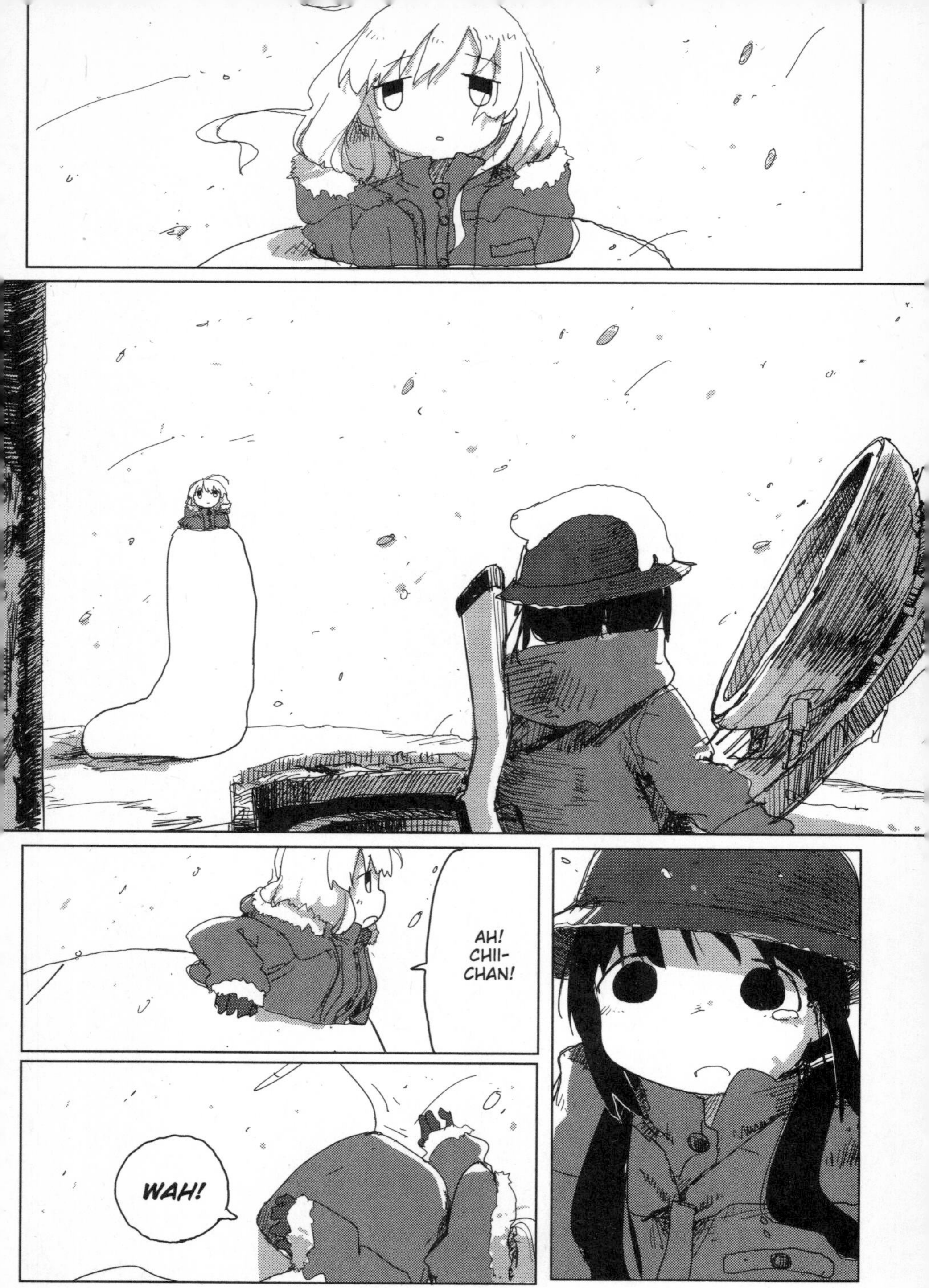
AH! CHII-CHAN!
WAH!

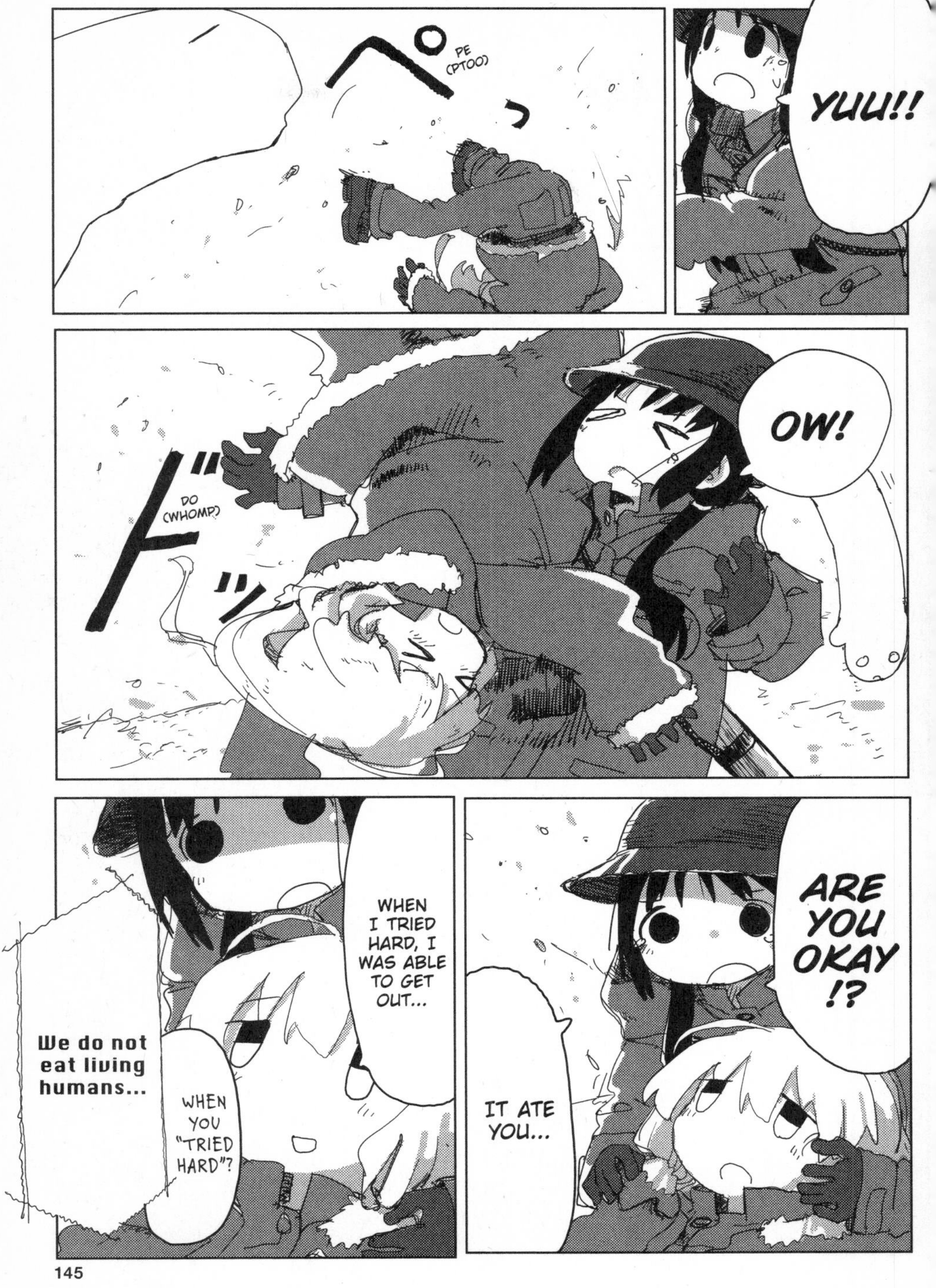
YUU!!
PE (PTOO)
OW!
DO (WHOMP)
ARE YOU OKAY!?
IT ATE YOU...
WHEN I TRIED HARD, I WAS ABLE TO GET OUT...
WHEN YOU "TRIED HARD"?
We do not eat living humans...

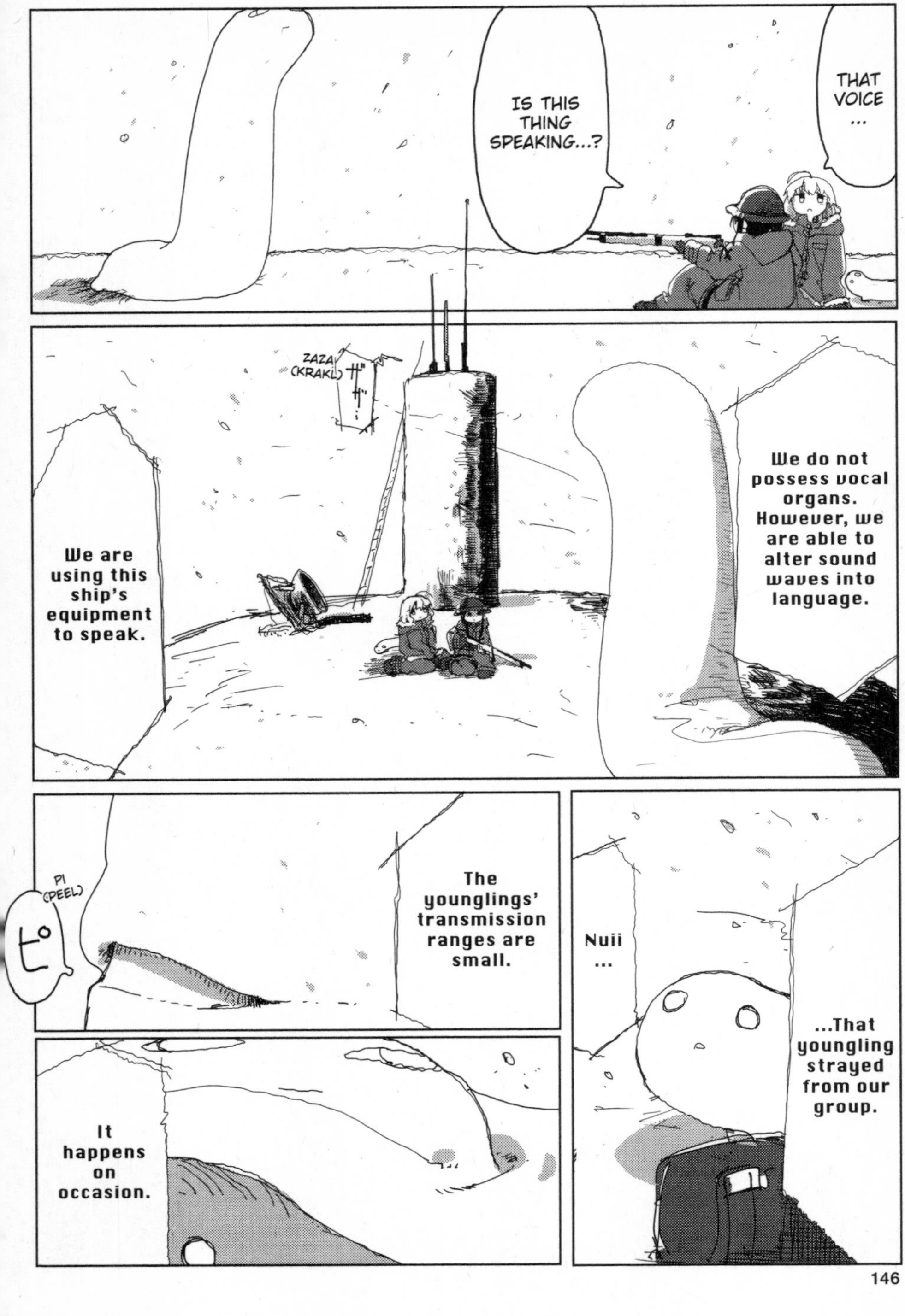
THAT VOICE ...
IS THIS THING SPEAKING...?
We do not possess vocal organs. However, we are able to alter sound waves into language.
ZAZA (KRAKL)
We are using this ship's equipment to speak.
Nuii ...
...That youngling strayed from our group.
The younglings' transmission ranges are small.
PI (PEEL)
It happens on occasion.

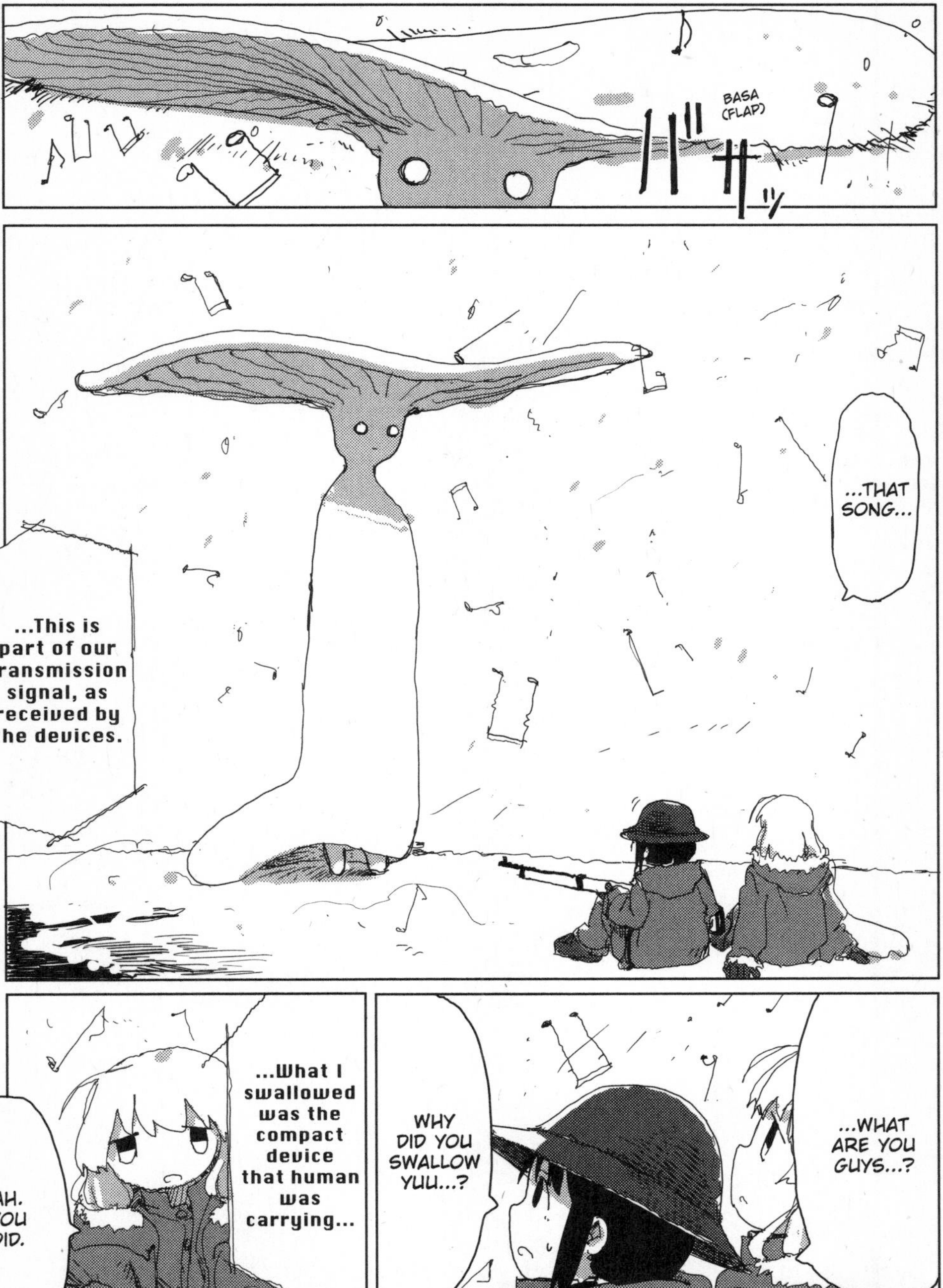

バサッ
BASA (FLAP)
...THAT SONG...
...This is part of our transmission signal, as received by the devices.
...WHAT ARE YOU GUYS...?
WHY DID YOU SWALLOW YUU...?
...What I swallowed was the compact device that human was carrying...
AH. YOU DID.

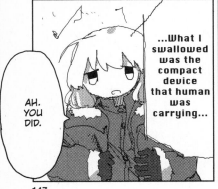

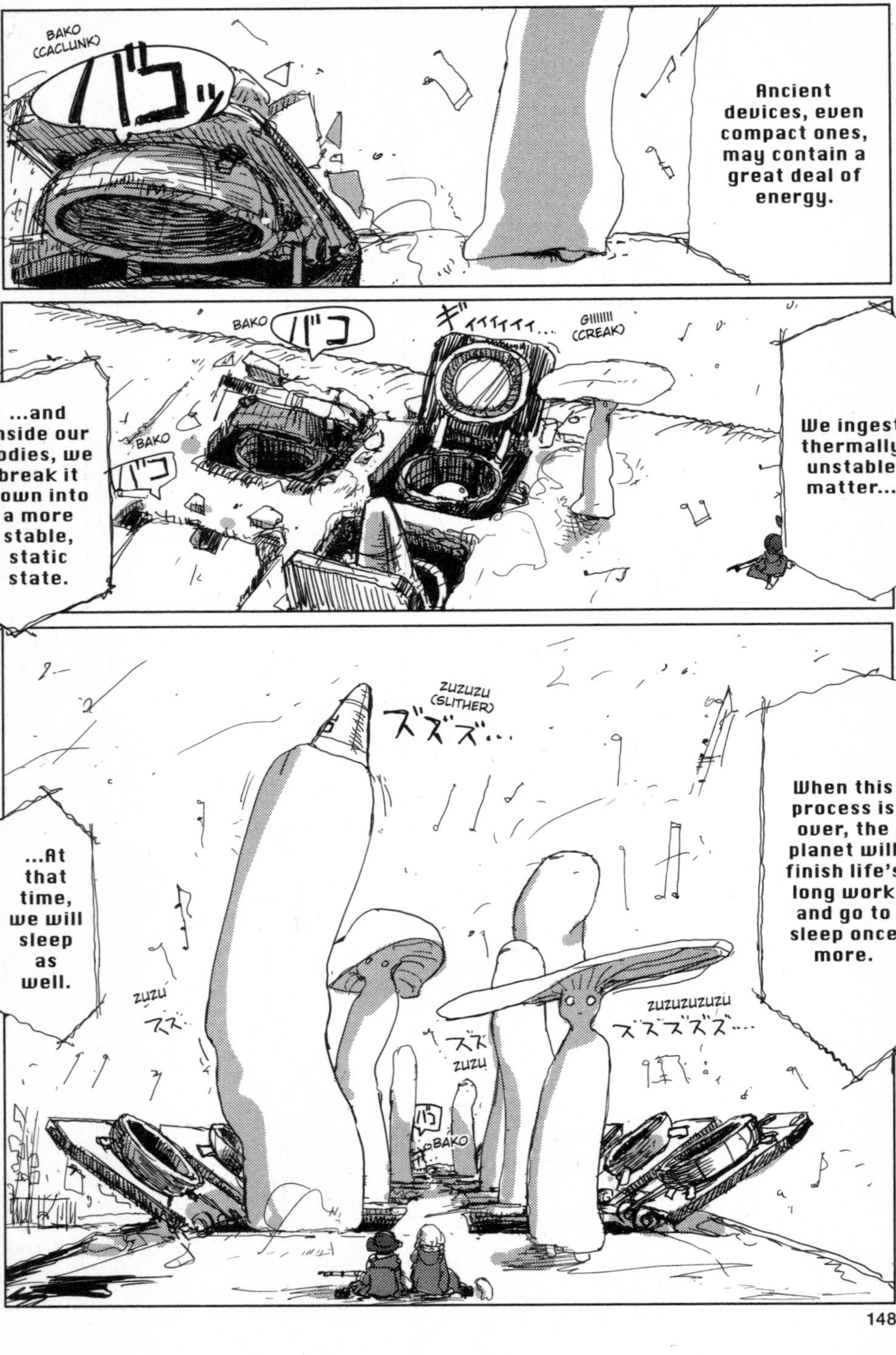

Ancient devices, even compact ones, may contain a great deal of energy.
BAKO (CACLUNK)
バコッ
We ingest thermally unstable matter...
GIIIIII (CREAK)
ギィィィィィ...
BAKO
バコ
...and inside our bodies, we break it down into a more stable, static state.
BAKO
バコ
When this process is over, the planet will finish life's long work and go to sleep once more.
ZUZUZU (SLITHER)
ズズズ...
ZUZUZUZUZU
ズズズズズ...
ZUZU
ズズ
バコ
BAKO
...At that time, we will sleep as well.
ZUZU
ズズ

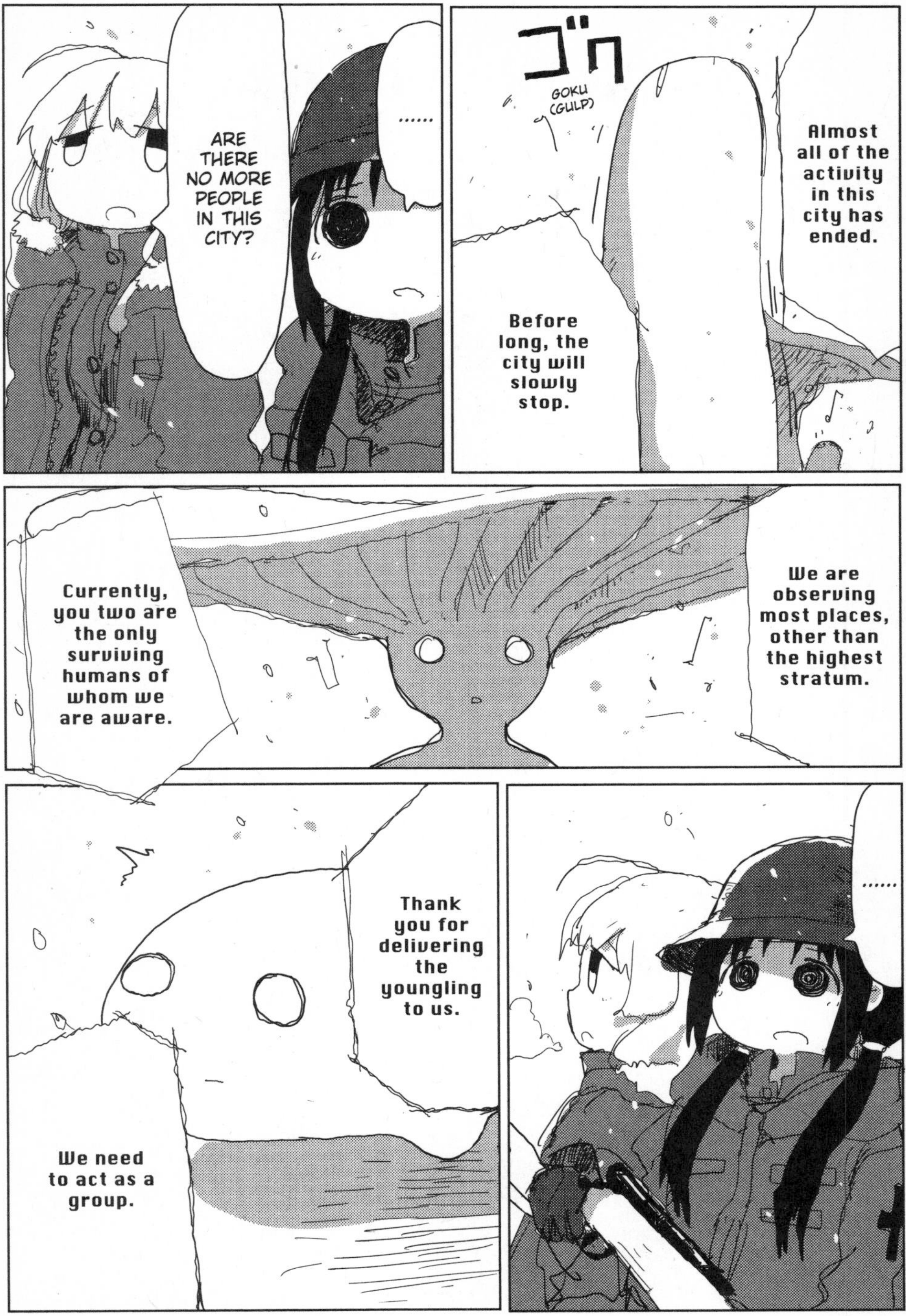
ゴク
GOKU (GULP)
Almost all of the activity in this city has ended.
Before long, the city will slowly stop.
......
ARE THERE NO MORE PEOPLE IN THIS CITY?
We are observing most places, other than the highest stratum.
Currently, you two are the only surviving humans of whom we are aware.
......
Thank you for delivering the youngling to us.
We need to act as a group.

Nui...

WHY ARE YOU SCARED, KET?

SHU (WRAP)

OH!

シュッ

フル
FURU

FURU (SHAKE)

フル

スイ...
SUI (SLIP)

......

Good-bye.

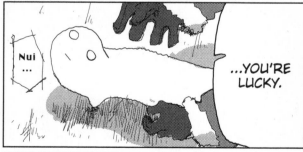

Nui...

...YOU'RE LUCKY.

YOU HAVE LOTS OF COMPANIONS.

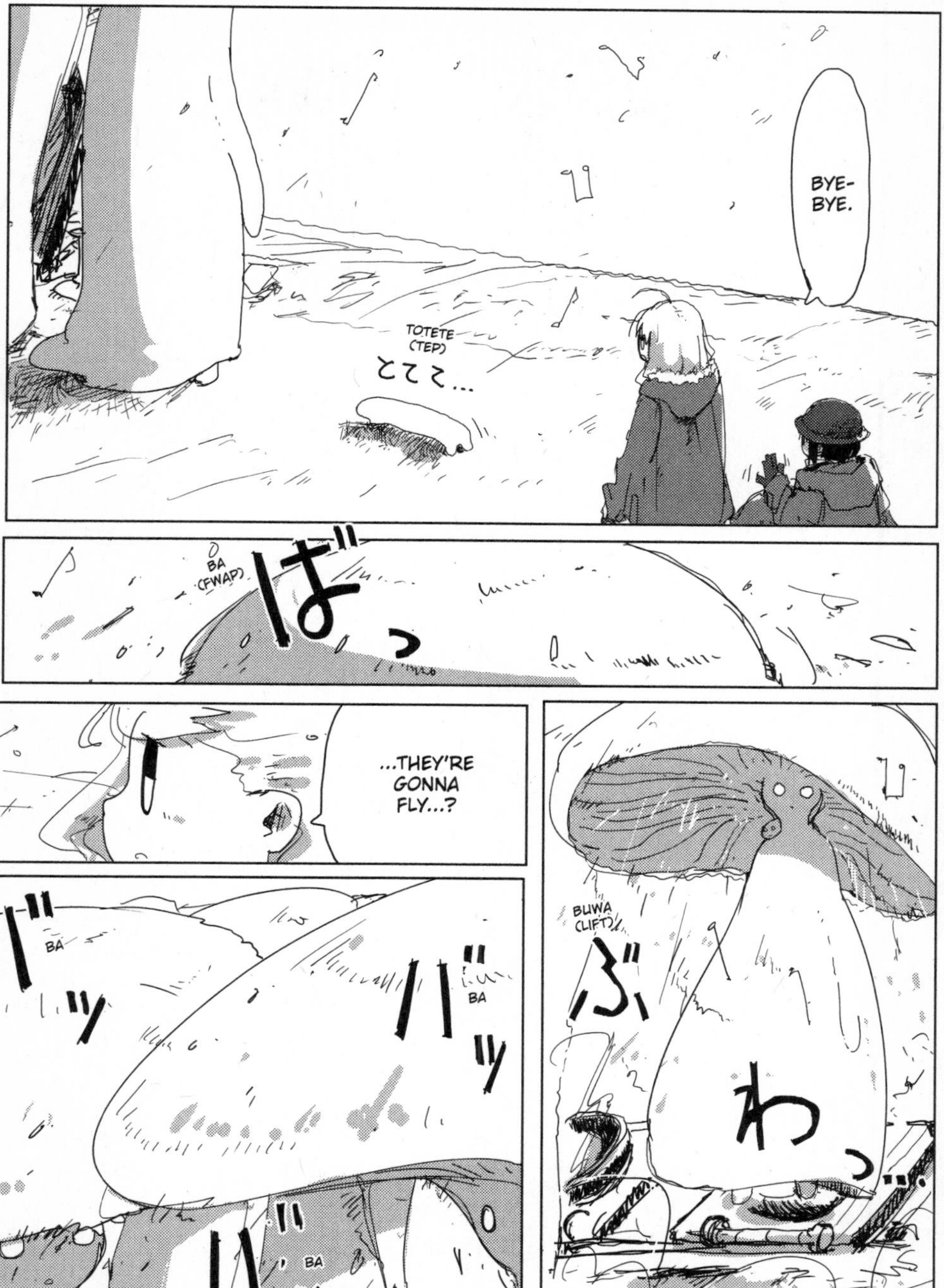
BYE-BYE.
TOTETE (TEP)
とてて…
BA (FWAP)
ばっ
BUWA (LIFT)
ぶわっ…
...THEY'RE GONNA FLY...?
BA
バッ
BA
バッ
BA
バッ

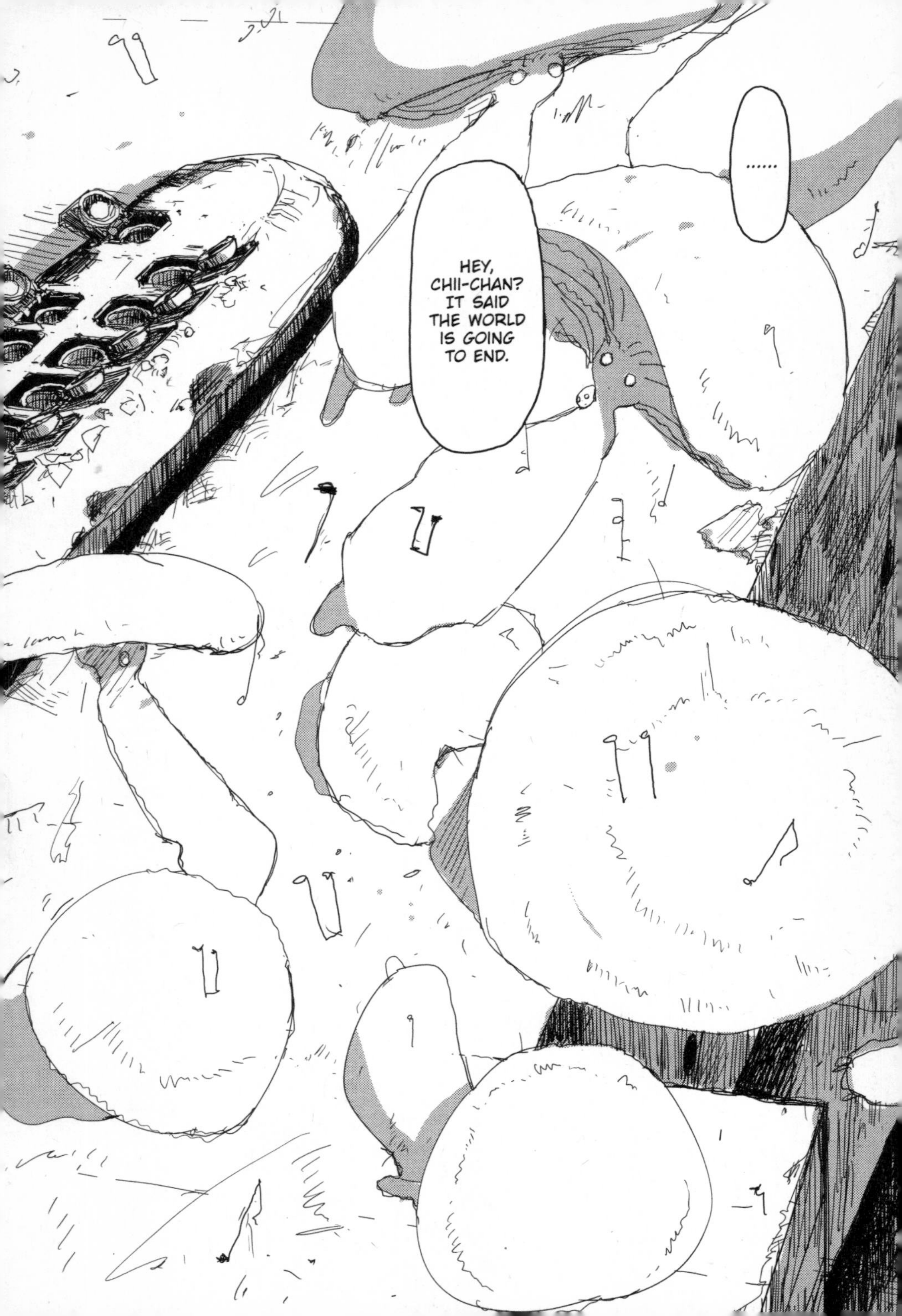
......
HEY, CHII-CHAN? IT SAID THE WORLD IS GOING TO END.

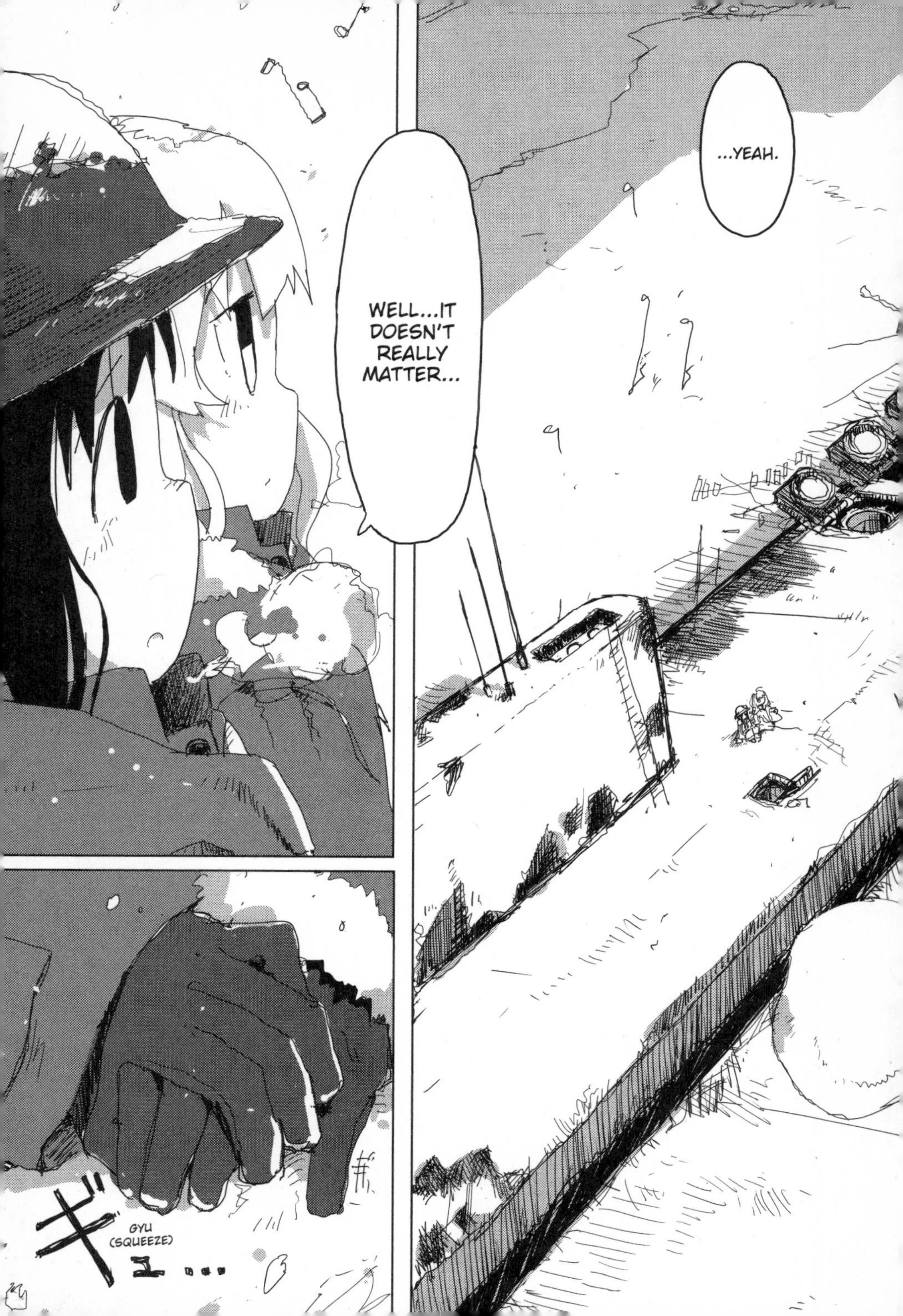
...YEAH.
WELL...IT DOESN'T REALLY MATTER...
GYU (SQUEEZE)

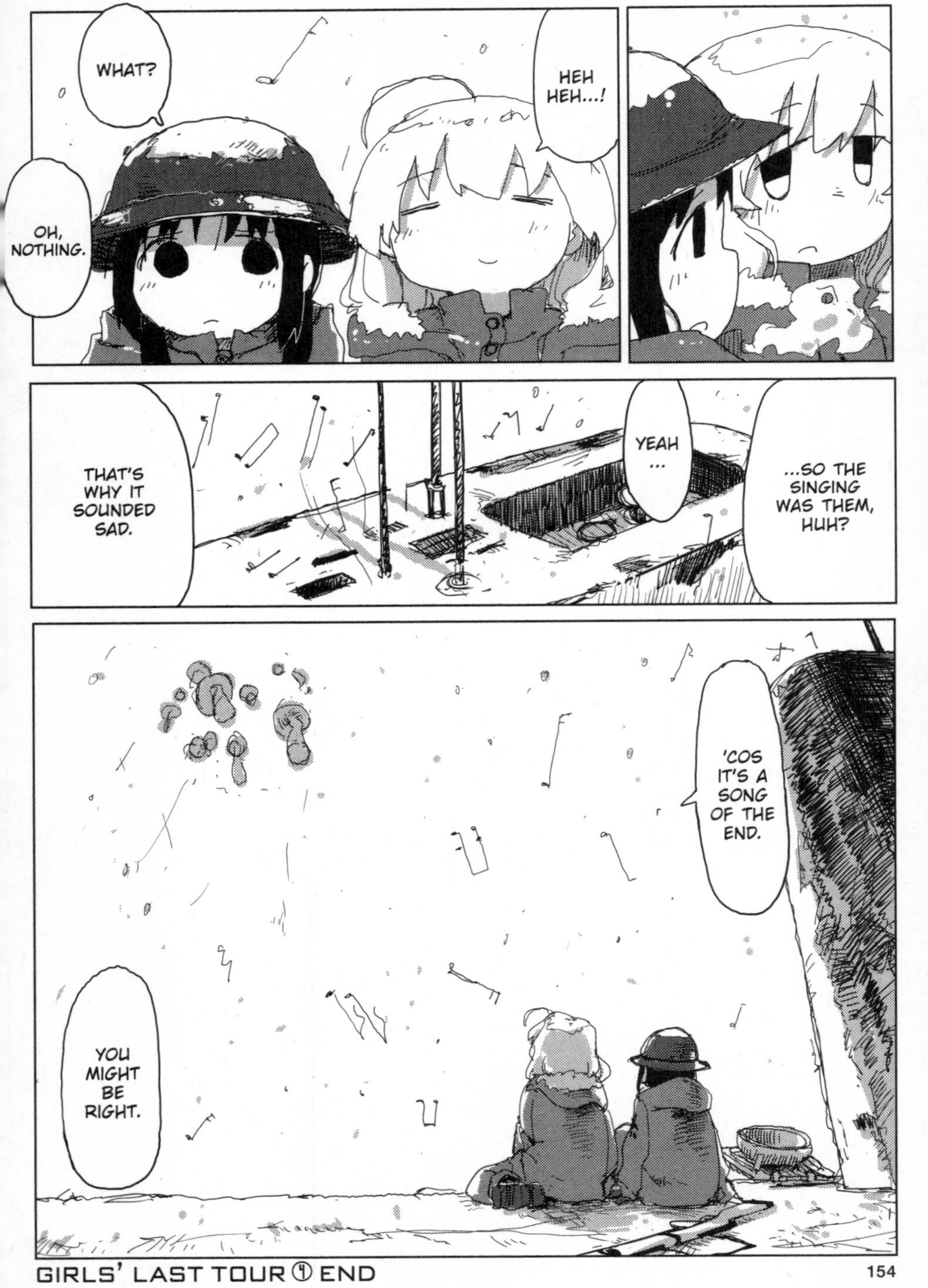
HEH HEH...!
WHAT?
OH, NOTHING.
...SO THE SINGING WAS THEM, HUH?
YEAH ...
THAT'S WHY IT SOUNDED SAD.
'COS IT'S A SONG OF THE END.
YOU MIGHT BE RIGHT.

GIRLS' LAST TOUR ④ END

(CROSSING
THE
OCEAN...)

CHITO'S PICTURE JOURNAL

TODAY, I GOT THE IDEA OF MAKING YUU DRIVE. IT'S NOT FAIR THAT I'M ALWAYS THE ONE STUCK DRIVING. BUT OF COURSE SHE TOOK US IN A WEIRD DIRECTION AND GOT US STUCK IN A DITCH. I DON'T THINK I'M GOING TO HAVE HER DRIVE AGAIN.
WE MANAGED TO GET OUT OF THE DITCH BY WEDGING A PLANK IN AND TURNING THE TRACK.

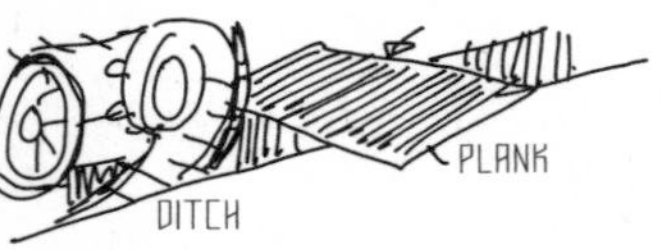
PLANK
DITCH

IT'S THANKS TO OUR VEHICLE THAT WE'RE ABLE TO TRAVEL. WITHOUT IT, WE'D GO HUNGRY AND USE UP ALL OUR STRENGTH IN NO TIME. WE CAN MOVE WITH THE ENERGY FROM FUEL INSTEAD OF FROM FOOD.

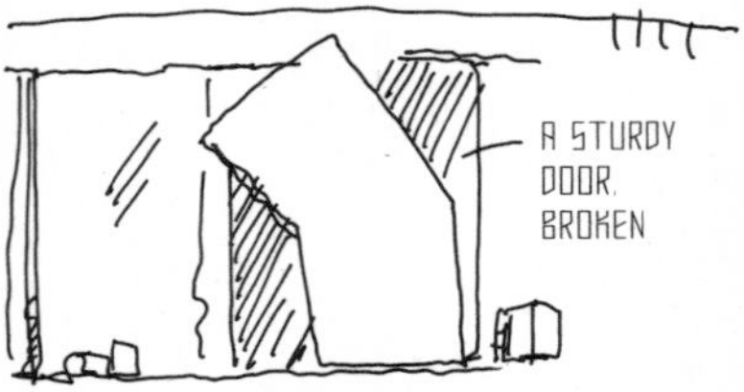
A STURDY DOOR, BROKEN

THERE WAS A HOLE IN A RARE TYPE OF DOOR. YUU SAID WE SHOULD GO INSIDE. IT WAS PRETTY DARK IN THERE, SO I DIDN'T REALLY WANT TO GO IN, BUT WE DECIDED TO ANYWAY. YUU'S INTUITION IS ACTUALLY RIGHT MORE OFTEN THAN NOT. A STURDY DOOR. MIGHT BE A CITY SUBSTRUCTURE IN THERE.

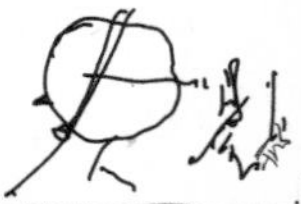

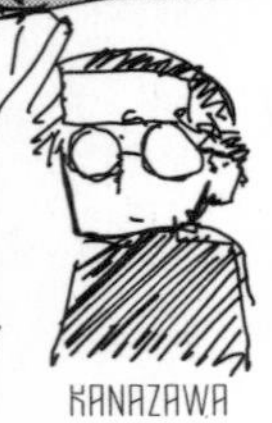
KANAZAWA

WE MET ANOTHER PERSON FOR THE FIRST TIME SINCE LEAVING TOWN. HE SAYS HIS NAME IS KANAZAWA, AND HE WALKS AROUND MAKING MAPS. AS WE WERE GOING UP, HIS MAPS FELL AND WERE LOST. THE WIND WAS STRONG TOO, SO EVEN IF HE'D GONE BACK DOWN, I DOUBT HE COULD HAVE PICKED THEM ALL UP AGAIN. HE SEEMED SAD. I WAS WORRIED THAT HE WOULD WANT TO COME WITH US, BUT WE QUICKLY PARTED WAYS.
THE KETTENKRAD WAS STRUGGLING CARRYING THREE PEOPLE PLUS OUR THINGS, AND I CAN'T HELP BUT BE SCARED OF MEN, EVEN THOUGH HE WAS PROBABLY A GOOD PERSON. WHEN WE PARTED WAYS, HE GAVE US A CAMERA. I THINK I'LL USE IT A LITTLE BIT HERE AND THERE. I'M GLAD I HAVE A METHOD OF KEEPING RECORDS OTHER THAN JUST THIS JOURNAL.

THE STRATUM ABOVE HAD LIGHTS. IT WAS NIGHT, BUT A BRIGHT NIGHT.

TODAY, I HAD ANOTHER DREAM. YUU AND I WERE DRIVING LIKE ALWAYS, ONLY THERE WAS NO CITY ABOVE US, AND WE WERE SURROUNDED BY BLUE SKIES AS FAR AS THE EYE COULD SEE. WE KEPT MOVING FOR A LONG TIME, LIKE WE ALWAYS DO.

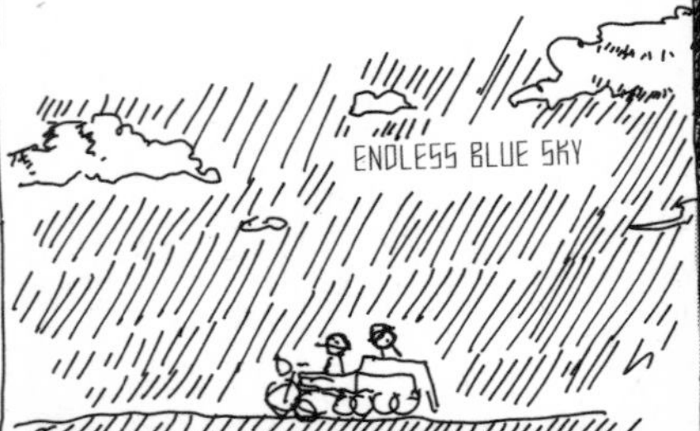
ENDLESS BLUE SKY

In her journal, Chito describes the things she's seen and what she thinks, accompanied by simple sketches. She can't write every day, of course, so she writes in it when she can. At first, she kept track of the number of days since they left on their journey, but she lost count somewhere along the line and gave up. Here are some excerpts.

WE FOUND GOD STATUES INSIDE A TEMPLE-LIKE BUILDING. THEY WERE MUCH BIGGER THAN THE STATUES OUTSIDE. IT WAS A LITTLE SCARY HOW THE PATTERNS BEHIND THEM WERE SHINING. I DON'T KNOW IF THERE'S A LIFE AFTER DEATH, BUT I LIKED THAT THERE WERE A LOT OF PLANTS AND FISH. THERE WERE SMALL STATUES OUTSIDE TOO. SOME OF THEM ONLY CAME UP TO OUR WAISTS. FOR SOME REASON, SOME OF THEM HAD STONES STACKED ON THEIR HEADS TOO. YUU WAS STACKING EVEN MORE STONES ON THEM. MAYBE IF YOU STACK STONES ON THEM, SOMETHING GOOD WILL HAPPEN?
I THINK I'VE READ ABOUT GOOD LUCK CHARMS LIKE THAT.

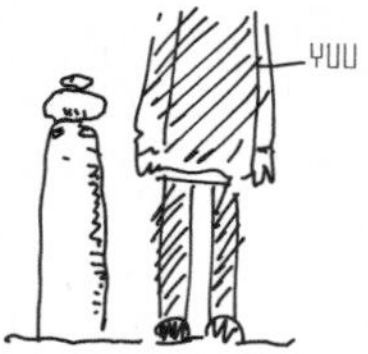
YUU

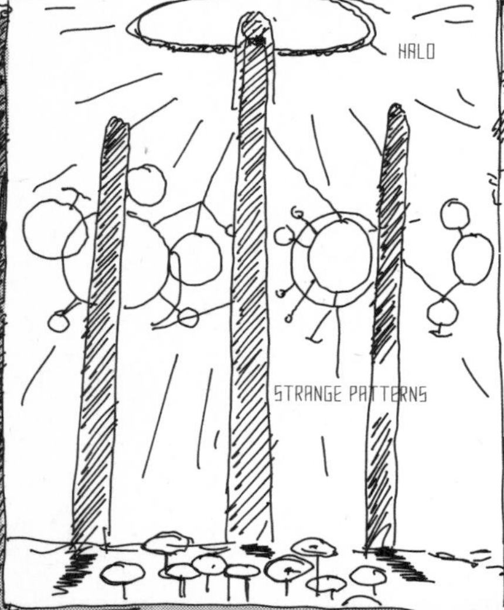
HALO
STRANGE PATTERNS

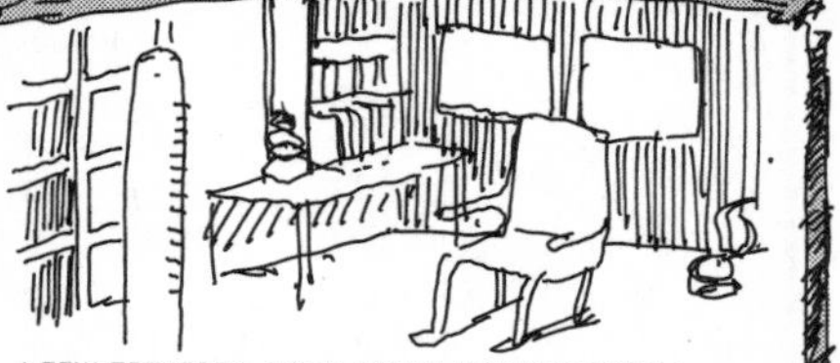

I SAW GRANDPA'S ROOM HAZILY, BUT NOW THAT I THINK ABOUT IT, THERE WAS SOMETHING THERE THAT SHOULDN'T HAVE BEEN.

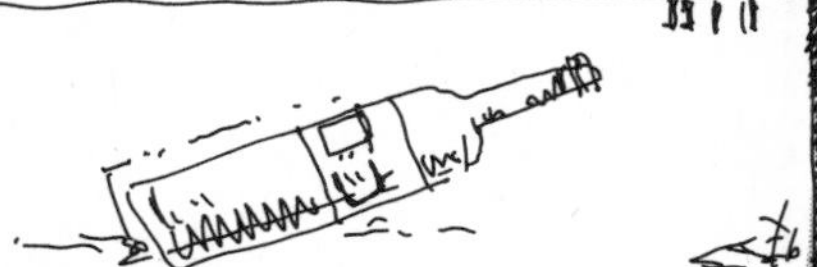

ON A BRIGHT, MOONLIT NIGHT, WE FOUND A STRANGE DRINK. THE LABEL SAID "VIU." I DON'T REMEMBER EVERYTHING THAT HAPPENED AFTER WE DRANK IT. WHEN I WOKE UP, I HAD A TERRIBLE HEADACHE. WHAT WAS THAT STUFF? BUT IT FELT KIND OF NICE.

TODAY, WE DIDN'T FEEL LIKE MOVING, SO WE RESTED INSTEAD. SOMETIMES WE HAVE DAYS LIKE THAT.

WE CAN SEE A TOWER A LITTLE FARTHER IN. I BET WE CAN GET TO THE NEXT STRATUM IF WE CLIMB IT.

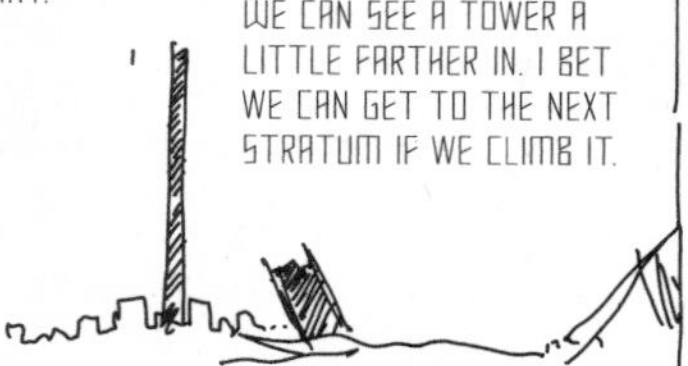

WE NAPPED. I DREAMED OF THE TOWN WHERE WE WERE BORN. SOMETIMES I DREAM OF THE PAST, AND WHEN I WAKE UP, I FEEL A LITTLE SAD. IS IT BECAUSE I REMEMBER THAT IT'S A PLACE I'LL NEVER BE ABLE TO SEE AGAIN?
YUU AND I WERE BOTH STILL SMALL, AND GRANDPA WAS THERE.

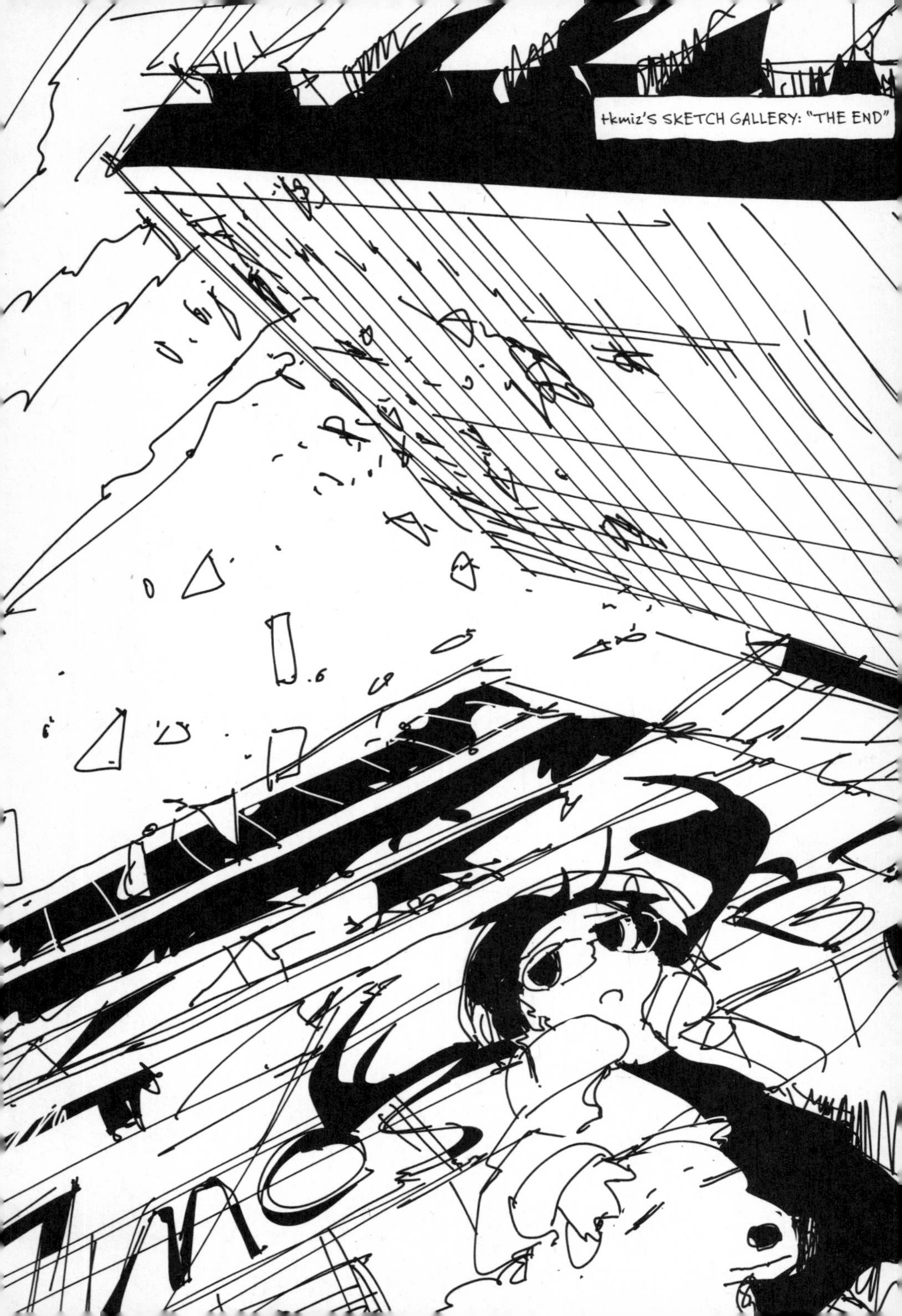
tkmiz's SKETCH GALLERY: "THE END"

AFTERWORD

Why are there always wars...? Why can't everybody have
 equal lives...?
I read a lot of books and think about this.
I'll make attempts to get to the bottom of it...or I'll dream
about my ideals...
But I don't get it. I start to hate everything.
Thinking wears me out.
Maybe thinking too "big picture" doesn't make people very happy.
The only feeling I want in life is the texture of the persimmons
from the persimmon tree in my family's yard.

TSUKUMIZU

GIRLS' LAST TOUR 4

TSUKUMIZU

Translation: Amanda Haley
Lettering: Xian Michele Lee

SHOUJO SHUUMATSU RYOKOU Volume 4 © 2016 Tsukumizu. All rights reserved. English translation rights arranged with SHINCHOSHA PUBLISHING CO. through Tuttle-Mori Agency, Inc., Tokyo.

English translation © 2018 by Yen Press, LLC

Yen Press
1290 Avenue of the Americas
New York, NY 10104

Visit us at yenpress.com
facebook.com/yenpress
twitter.com/yenpress
yenpress.tumblr.com
instagram.com/yenpress

First Yen Press Edition: February 2018

Yen Press is an imprint of Yen Press, LLC.
The Yen Press name and logo are trademarks of Yen Press, LLC.

The publisher is not responsible for websites (or their content) that are not owned by the publisher.

Library of Congress Control Number: 2017932043

ISBNs: 978-0-316-41598-9 (paperback)
        978-1-9753-2611-1 (ebook)

10 9 8 7 6 5 4 3 2 1

WOR

Printed in the United States of America